UNDERGRADUATE TEXTS IN COMPUTER SCIENCE

Editors
David Gries
Fred B. Schneider

Springer

New York
Berlin
Heidelberg
Barcelona
Budapest
Hong Kong
London
Milan
Paris
Santa Clara
Singapore
Tokyo

UNDERGRADUATE TEXTS IN COMPUTER SCIENCE

John Beidler

DATA STRUCTURES AND ALGORITHMS

An Object-Oriented Approach
Using Ada 95

With 29 Illustrations

 Springer

John Beidler
Department of Computing Sciences
University of Scranton
Scranton, PA 18510-4664
USA

Series Editors
David Gries
Fred B. Schneider
Department of Computer Science
Cornell University
Upson Hall
Ithaca, NY 14853-7501
USA

Library of Congress Cataloging-in-Publication Data
Beidler, John, 1941–
    Data structures and algorithms : an object-oriented approach using
Ada 95 / John Beidler.
        p.   cm. — (Undergraduate texts in computer science)
    Includes bibliographical references and index.
    ISBN 0-387-94834-1 (hardcover : alk. paper)
    1. Object-oriented programming (Computer science)   2. Ada
(Computer progam language)   3. Data structures (Computer science)
4. Computer algorithms.   I. Title.   II. Series.
QA76.64.B43   1996
005.13′3 − dc20   96-23982

Printed on acid-free paper.

Production managed by Bill Imbornoni; manufacturing supervised by Joe Quatela.
Camera-ready copy prepared using the author's WordPerfect files.
Printed and bound by R.R. Donnelley and Sons, Harrisonburg, VA.
Printed in the United States of America.

9 8 7 6 5 4 3 2 1

ISBN 0-387-94834-1 Springer-Verlag New York Berlin Heidelberg   SPIN 10523571

(Pauling-Bass) Lois Music
As performed by the Shirelles
transcribed by Joan Roccasalvo, CSJ

Preface

Picture this: sitting in a cottage by a peat fire in a small farm village just outside of Limerick City in Ireland, with a pint of Guinness, a copy of Booch's software components in Ada book, and a laptop computer. That picture describes how I spent part of my sabbatical during the 1989–1990 academic year, after spending the summer of 1989 working with an Ada programming group at the Naval Surface Warfare Center in Dahlgren, Virginia. This was preceded by many years of looking at ways of improving the Data Structures and Algorithms course as more and more material filtered out of that course and into the CS 2 course. That year in Limerick provided the opportunity to think through the variety of issues that led to this book.

The Data Structures and Algorithms course is commonly referred to as the ACM CS 7 course. During the past decade, a large amount of material has moved from the CS 7 course to the CS 2 course. I viewed this relationship between the CS 2 and CS 7 courses as an opportunity to enhance the CS 2 course and modernize the CS 7 course. Two elements that played key roles in this process are software reuse and object-oriented programming.

My experiences at Dahlgren, during the summer of 1989, convinced me of Ada's value as an educational tool. I found Ada's features to be great tools for enhancing and presenting software development concepts. Of particular importance, I found Ada's encapsulation features and the ability to present specifications without even a hint of implementational details an extremely important software abstraction feature.

While I was on my sabbatical, my colleagues back at the University of Scranton made the decision to select Ada as the core programming language for the CS 2 and CS 7 courses. We had been using Modula-2 since 1980. Dr. Dennis Martin played a lead role in making the case for the transition to Ada. In fact, the year I was away was a significant year for our department, as we moved to new quarters with new laboratories and a fully networked environment. I'd like to recognize the key role Rich Plishka played in putting it all together.

Between 1990 and 1992 we received two Software Engineering and Ada grants for the development of support resources for the CS 2 and CS 7 courses. This provided us with an opportunity to build upon the resources that were constructed during my sabbatical. In 1992 we started refocusing our materials toward the coming transition to Ada 9X, today we know as Ada 95. I must acknowledge the direct and indirect roles Bob McCloskey played in the development of the data structure suites that I use to support both courses.

This transition to an Ada 95–based resource lead, in the fall of 1994—to experimentation with packages that employed type extension in lieu of generic instantiation as the method of interfacing reusable software components to the needs of clients—eventually led to the construction of a second suite of data structure components that has a very distinct object-oriented flavor.

The Course

The course implied by this book requires substantial software support. I spent my 1989–1990 sabbatical constructing an outline for the course and course support materials, including a component suite, based upon the Booch components, intended to meet educational needs, but with industrial-strength features. I wanted these components to provide good object-oriented support and software reuse experience for students in the CS 2 and CS 7 courses.

It is assumed that the reader of this book is familiar with the topics normally covered in a strong CS 2 course. We expect the CS 2 course to be a broad-based introduction to the discipline with a strong emphasis on analysis, design, abstraction, and the basics of formal specifications, and with a software engineering flavor. In the CS 2 course the students gain a fundamental understanding of the essential concepts of the basic logical data structures, like stacks, queues, lists, and trees. This book moves forward from that foundation with an in-depth presentation of representation, encapsulation, and measurement issues.

There are four recurring themes in this book: abstraction, implementation, encapsulation, and measurement. One significant difference you may find between this book and others is that this book addresses a great variety of encapsulation issues and separates representational issues from encapsulation issues.

There is more than enough material in this book to support a CS 7 course. My preference is to cover the first six chapters in the first half of the semester. My experience has been that the first two chapters must be addressed carefully. Students never seem to fully grasp the implications of static representations, the fundamental reasons behind the need for both `private` and `limited private` types, and the subtleties of tagged and controlled types. While covering Chapters 3 through 6, I emphasize encapsulation and the variety of implementation and measurement issues.

During the second half of the semester, I cover about 80 percent of the material in the remaining chapters, leaving the uncovered material as the basis for individual and team projects. For example, in Chapter 7 I may cover the AVL tree restructuring in depth, then give a cursory presentation of B-trees, leaving the construction of B-tree algorithms as an assignment. Another year I will switch and do B-trees in depth and give various AVL-based assignments.

Support

This book describes, and is supported by, two approaches to encapsulation, the traditional encapsulation of reusable Ada resources in generic packages and a polymorphic approach that makes use of Ada 95's object-oriented features. Both suites may be obtained across the World Wide Web from

> `http://academic.uofs.edu/faculty/beidler/`

by following the Ada link. The packages may also be obtained through an anonymous ftp from

> `ftp.cs.uofs.edu`

in the `pub/Ada` directory. For those without network access, the data structure component suites may also be obtained by contacting the author at (717) 941-7774.

Gratia Tibi Ago . . .

So many people contributed in so many ways to this manuscript. Of particular note are the many students who suffered through many variations of course notes in Cmps 240 from 1991 to 1996. They were the biggest contributors. They pushed, and questioned, and made being an educator a real treat.

I'd like to thank my departmental colleagues. I could not forget our departmental support staff of Mary Alice Lynott and Bill Gunshannon. Without Mary Alice's assistance at critical times, and Bill's work in keeping our "ancient" UNIX systems alive, I wonder if this book would ever have been completed. If it was not for our department's unofficial open-door policy, I could not have tried out many ideas on Rich, Bob, Paul, Bi, Dennis, and Dick. I would also like to thank Chip for allowing me to try to improve his racquetball game.

My sabbatical in Ireland played an important role in getting this book started. If Mary Engel, the associate dean of the College of Arts and Sciences, had not met with Barra O'Cinneadie of the University of Limerick, my sabbatical would not have come to be. The year at Limerick was made both a pleasure and an academic success by such good folks as Wally Ryder, Tony Cahill, Norah Powers, and Mike Coughlin. Nor can I forget the invaluable contribution of Fionbarr McLaughlin and Liam O'Brien in teaching me to play squash.

In the last few years, numerous discussions with three good "Ada" friends helped this project along. They are John McCormack, Mike Feldman, and Nick DeLillo. Nick and I, along with our wives, share a full appreciation of the other CIA, The Culinary Institute of America. Now if only he could learn to make a good cappuccino.

Of course, what makes this venture so worthwhile is the support and love of my family. They may be added to the dedication, if you figured it out, by replacing the word "one" with the word "ones" when you sing the song. Now that this book is completed, you may find it difficult getting in touch with me. I'm busy playing with my grandchildren.

Jack Beidler
Summer 1996

Contents

1

Preliminaries

This book presents data structure techniques in the context of object-oriented software development with the eventual implementation of algorithms in Ada 95. Object-oriented software development is a contemporary approach to the design of reliable and robust software. The complexity of the implementation of software systems is a combination of the complexity of the representations of information and the complexity of the algorithms that manipulate the representations. **Data structures** is the study of methods of representing objects, the design of algorithms to manipulate the representations, the proper **encapsulation** of objects in a reusable form, and the **evaluation** of the cost of the implementation, including the measurement of the complexity of the time and space requirements.

Programming languages play an important role in representing the solutions to problems in an efficient, reliable, and maintainable manner. Many modern programming languages support the layered representation of information and algorithms, frequently referred to as abstraction. **Abstraction** is the separation, or layering, of software to distinguish between **what** a data structure represents, or **what** an algorithm accomplishes, from the implementational details of **how** things are actually carried out. Abstraction is very important because frequently there are several competing methods for representing a structure. Usually, there are tradeoffs among competing representations and their algorithms. These

1

tradeoffs must be measured in light of the goals of the system under development, or the problem being solved.

Important software design features that derive from good abstraction and algorithm design are loose coupling, strong cohesion, and provably correct software. **Loose coupling** is the clear indication of the flow of information in a software system. Coupling has to do with how information is passed among modules in a software system. Loose coupling is usually achieved by reducing access to global variables and restricting the passing of information between modules through the use of procedure parameters and other obvious methods of passing information.

Strong cohesion is achieved by placing within a software module only the code that helps the module achieve its task. Any code that is not related to the task of the module is not in the module. Good use of loose coupling and strong cohesion assists in making it easy to follow how a system achieves its goals, hence assisting in verifying the **correctness** of the software.

Proving the correctness of a system is far beyond the scope of this book. However, correctness issues should always be addressed. Correctness issues are addressed here with carefully stated assertions using a **Z**-like (pronounced zed-like) notation. The notation addresses the issues of values in variables before and after the execution of a statement sequence. For example, the statement sequence

```
Sum:= 0;
for i in 1..n loop
   Sum:= Sum + i;
end for;
```

could be written with assertions as

```
Sum:= 0;
-- Precondition: Sum = 0
for i in 1..n loop
   Sum:= Sum + i;
   -- Invariant: Sum' = 1+2+...+i = Sum + i
end for;
-- Postcondition: Sum' = 1 + ... + n
```

where a variable followed by a prime mark indicates the value in the variable, Sum', after the statement, or statement sequence, associated with the assertion. For example, the loop invariant in the above code refers to the change in Sum during execution of the statements within the loop. The postcondition of the loop refers to the value of Sum when the loop terminates. Assertions appear throughout this book to describe subprogram preconditions and postconditions and other assertions. Assertions can also be used to analyze code within the bodies of subprograms.

A good programming language supports an assortment of features that aid in the formation of efficient, reliable, and maintainable software systems. Also, contemporary programming languages support various means of encapsulating representation in various ways, allowing clients who use these abstractions to select the encapsulation that best meets their needs. As a result, software developers may use these features to represent relationships between the original problem and the solution being represented by the software. One programming language that does this quite well is Ada 95.

1.1 Object-Oriented Software Development

Over the past decade, significant advances have been made in describing how a software system represents the solution to a problem. The object-oriented approach to software development plays an important role in improving the software development process. From the data structures point of view, the object-oriented approach provides a balance between objects and actions. This balance yields important insight into the design and implementation of software systems, resulting in efficient, reliable, robust, and maintainable software systems built from reusable encapsulations of object classes.

This book supports the object-oriented philosophy of software development. The book is not committed to any one object-oriented approach, or to the issues concerning the multiplicity of methods used by various object-oriented programming languages. It is more concerned with using the object-oriented philosophy as a means of presenting and carry out good software development practices.

1.1.1 The Object-Oriented Concept

Object-oriented software development is an approach to software development that has the potential to produce reliable, efficient, and maintainable software systems, object-oriented software development is a topic whose scope is beyond this text; however, some understanding of the terminology and philosophy of the object-oriented approach is essential. This section touches on the terminology and concepts as they relate to data structures.

1.1.2 Objects and Their Attributes

Some traditional approaches to software design emphasize actions first and view variables as a means of reporting on the results of actions. Informally, one may view the object-oriented approach as being more balanced, placing an appropriate emphasis on objects and actions as information, or messages, are passed among objects.

Object-oriented software design begins with an analysis of the problem that classifies the families, or classes, of objects that describe the problem's environment. Each family of objects is classified by the attributes that combine to form the states, or values, of objects in the family. Object-oriented design classifies the actions and operations surrounding each object type. Additional object types may be formed to assist in the design of a solution. Each time a new object type is developed, its attributes, values, and operations are catalogued.

Abstraction, the hiding of details, plays a fundamental role in the object-oriented approach. In data abstraction, complex object types are constructed from simpler object types. Similarly, procedural abstraction distinguishes between **what** an operation does from the details of **how** the subprogram is carried out. This leads to the natural building of complex algorithms from simpler ones.

Since layering, or stratification, is natural in the object-oriented approach, it lends itself to a natural progression from the specification of a problem to the implementation of a solution through the careful control of the visibility and interaction between objects.

Frequently, those who are unfamiliar with the object-oriented approach to software development confuse the notions of **object classes** and **objects** with the programming language notions of **types** and **variables**. Variables in a programming language should not be viewed as being equivalent to objects. One or more variables are brought together to describe the attributes of objects. In many procedure-oriented programming languages, like Ada, the representation of the value of an object is constructed from a collection of variables. Type declarations assist in describing the attributes common to all objects in a class of objects. In turn, a class of objects is completely described by the attributes of objects, the relations between the attributes of objects in the class, and the collection of constructors and observers that may act upon objects in the class.

To illustrate these notions, let us consider the description of figures in a Cartesian coordinate system. All objects in the class of figures in a Cartesian coordinate system have the attribute of **position**. Objects in the class of figures may be acted upon by constructors that position figures on the plane, move them, and remove them from the Cartesian system. The class of figures also has observers that return location, size, and other information. The **location**, or anchor, attribute is a Cartesian coordinate. Cartesian coordinates themselves are a class of objects. The attribute of each object in that class is described by a pair of real numbers, called the x-coordinate and the y-coordinate. In turn, the x- and y-coordinates are described by the class of objects called **real numbers**.

The object class of Cartesian coordinates is described by the typical attributes of Cartesian coordinates and the usual operations and relationships between coordinates, such as position and distance between coordinates.

Sometimes a class of objects might not be rich enough to describe the objects in a problem. The extension of a class of objects to include additional attributes and operations is called a **polymorphism**. For example, the terms **rectangle**, **circle**, and **square** describe classes of objects that are polymorphisms of the class **figures**. Each class has a set of attributes that describe the values of objects in that class, and a collection of constructors and selectors that operate on objects in the class. The derived class may also inherit from the original class attributes and operations that were defined for the original class. For example, each object in the class **rectangle** may be described with four attributes, the three new attributes, **width**, **height**, and **orientation**, along with the inherited attribute, **position**. Each object in the class **circle** is described with two attributes, the new attribute, **radius**, and the inherited attribute, **position**. Each object in the class **square** is described with two new attributes, length of a **side** and **orientation**, along with the inherited attribute, **position**.

Frequently, simpler classes of objects are used to describe the attributes of more complex classes. For example, the attributes width, height, radius, and side are values from the class of objects known as the **real number** system, or class. The attribute **orientation** comes from the class of objects called **angles** that describes the relationship between a specified straight line and the horizontal axis. The attribute **position** is a value in the class of objects called **Cartesian coordinates**, which are composed of ordered pairs of values from the class of **real numbers**.

An attribute is **compound** if it can be decomposed into two or more values from one or more object classes. An attribute that cannot be decomposed is called **primitive**. A class is said to be primitive if objects in the class are described with a single, nondecomposable attribute. The class of real numbers is an example of a primitive class of objects. This class, along with its set of constructors and selectors, is very rich. The class Cartesian coordinates is not primitive, because it is composed by combining a pair of real numbers.

The attributes that describe the values of objects in a class may be composed of other objects from simpler classes, possibly primitive objects. For example, the relationship between a compound class, like rectangles, and a more primitive class, like real numbers, is frequently exploited in the construction of algorithms that manipulate objects in the more complex classes.

1.1.3 Operations

There are two categories of operations on object classes, **constructors** and **observers**. A **constructor** is an operation that may change the value of an object. An **observer** is an operation that does not change the value of an object, it simply reports on the object's value. Some books refer to observers as **reports** or **selectors**.

To illustrate, consider the Cartesian coordinate problem presented in Section 1.1.2. Typical constructors for the class rectangle might include Initialize, Display, Undisplay, Move, Reorient, Change_Width, and Change_Height. Typical observers for the class might include Is_Initialized, Is_Displayed, Orientation_Of, and Area_Of. The observer Area_Of uses the multiply operation for **real numbers** to report the object's area.

1.2 Problem Analysis

The object-oriented approach to software development complements the well-known mathematician George Polya's four-step problem-solving process. Table 1.1 illustrates an elaboration of Polya's four-step problem-solving process that includes an object-oriented approach and expands upon the design phase. The elaboration of the design phase into problem-oriented (high-level) and solution-oriented (low-level) phases corresponds in a natural way to recursively applied stepwise design during the software development process.

The software development process involves the formation of a solution to a problem and the mating of the solution with the capabilities and limitations of the target computer system. The fundamental problem of software development is the smooth transition from the problem through the design to the representation of the solution. A danger in the software development process is placing too early and too much emphasis on the software system and its capabilities. The object-oriented approach helps overcome this danger by providing a regular progression through the various phases of the problem-solving process.

A simple analogy between software development and basic physics may help in understanding the role of the object-oriented paradigm in the software

Table 1.1. The Software Development Phases

PHASE	ACTIONS	
Analysis	What are the objects? Attributes? Operations. Constructors. Observers. Iterators. Messages. What relations exist between object classes/Objects?	A b s t r a c t i o n
D E - High Level S	What is to be accomplished? Partitioning of events. Order. Object types, attributes, operations, assertions (Preconditions, postconditions)	
I G - Low Level N	Representation of objects Stepwise refinement of representations and algorithms. Coupling. Cohesion. How is it done?	I m p l e m e n t a t i o n
Implementation	Code, debug, test (various cases), verify, and validate assertions Integrate Optimize Error handling	
Evaluation Maintenance	Monday morning quarterbacking Evaluation, collate documentation, locate potential weaknesses, improvements, enhancements. Maintenance, locate errors	

development process. In basic physics, there are two primitives, force and mass. Force acts on mass and mass is changed by the force. In software development, the analogy to mass is objects and the analogy to force is operations, or algorithms.

The term "object-oriented" means various things to different groups of software developers. To some it may imply the use of a particular object-oriented programming language, like Smalltalk, Actor, or C++. To others it could mean the step before system implementation, or coding, in the software development process, an object-oriented approach to design. Object-oriented purists may view this book as one on object-based programming, using object-oriented analysis and design with implementation in Ada 95. In any case, whether we call it object-oriented or object-based, the approach transcends the specifics in any particular programming language.

During the analysis phase, solution details are not important; the overriding concern is understanding the problem. An object-based approach to analysis concentrates on understanding the object types, along with their attributes and operations, and how the problem creates and manipulates the values of objects. Relationships between objects are observed and the operations on objects are defined and classified.

Informally, object-based analysis helps us lay the pieces of the jigsaw puzzle face up on the table. In so doing, patterns begin to emerge, providing clues to possible solutions, which prepare the software developers for the next step, high-level design. For example, consider the example, described in Section 1.1.2, of displaying regular figures on a Cartesian plane. An object-oriented analysis of this problem would begin with a complete description of each object class, including the constructors and observers for each object class, and the decomposition of the attributes down to the primitive object classes, upon which the others are built. This analysis would lead to other questions regarding the interactions between objects, like what should be done with the display when two figures overlap? Simply stated, if object-oriented analysis is aggressively pursued, the results of that analysis produce much information and many clues about how to address issues that arise in later stages of the software development process.

1.3 Solution Design

One method of solution design is called **top-down design**. Top-down design is a solution development technique that starts with the big picture. Sometimes the terms "strategic planning", "tactical planning", and "operational planning" are used to indicate levels of planning. Top-down design is the software equivalent of emphasizing strategic planning first. Like the analysis phase, the design should not be overly influenced by a particular software environment or programming language. This is not to say that software constructs are not described or implied, but rather the initial guiding force behind a solution design is how the system being designed solves the problem - without a concern for the particulars of the programming language or operating system that will be used.

Five keys to the production of well-designed software are

1. **Logical partitioning and modularization** — Breaking the solution into manageable pieces, each piece being somewhat logically self-contained. Each piece solves a subproblem of the bigger problem that is under consideration. Loose coupling and strong cohesion assist in this process.
2. **Abstraction** — Both data and procedural abstraction, are important. The name of a procedure tells us **what** the procedure does; the code inside

tells us **how** the procedure arrives at its result. A type declaration describes **what** class is formed by objects of this type. The details of the declaration describe **how** values of objects of this type are defined. The more complex a procedure, the greater the possibility that the procedure might call other procedures, hence hiding implementational details. The more complex the description of the attribute of objects in an object class, the more chance that the object class is constructed from other object classes that, in turn, hide more implementational details.

3. **Correctness** — Formally proving the correctness of algorithms or the correctness of linkages between pieces of the problem. It begins by simply using the preconditions and postconditions on subprograms to determine that subprograms are called in the correct order to solve the problem. Correctness may be applied to layers of detail that can eventually involve assertion surrounding every control structure and the use of loop invariants.

4. **Loose coupling** — Reducing, or controlling, the interaction between subprograms or modules. Make each procedure as self-contained as possible with clearly defined and minimized interactions with other procedures. Avoid global access - in particular, modification - of the values in objects. Encourage the standardized passing of information between subprograms or modules, usually through parameters, with clearly defined indications of where the values of objects are modified.

5. **Strong cohesion** — Keeping together all code that supports a particular goal. A simple rule might be "One procedure equals one goal." Any part of an algorithm that supports that goal, and no other goal, stays in that procedure. Any part of an algorithm that does not help achieve the subprogram or module's goal should not be in the subprogram or module.

There are many interactions between these keys to good software construction. In many respects, the design is driven by the need to sequence the actions applied to objects, leading to a correct and efficient solution to the problem. The term "partition" is used here in a strict mathematical sense. A **partition** is a collection of subdivisions with two unique characteristics:

1. The total collection of algorithms covers everything that must be done to solve the problem.
2. Everything that is to be done is done in one and only one subdivision; nothing is duplicated.

It is to the advantage of the software developer to make the partitioning of the problem **logical**, in the sense that things that logically belong together are placed in the same subdivision. This helps address the issues of loose coupling and strong cohesion, which make the resulting system easier to understand and maintain.

The danger during the design phase is the early consideration of coding details. This danger may be avoided by concentrating properly on the **"what"** side of the solution abstraction. That is, top-down design starts by emphasizing *what* is to be accomplished or represented, not *how* it is to be carried out or represented. Just as abstraction produces layers of information hiding, the layers of abstraction may be used to nest several layers of design. One may consider that high-level design loosely associates to the "what" level of abstraction and low-level design associates to "how" level of abstraction. By associating design layers to abstraction, the low-level design at one layer equates to the high-level design of the next nested layer. With a firm and clear analysis of the problem in hand, the software developer has laid the proper foundation for top-down design. The complementary component in top-down design is stepwise refinement, the application of the analysis and design methodology to each of the components in the design, leading, through further refinement, toward implementational details.

An important consideration is proving the correctness of the solution. Minimally, the descriptions of all operations, and groups of operations, should include clear statements of their preconditions and postconditions. The correctness statements should associate to the design levels. As the design takes shape, a concern for program correctness should lead to **assertions**. Assertions are provable statements that can be placed at specific points in a program. As the design is nested, the statements of preconditions and postconditions for each design level should provide clues regarding the correct ordering and associations between design modules and lead directly to the assertions that guide the construction of the eventual implementation. The preconditions of one statement sequence are made true by the postconditions of the statements and statement sequences that precede it.

1.4 Design to Implementation

Stepwise refinement may be viewed as the reapplication, or recursive use, of top-down design to further refine the descriptions of the various components in the problem's solution. Specifically, the partitioning, or modularization, that occurs during the previous level of design starts with the original problem and forms a solution that is described in terms of several smaller problems, each of which must now be solved.

The assumption is that it is usually easier to solve several smaller problems than one larger one.   Further, as each smaller problem is viewed, the preconditions and postconditions for that component of the solution state the assumptions and results for that part of the solution.   The assertions for the smaller problems should demonstrate how the preconditions of the larger problem lead to the larger problem's postconditions. Most of the objects, their attributes, and their operations are also defined. However, in solving each of these smaller problems, it may be necessary to define additional object types that help solve the smaller problem.

Also, the separation that abstraction provides in the object-oriented approach between what is accomplished and how it is accomplished leads in a stepwise fashion to the eventual detailing of the objects and the algorithms in an appropriate programming language. But it is not just the language — it is the environment that surrounds the language — that helps produce reliable, efficient, and effective software.   It is the combination of language features and environmental considerations that makes Ada a good choice for the development of large, complex software systems.

1.5 Software Maintenance

Unfortunately, many software developers look at the delivery of the software as the end of the software development process. In many respects it is only the beginning, in the sense that good software may have a long life expectancy relative to the time it took to analyze, design, and implement the system. Software maintenance is not just long-term debugging. Granted, a large software system might contain flaws that remain undetected until the system is heavily used. However, there is another aspect, the evolution of the system. An equally, if not more, important aspect of software maintenance is the following:

> In solving a problem, a software system modifies the environment for which it was created. That modification and the new information brought forth by the software system, along with external factors, change the environment.   Those changing circumstances bring forth new problems and hint at new information and solutions.

Frequently it is the solution of these new problems that makes the real difference in the long-term value of the software system.

The ability to evolve, or create, a new system based upon an existing one is assisted, or hampered, by the quality of analysis, design, implementation, and documentation of the existing system. There is no question that good documentation is essential regardless of the software development methodology. Without good documentation, any good application of a methodology is lost in the process. Unfortunately, software maintenance issues are beyond the scope of this text.

1.6 Data Structures and Algorithms

As stated in Section 1.1, **data structures** is the study of methods of representing objects, the safe, reliable encapsulation of structures, the development of algorithms that use these representations, and the measurement of both the time and space complexity of the resulting systems. The object-oriented approach emphasizes the role of objects, along with their attributes and operations, that form the nucleus of the solution. The attributes and operations provide clues to the functionality of the components that must be brought together to create a solution. A knowledge of data structures provides a software developer with an understanding of the tradeoffs that must be considered as the solution proceeds from the analysis phase, through the design phase, to the solution.

From the point of view of deciding which data structure should represent the attributes of objects in a specific class, the emphasis that the object-oriented approach places on abstraction is very important to the software development process. *Abstraction* means hiding unnecessary details. **Procedural abstraction**, or algorithmic abstraction, is the hiding of algorithmic details, which allows the algorithm to be seen, or described, at various levels of detail. Building subprograms so that the names of the subprograms describe **what** the subprograms do and the code inside subprograms shows **how** the processes are accomplished is an illustration of abstraction in action.

Similarly, **data abstraction** is the hiding of representational details. An obvious example of this is the building of data types by combining together other data types, each of which describes a piece, or attribute, of a more complex object type.

An object-based approach to data structures brings together both data abstraction and procedural abstraction through the packaging of the representations of classes of objects. The package specification encapsulates the types that describe the attributes of objects in the class being encapsulated as well as the fundamental algorithms that manipulate and report on object values.

Once an appropriate abstraction is selected, there may be several choices for **representing** the data structure. In many cases there is at least one static representation and at least one dynamic representation. The typical tradeoff between static and dynamic representations is between a bounded or unbounded representation versus the added storage and time requirements associated with some unbounded representations.

After an abstraction and representation are chosen, there are competing methods to **encapsulate** data structures. The choice of an encapsulation is another tradeoff, between how the structure is made available to the user and how the user's instantiating objects may be manipulated by the package. The encapsulations have an effect on the integrity of the representation, and time and space requirements associated with the encapsulation.

Once specified, one or more competing methods of representation may be carried out, and the structure, its representations, and its encapsulation may be **evaluated** relative to the problem being solved. The time and space requirements of each method must be measured against system requirements and constraints.

This book contains a collection of classical methods for representing various object types frequently encountered in the solution of problems. In most cases a variety of competing representations are described. Each method should be carefully studied to attain a thorough understanding of the strengths and weaknesses of each approach. Therefore, it is as important to know the various methods of representation as it is to understand the timing characteristics of the algorithms that correspond to each method.

The hidden danger for a software developer is becoming enthralled with a particular data structuring method. A method of representation cannot stand on its own. It must always be measured against how well it meets the needs of a specific system under development. The evaluation of a specific representation for a particular problem is usually not easy. It is a matter of measuring the time and space requirements of competing approaches, evaluating the limitations imposed by each approach, and weighing the tradeoffs between approaches and other factors that may affect system performance. Frequently, this does not lead to a simple choice among competing approaches.

There are very few absolutes in programming. However, certain universal observations may be made. In general, the more directly and naturally the software represents the problem being solved, the more reliable the software is. The efficiency of the software is dominated by two items, the efficiency of the algorithm and the extent to which the algorithm efficiently utilizes a system's resources. A good programming language plays a fundamental role in software reliability. It does this by providing direct and efficient means for representing and maintaining high-level design information while supporting efficient implementation of algorithms.

1.7 Ada 95

There are many reasons for selecting Ada 95 for software implementation, including standards and environments. The history of the development of Ada is chronicled elsewhere. It was an exhaustive process involving many interested parties. The definitions of Ada, both Ada 83 and Ada 95, represent important milestones in the development of programming languages. There has been much criticism of Ada. There were dire predictions about the computing resources necessary to support an Ada compiler. However, compiler developers have been up to the task and have developed efficient Ada compilers for a large variety of computing systems.

Fortunately for Ada, those individuals with the narrow concerns for compiler efficiency did not dominate the design of the language. Software engineering factors were given fair consideration in the language's design. The design of any software system includes a collection of compromises and tradeoffs. The design of a programming language is no exception. When it comes to evaluating those tradeoffs relative to safe, efficient, reliable, and maintainable software, Ada measures up quite well as a programming language. As one will see in reading this book, the features in Ada come together time and again to provide the software developer with direct and efficient representations of algorithms. Ada tends to be a programming language that you design *with*, not design *around*.

Other factors besides a programming language contribute to the successful development of software. An environment that supports the design of software has a major impact; it influences the efficiency, reliability, and maintainability of the software. An important component in any quality software development environment surrounding a programming language is a library, a means of supporting software reusability. When looking at Ada, or any programming language for that matter, one should not look just at the language, but at the program support environment surrounding the language. For Ada, this is called an **APSE**, an **A**da **P**rogram **S**upport **E**nvironment. Programming support environments can range dramatically and have a major impact on the software development process. Access to a good programming support environment enhances your ability to expand upon the material presented in this book.

The transition from the initial version of Ada, called Ada 83, to the current version has been relatively smooth, but slow. Ada 95 does two important things. First, it corrects several flaws found in Ada 83. Second, it incorporates into the language additional features that address important software design issues and new software development methodologies, especially object-oriented programming.

1.8 Simple Static Types

Like most modern programming languages, Ada supports a variety of features for representing object types. Figure 1.1 illustrates one possible organization of classes of data types. The first dichotomy is between static and dynamic representations. The representation of an object is **static** if the size of memory required to represent the object is known when the object is defined. The representation of an object is **dynamic** if the amount of memory required to represent the value of the object may vary during program execution time. Both static and dynamic representations may be subdivided further into the categories of **structured** and **simple**. The simple types are further subdivided into **ordinal** and **nonordinal** types.

The **ordinal** types are characterized by the ability to place the values of the type into a one-to-one correspondence with a subset of the integers. The countability of the values of an ordinal type is the foundation of a number of attributes shared by ordinal types, including correspondences between the possible values of an ordinal type and the representations of these values. On the other

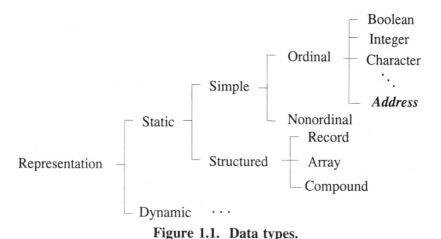

Figure 1.1. Data types.

hand, the representations of nonordinal types, like the nonordinal real arithmetic values with which they are typically associated, do not have a one-to-one correspondence to integers. Hence the nonordinal types are characterized by the inexact (i.e. approximate) representations of values.

There are three classifications of **structured** types - records, arrays, and compound types. Records and arrays are fundamental building blocks. Compounds types are created by combining records, arrays, and the simple types. A solid understanding of the static representations of objects using structured data types is essential before studying dynamic representations.

The building of objects whose representations are dynamic and the applications and measurement of dynamic representations are major objectives of this book. The fundamental tools for building **dynamic** data structures are few, but powerful. Section 1.8.2 presents these basics. The key to dynamic data types is address variables, called **access** types in Ada. The power of access types also represents a potential danger. Access types have been referred to as the potential `go tos` of data structures. The reference to `go tos` is an analogy to the potential danger programmers face when they build ad hoc control structures using `go to` statements in some programming languages instead of the looping and conditional execution (if, case) in any programming language. Access types form the logical links between data in various parts of a computer's memory. If those addresses are not carefully created and employed, the result is incorrect access to various parts of the computer's memory.

The potential danger with `go to` statements in some programming languages is the difficulty in following the flow of control within a program. Similarly, the misuse of access types leads to a comparable difficulty in comprehending how the dynamically allocated memory represents the value of an object. Just as control structures hide `go tos`, data abstraction and the correct encapsulation of object types must hide access variables. Restricting the visibility of access variables helps guarantee the reliability of dynamic representations of values.

Ada attributes provide access to a variety of information about an object's representation. These attributes appear in Table 1.2. For any object A, `A'address` is the `system.address` of the object and `A'Access` is an access type that "points" to the object. Throughout this chapter several tables delineate the attributes available for a specific object type or class of object types. Some attributes, like `'address` and `'Access`, provide information for practically all objects or object types. The attribute `'Access` may be made compatible with an access type in the sense that a value defined as `'Access` may be placed in appropriately defined access type variables.

Table 1.2. Generic attributes

Attribute	Result
V'address	The system.address of V
T'size	The number of bits required to hold an object of type T
T'storage_size	The number of memory storage units (bytes) required to hold an object of type T

In the above descriptions, T is a type, V a variable of type T.

1.8.1 Ordinal Objects

A one-to-one correspondence with a subset of the natural numbers characterizes all ordinal types. Through this correspondence, the ordinal types inherit certain attributes and operations, including

1. **The well ordering relation** - The inheritance of the less than (<) relationship and its derivatives, equality (=), inequality (/=), less than or equal to (<=), greater than (>), and greater than or equal to (>=), are frequently used relationships of all ordinal types.
2. **Predecessor and successor attributes** (`pred` and `succ`) - An immediate result of well ordering are the predecessor and successor attributes. Except for the boundary values, all other values have both predecessors and successors. The lower bound has no predecessor, but it does have a successor, while the upper bound has no successor but does have a predecessor.
3. `for` **and** `case` **control structures** -- Subranges of ordinal variables, and only ordinal objects, may control both the `for` and `case` structures.
4. **Ranging** - New types, `subtypes`, may be derived from all ordinal types by limiting the range of values to a constrained subrange of the type.

There are seven predefined ordinal types: `boolean`, `integer`, `character`, `wide_character`, enumerations, modular, and `address` types. Readers should be familiar with the `boolean`, `integer`, `character`, and enumeration types. Ada supports all the typical ordinal types. Besides supporting the `boolean` and `character` types and user-defined enumerations, Ada supports three integer types, `integer`, `natural`, and `positive`. The `natural` and `positive` types are predefined subtypes of `integer` and may be thought of as being defined as

```
subtype natural  is integer range 0 .. integer'last;
subtype positive is natural range 1 .. natural'last;
```

Modular types define an arithmetic type where the arithmetic operations are defined using modular arithmetic. For example, the type declaration

```
type Hexadecimal is mod 16;
```

defines a type whose set of values is the integers in the range 0..15, inclusive.

The ordinal types share several common traits. In particular, variables of any ordinal data type may control **for** and **case** structures. In addition, the ordinal data types share the Ada attributes listed in Table 1.3.

Subtypes may be derived from ordinal types by applying Range constraints. The format for range constraints is

```
subtype New_Type is Ordinal_Type range Low .. High;
```

where Low and High are values in the Ordinal_Type that define the bounds of the new subtype New_Type. There are two main reasons for constraining ordinal types in this fashion. First, object types, or attributes of an object type, evolving from a problem might be described by constraining a type limiting the range of

Table 1.3. Ordinal attributes

Attribute	Result
V'address	The system.address of V
T'base	The base type for type T. It cannot stand alone. Typically used in accessing another attribute. For example, T'base'first returns the first value in the base type from which the type T is derived.
T'digits	The number of digits of accuracy in the representation of values in type T
T'first	The first value of type T.
T'image	T'image(V) is a string representation of the variable V.
T'last	The last value of type T.
T'pos	Returns the ordinal position of the value in V, T'pos(V). If T is noninteger, ordinal positions start with 0, T'pos(T'first) = 0. T'pos(i) = i for integer value i.
V'pred	Returns the value that precedes the current value of V.
T'size	The number of bits required to hold an object of type T.
V'succ	Returns the value following the current value of V.
T'val	Inverse of T'pos. For integer i, T'val(i) returns the value of V that corresponds to i. T'val(V'pos)=V.
T'value	If the string S contains a representation of a value in T, then T'value(S) returns that value

In the above descriptions, T is a type, V a variable of type T.

values to those that represent the object or attribute values. Second, constrained ordinal types frequently form the ranges for arrays. The use of ranges in defining arrays is discussed in Section 1.9.1.

The ordinal types share a large collection of Ada attributes. The attributes appearing in Table 1.3 provide access to low-level information and basic manipulations of values in that ordinal type. Included are the 'succ and 'pred attributes for sequencing through the values in an object type and 'first and 'last attributes for determining the values that bound the range of values in an ordinal type.

Access types are the key to representing dynamic data types. Section 1.8.2 discusses the basics of building object representations with access types.

1.8.2 Access Types

The space allocation for static data structures remains fixed during the execution of a software system. For example, static arrays are fixed-size, sequential, homogeneous data structures with no access limits. Static records are fixed-size, sequential, heterogeneous data structures with no access limits. In both cases the terms "fixed-size" and "no access limits" are fundamental to arrays and records. *Fixed-size* means the size of the structure is determined when the structure is created. *No access limits*, also called the **random access property**, means that any object within these structures may be accessed at any time, regardless of either where it is located within the structure or whatever object had been previously accessed within the structure.

The solution to some software development problems requires the unbounded representation of object values. As the software system executes, the space required to represent the object is determined dynamically. However, with many of these structures, there are acceptable tradeoffs between the representation of the structure and the time required to access the values of objects within the structure.

Figure 1.1 illustrates one way of viewing dynamic data types from the viewpoint of view of the method of representation. It lays out the low-level features upon which dynamic structures are built. There is another point of view, that of high-level design considerations. High-level design hides the implementational details through data abstraction. This is the view presented in the subsequent chapters. Included in those chapters are the details of binding the high-level logical structure requirements with the low-level representation details.

In Ada, the key to dynamic storage allocation is address variables, called **access** variables in Ada. **Pointers**, or **pointer variables**, also refers to address variables. The term "pointer" refers to the fact that these variables do not contain data themselves, but indicate, or point to, the location where the information is located.

Access types provide access to dynamically allocated structures. Dynamic structures not only expand, but they contract as well. If a structure shrinks in size, something should be done with the space that the structure no longer uses. If access to that memory is lost, by losing or ignoring the access to that space, it is possible that a system might unnecessarily run out of memory. That is, although there is memory that is not being used, the access to that memory has been lost or is no longer available and normal requests for access to new space raise an exception because no memory is available to satisfy the space request.

The basic element of dynamic data types are address variables, called access types in Ada. One way to view the difference between dynamic and static data types is binding time. Static data types are bound to memory location before the procedure or package in which they are defined begins execution. For example, as a procedure is called, its static variables are allocated and then the procedure begins execution.

Dynamic data types are allocated as they are needed while a program executes. At least one static access type must be defined to provide access to a dynamic structure. Access types are created through a typical type declaration, as in

```
type Access_Type is access Dynamic_Object_Type;
```

`Access_Type` variables may then be declared,

```
Able, Baker: Access_Type;
```

and during program execution the address of a dynamically allocated object is placed in the access type with an assignment statement of the form

```
Able:= new Dynamic_Object_Type;
```

There are no limits to the number of objects that may be dynamically allocated. However, in most cases, the dynamically allocated object must contain at least one access component so that an arbitrary number of objects can be linked together. Typically, the `Dynamic_Object_Type` is a record, which contains one or more components for holding information and one or more components for additional access variables for extending the structure. It is through these additional access components that variable-size structures may be built during program execution.

Listing 1.1. Example dynamic allocation declarations

```
type Linked_Object;
type Record_Ptr    is access Linked_Object;

type Linked_Object is
   record
      Value    : integer;
      Next_Link: Record_Ptr;
   end record;
```

Since dynamic objects are typically represented by linking together other objects, the Ada notation for accessing dynamic objects is the same dotted notation that is used to access records. To illustrate, consider the declarations that appear in Listing 1.1. These declarations define two data types. Objects of the access type, called `Record_Ptr`, contain the addresses of a record type called `Linked_Object`. All records of type `Linked_Object` contain two components, an integer value and an access type to another `Linked_Object` record. These declarations are all that is necessary to form a dynamically allocated linked collection of records.

Figure 1.2 illustrates one way of viewing a dynamic structure. Lines with arrows indicate the roles of access types that point to other data spaces. Assume the type declaration

```
Start: Record_Ptr;
```

The single static access variable `Start` provides access to a dynamic structure. There is no predetermined limit to the number of objects in the structure. `Start` addresses, or points to, the first object in the structure, and the access component in each record addresses, or points to, the next record in the structure. The address component in the last object is null, to indicate that there are no more records in the structure. The reserved value **null** indicates that the access variable does not contain a memory address.

The linked collection of numbers illustrates the fundamental tradeoffs between static and dynamic allocation. Any component in a static record is directly accessed by referencing the name of the component. Any object in a static array may be directly accessed by referencing the array with the appropriate index.

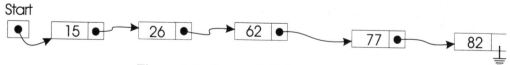

Figure 1.2. Dynamic linked structure.

However, when a structure is allocated dynamically, a series of addresses must be followed from one record in the structure to the next until the dynamic record containing the desired item is found. Therefore, the tradeoff, or price paid, for dynamically allocated structures is the additional computer time required to follow access variables and locate the desired item.

It is worthwhile to take a few minutes and become comfortable with the dotted notation that is used for dynamic allocation. Given the declarations in Listing 1.1, consider the references `Start`, `Start.all`, `Start.Value`, `Start.Next_link`, `Start.Next_Link.all`, and `Start.Next_Link.Value`. `Start` is an access type; it accesses a `Linked_Object`. If `Start.all` is not null, then `Start.all` is the `Linked_Object` accessed by `Start`. `Start.Value` is the `integer` component in the `Linked_Object` accessed by `Start`, and `Start.Next_Link` is the access type in that same record. `Start.Next_Link.all` is the record accessed by the access type in the record accessed by `Start`, and `Start.Next_Link.Value` is the integer value in that component. In Figure 1.3, the number 14 is `Start.Value` and 26 is `Start.Next_Link.Value`. `Start.all` is the record that contains the `Value` component 14 **and** the access type that points to the record containing 26.

Dynamic allocation also costs additional space. As a dynamic structure is allocated, space must be provided for the access components within each record that link together the dynamically allocated pieces of the structure. The access variables require additional space not required for static data types.

To illustrate the use of access types, the declarations that appear in Listing 1.1 may be used to create a dynamic structure of numbers with the structure linked so that the numbers appear in the structure in ascending order. Assume `Start` is a `Record_Ptr`:

```
Start: Record_Ptr:= null;
```

Start is initially null to indicate that initially there are no objects in the structure. A sorting process uses a procedure

```
procedure Linked_Sort (Start : in out Record_Ptr;
                        Number: in      integer);
```

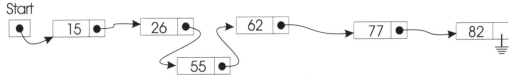

Figure 1.3. Dynamic sort illustration.

to place the numbers, one at a time, into their proper positions in the structure so that the records in the structure are logically ordered, through the access types, from the record containing the smallest number to the record containing the largest number.

Figure 1.3 illustrates the result of the Linked_Sort procedure assuming the particular set of numbers that appear in Figure 1.2 have already been linked into the structure and a new value, 55, must be placed into the structure. The result is achieved by changing the values of access components in the record to logically place a record between the two records containing the number just smaller than and just greater than or equal to 55.

Listing 1.2 contains the source for Linked_Sort. This procedure recursively visits the records in the dynamically allocated structure one at a time, until the correct location within the linked structure for New_Object is found. The three-way selection structure tests for the two possible terminating situations. First, the procedure checks to see if The_Link is null. That would indicate that the procedure is at the end of the structure, in which case Insert_Object is called to place a record with the new number at that end of the linked structure. Next, the procedure compares the value of New_Object to the value in the record currently being pointed to, Pointer.Value,

> elsif New_Object <= The_Link.Value then.

If the comparison is successful, New_Object is inserted into the structure before the record containing The_Link.Value. If neither test is successful, the

Listing 1.2. Linked sort procedure

```
procedure Linked_Sort (The_Link   : in out Record_Ptr;
                       New_Object: in      integer  ) is
   procedure Insert_Object (Here: in out Record_Ptr) is
      New_Ptr: Record_Ptr:= new Linked_Object;
      begin -- Insert_Object
         New_Ptr.Value    := New_Object;
         New_Ptr.Next_Link:= Here;
         Here             := New_Ptr;
      end Insert_Object;
   -------------------------------------------------
begin -- Linked_Sort
   if The_Link = null then
      Insert_Object (The_Link);
    elsif New_Object <= The_Link.Value then
      Insert_Object (The_Link);
    else
      Linked_Sort (The_Link.Next_Link, New_Object);
   end if;
end Linked_Sort;
```

`New_Object` must be placed further along in the structure. This leads to the recursive call

```
Linked_Sort (The_Link.Next_Link, New_Object);
```

which continues the search by proceeding to the next record in the structure.

The structure of the algorithms is typical of recursive subprograms that access dynamically allocated structures. The recursive call in the procedure `Linked_Sort` is typical of the recursive algorithms that access dynamic structures. It contains a multiple selection structure with two or more alternatives. At least one of these alternatives leads to a recursive call. The passing of a parameter in that recursive call, `The_Link.Next_Link`, provides access to the next object in the structure.

The procedure demonstrates a typical linking process. The declaration

```
New_Ptr: Record_Ptr:= new Linked_Object;
```

obtains access to a new dynamic record. The record is initialized,

```
New_Ptr.Value:= New_Object;
```

then linked into place. The relinking process is an example of what is frequently called parallel assignment. **Parallel assignment** is when it is desirable to reassign the values of two or more variables simultaneously. However, computers are sequential devices, and if the sequence of actions is not properly ordered, the original value in one variable might be lost before it is placed in another variable.

An example of parallel assignment occurs in the procedure `Insert_Object` in Listing 1.2. In this procedure it would be desirable simultaneously to place both the value in the parameter `Here` into `New_Ptr.Next_Link` and the value `New_Ptr` in `Here`. Care must be taken in carrying out the parallel assignment with the correct sequence of actual assignments. If the assignments are listed using the zed-like prime mark to indicate the results after the parallel assignment,

```
New_Ptr.Next_Link' <- Here  &  Here' <- New_Ptr.
```

The original value of `Here` is placed elsewhere and a new value is placed in `Here`. Thus, the old value must be copied to the new location **before** a new value is placed in `Here`. Hence,

```
New_Ptr.Next_Link:= Here;
Here               := New_Ptr;
```

is the correct sequence for achieving the parallel assignment.

In some cases of parallel assignment, temporary variables must be introduced. This occurs in cases where all variables involved in the parallel assignment have their old values placed elsewhere and have new values assigned to them, as in

```
A <- B  &  B <- C  & C <- A.
```

In this case, a temporary variable must be created to hold the old value of one of the variables in order to save the old value while making the variable available for reassignment:

```
Temp := A;
A    := B;
B    := C;
C    := Temp;
```

Note the way each variable appears on the right side of an assignment statement before it appears on the left side of the next assignment statement. Look for this pattern when manipulating the values of access types. It is a good double-check on the correct order of assignment statements.

The Linked_Print procedure copies the access type passed in the parameter into the variable Current. This access type controls the while loop that iterates through the structure. The Value in the record pointed to by Current is printed; Current_Column is incremented to keep track of the number of columns displayed on the current line; the if selection determines whether the current line should be terminated; and then Current is reset

```
Current:= Current.Next_Link;
```

to point to the next record in the linked sequence (see Listing 1.3). The loop iterates until Current becomes null, which indicates that there are no more records in the sequence.

Although the discussion in this section centers around the assumption that all access types point to records, the fact is that access types may be defined for any type of object:

```
type integer_Ptr_Type is access integer;
```

When a variable of this type is defined,

```
Int_Ptr: integer_Ptr_Type;
```

and the access type is initialized,

Listing 1.3. Linked print procedure

```
procedure Linked_Print ( The_Link: in      Record_Ptr) is

   Current         : Record_Ptr       := The_Link;
   Width           : constant positive:= 7;
   No_Of_Columns : constant positive:= 10;
   Current_Column: natural            := 0;

   begin
   while Current /= null loop
      I_IO.Put (Current.Value, Width);
      Current_Column:= Current_Column + 1;
      if Current_Column = No_Of_Columns then
         Current_Column:= 0;
         Text_IO.New_Line;
      end if;
      Current:= Current.Next_Link;
   end loop;
   end Linked_Print;
```

```
          Int_Ptr:= new integer;
```

the integer object pointed to by `Int_Ptr` is accessed and manipulated as `Int_Ptr.all`, as in the assignment statement

```
          Int_Ptr.all:= -572;
```

The qualifier .all may be used with all access types to refer to the entire object being addressed by the access type.

1.8.3 Nonordinal Objects

Nonordinal objects are simple objects whose possible values are uncountable. Many computer systems support more than one representation of real numbers, a nonordinal type. Real numbers have one attribute that distinguish them from integers, specifically, uncountability. A consequence of this is the lack of finite representations of all reals. Finite representations are essential in computers. Therefore, a compromise must be made to represent real values in computers. The compromise is that real values are approximated. The method of approximation is a scientific notation-like representation of real values.

Some direct results of the fact that reals cannot be represented exactly are the following:

1. The addition of approximate values is not associative:

$$((A + B) + C) \neq (A + (B + C)).$$

2. During the course of computation, if the values in two real variables are suppose to be equal, A = B, it is possible that the expression (A = B) might be `false`.

The specific details of the representation of reals is beyond the scope of this book. An awareness of the problem is essential for software developers. The problem may be summarized with the statement that all real objects should be handled as if the representations of the values of real objects is, at best, an approximation of the actual value of the object.

The problem of working with reals is complex. In fact, there are several methods, studied in the area of mathematics called numerical analysis, for overcoming some of the problems of working with approximate values. One of the basic tools is a device for testing "equality" between approximate values.

For many problems, two approximations of real values are considered equal if they agree for a certain number of digits. The test for this is the relative difference calculation,

```
abs ((A-B)/A).
```

Since the calculation requires a division, if A is close to zero, there is the potential for arithmetic overflow. Therefore, the calculation must be preceded by a test of the divisor. If the divisor is close to zero, then the calculation

```
abs (A-B)
```

tests for "equality."

Listing 1.4 contains a boolean function, `Almost_Equal`. The function returns a value of **true** if the parameters A and B pass the test for equality. The function is instantiated with a value for `Near_Zero`. The value `Near_Zero` cannot be less than the real value accuracy for the computer system at hand. When `Almost_Equal` is instantiated, select `Near_Zero` so that at least a digit or two is left between the value of `Near_Zero` and the smallest possible positive real that may be formed, `float'epsilon`.

Ada supports two types that approximate the values of objects float types and fixed-point types. Float directly uses the floating point hardware on a system and should be viewed in terms of scientific notation-like representations. Fixed-point types are defined as

```
type Fixed_Type is delta Precision range Low .. High;
```

where `Precision` is the precision desired by the user and `Low` and `High` bound the range of admissible values. `Precision` is the minimum difference the user will accept between the values in the representation. Normally, the system does not provide the exact accuracy requested, but provides an accuracy that is machine dependent and slightly smaller than requested. The floating-point and fixed-point types share a large collection of attributes that give access to machine- and implementation-dependent information about the type. Table 1.4 lists the fixed and float attributes.

1.9 Structured Data Types

Frequently, the requirements for representing data objects in an abstract data type are beyond the capabilities of simple data types. Most programming languages include capabilities for creating new data types by combining data types and creating representations for more complex data objects. Ada supports two structured data types:

1. **Arrays** — Arrays are **physically sequential, fixed-size** collections of **homogeneous** objects. Further, objects within the structure have the **random access property**. Arrays are physically sequential in that the

Listing 1.4. `Almost_Equal` **function**

```
generic

   Near_Zero: in float:= 0.0001;

function Almost_Equal ( First, Second: in      float) return boolean;

function Almost_Equal ( First, Second: in      float) return boolean is
   begin
   if abs (First) <= Near_Zero then
      return (abs (First-Second) <= Near_Zero);
     else
      return (abs ((First-Second)/First) <= Near_Zero);
   end if;
   end Almost_Equal;
```

Table 1.4. Float attributes

Attribute	Result
V'aft	The number of digits after the decimal point required to represent values without an exponent and without trailing zeros given the delta declared for T.
T'delta	The smallest increment between representations of values in the fixed-point type T.
T'digits	The number of digits of accuracy in the representation of values in type T.
T'emax	Returns the maximum exponent for the real type T.
T'epsilon	Returns the smallest positive value that may be formed in the real type T.
T'first	The first value of type T.
V'fore	The number of digits before the decimal point required to represent values without an exponent for the declared delta.
T'image	T'image(V) is a string representation of the variable V.
T'large	Returns the largest value that may be formed in this universal real type.
T'last	The last value of type T.
T'machine_emax	The largest exponent the machine may form for the real type T.
T'machine_emin	The smallest exponent the machine may form for the real type T.
T'machine_mantissa	The number of digits in the machine in the mantissa for the real type T.
T'machine_overflow	Returns true if the machine checks for overflow on the type T.
T'machine_radix	The radix, or base, for arithmetic in the real type T; typically, 2, 8, or 16.
T'machine_rounds	Returns true if the machine rounds calculations performed in type T.
T'mantissa	Returns the size of the mantissa for the real type T.
T'safe_emax	Returns the safe exponent maximum value for real types.
T'safe_large	The largest value that may be safely formed in this universal real type.
T'safe_small	The smallest value greater than zero that may be safely formed in this universal real type.
T'size	The number of bits required to hold an object of type T.
T'small	The smallest value greater than zero that may be formed in this universal real type.
T'value	If the string S contains a representation of a value in T, then T'value(S) returns that value.
T'width	The width of the largest field required to hold character representations of the values in T.

In the above descriptions, T is a type, V a variable of type T.

random access property. Arrays are physically sequential in that the data objects are stored in consecutive memory locations. Arrays are homogeneous in that the array is made up of objects that are all the same type.

2. **Records** — Records are **physically sequential, fixed-size** collections of **heterogeneous** objects. Further, objects within the structure have the **random access property**. Records are heterogeneous in that the objects that make up the components in a record may be of different types.

The random access property means that the time it takes to access one object in the structure does not depend on what object in the structure had been accessed previously. For example, the time required to access the eighth object in an array does not depend on which other object in the array has been accessed before the eighth object. This may seem to be a trivial issue now, but as we build various types of logical structures, there will be a time dependence on the access to objects in a dynamic structure.

Records and arrays are the fundamental building blocks for the representations of structured object types, objects whose attributes are not simple. The attribute of an object is simple if it can be represented with a simple data type. Analysis and design considerations dictate that structured types be used to represent the attributes of many objects. It is important to recognize the keys that indicate when the attributes of an object type are represented with an array or a record. Usually, there is one of two fundamental keys:

1. When the fundamental units that combine to describe the value of an object are of different types, the object is probably best described with a record type.

2. When the objects that come together to describe the object type are all the same type of object and the fundamental objects themselves may be distinguished with a subrange of ordinals, the object is probably best described with an array.

Although we mention these two keys, it is easy to build situations where the key to the data representation either is not obvious or might also depend on solution design considerations.

1.9.1 Arrays

1.9.1.1 Constrained Arrays

An array type is appropriate for representing an abstract data type when the following three conditions are satisfied:

1. The data objects in the abstract data type are composed of homogeneous objects, objects that are all the same type, regardless of the values of the objects.
2. The solution requires the representation of a fixed, predetermined number of objects.
3. There is an ordering that can be placed on the objects in the abstract data type, a first object, a second object, and so forth. The ordering may be explicit, implied, or even irrelevant as far as the solution to the problem is concerned. The declaration of an array requires two steps of equal importance:

   a. Determine the exact specification of the data objects that appear in the array.
   b. Determine the sequential relationship between the data objects and form a suitable subrange of the appropriate ordinal data type to represent the sequential relationship.

Once the objects are determined in step a and the subrange is determined in step b, the array declaration may be created by first, if necessary, building the appropriate type or subtype to represent the `Object_Type` that appears in the array, and then building the subrange

```
subtype Array_Range is Some_Ordinal_Type range Low .. High;
```

and the array type

```
type Array_Type is array (Array_Range) of Object_Type;
```

Once the representation is determined, the operations for that type may be implemented.

Table 1.5 lists the attribute for array types.

To illustrate the steps leading from an abstract data type to its implementation as a data structure, consider the problem of finding all the prime numbers less

Table 1.5. Array attributes

Attribute	Result
A'first (n)	Returns the first index value in the nth index range of the constrained array A
A'first	Equivalent to A'first(1)
A'last (n)	Returns the last index value in the nth index range of the constrained array
A'last	Equivalent to A'last(1)
A'length (n)	Returns the number of index values in the nth index range of A
A'length	Equivalent to A'length (1)
A'range	Equivalent to A'range (1)
A'range (n)	Returns the nth index range in the array A

In the above descriptions, A is an array.

than a given number N. A prime number is an integer greater than one that is divisible only by itself, one, and their negatives.

A classical method of locating prime numbers is called the **sieve of Eratosthenes method**, which is attributed to the Greek mathematician-philosopher Eratosthenes. The method is described in the following algorithm:

1. List the numbers in order, starting with 2 and ending with the last number, N, to be tested.
2. Starting with the smallest number and proceeding to largest number, perform step 3. After processing the last number, go to step 4.
3. If the number is unmarked, it is prime, so circle the numbers and cross off all multiples of the number and continue with step 2.
4. List the circled numbers.

Figure 1.4 illustrates the sieve method in finding the prime numbers less than or equal to 21. Figure 1.4i demonstrates step 1, listing the numbers from 2 to 21. The first time through steps 2 and 3, as illustrated in Figure 1.4ii; 2 is circled and the multiples of two are crossed off. The next time through steps 2 and 3, in Figure 1.4iii, 3 is circled and the multiples of 3 are crossed off. Figure 1.4iv illustrates the final result.

The algorithm implies an abstract data type, a collection of objects with values, relationships between the objects, and operations on the objects. During problem analysis and the processing of the algorithm, a natural data abstraction evolves from the sieve method. An important attribute of a good system developer is not to force the natural data abstraction that evolves from a problem into the developer's preconceived notions of representations using particular data types, especially the predefined data types with their richness of operations.

Figure 1.4 hints at an abstract data type. Figure 1.4i clearly presents a fixed-size sequential relationship, the set of integers 2 through 21, inclusive, a **range** of natural numbers. In Figure 1.4, parts ii through iv, the markings placed on the numbers indicate a set of three markings, unmarked, circled, and crossed-off. Figure 1.4v-vi illustrates a method of representing the structure implied from the sieve method. Actually, unmarked and circled are redundant; they simply keep track of the prime numbers before and after, respectively, the prime number had been processed by the algorithm. Since the looping structure in the algorithm keeps track of the current prime being processed, the values unmarked and circled are redundant. Hence, only two values are needed to keep track of whether or not a number has been crossed_off. The declarations leading to the implementation of the sieve method's data representation appear in the **type** declarations in Listing 1.5.

The implementation of an abstract data type to find primes using the sieve method is completed by observing that there are three operations performed on

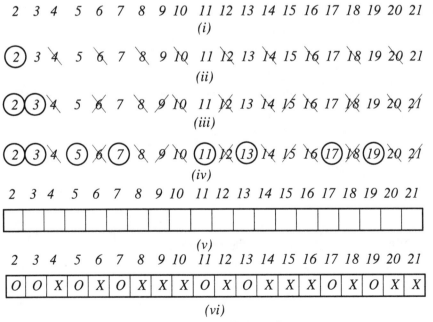

Figure 1.4. Sieve illustration.

Listing 1.5. Sieve algorithm for finding primes

```
with Text_IO;

procedure Sieve is
   -- 2*Last_Spot + 3 is last number checked
   Last_Spot: constant integer:= 1000;
   subtype    Text_Range is integer range 0 .. Last_Spot;
   type    Marking_Array is array (Text_Range) of boolean;

   Unmarked     : Marking_Array:= (others => true);
   No_Of_Primes: natural     := 0;
   Prime        : natural;
   X_Off        : natural;

   procedure Print (Image      : in     string;
                    This_Count: in     natural ) is
      Width  : constant natural:= 7;
      Columns: constant natural:= 11;
      begin
         for Index in image'last+1 .. Width loop
            Text_IO.Put (' ');
         end loop;
         Text_IO.Put (Image);
         if (This_Count mod Columns) = 0 then
            Text_IO.New_Line;
         end if;
      end Print;
   -----------------------------------------
   begin
   for Index in Unmarked'range loop
      if Unmarked (Index) then
         No_Of_Primes:= No_Of_Primes + 1;
         Prime:= 2*Index + 3;
         Print (integer'image(Prime), No_Of_Primes);
         X_Off:= Index;
         While (X_Off + Prime) <= Last_Spot loop
            X_Off:= X_Off + Prime;
            Unmarked (X_Off):= false;
         end loop;
      end if;
   end loop;
   Text_IO.New_Line;
   end Sieve;
```

this structure, the initialization of the structure, the sieve method algorithm, and the listing of the primes from the structure.

1.9.1.2 Unconstrained (Generic) Arrays

Frequently, when building array types, it is desirable to have a class of array types where all arrays in the class contain the same object type and the ranges of all arrays in the class are over the same ordinal type but over different subranges. Ada provides an ability to define an array type whose range is not specified when the type is declared. In Ada, such a class of array types may be defined with an **unconstrained array** declaration. Instances of this declaration may be used to define each array type with these characteristics.

Suppose the solution to a problem requires the representations of several object types represented with arrays that are identical in structure, except for the sizes of the various ranges over which the arrays are defined. Ada addresses this issue through unconstrained array types. For example, the solution to a problem requires arrays of floating-point representation of reals over various subranges of the positive integers. These object types are all described with unconstrained array declarations,

```
type Float_Array is array (integer range <>) of float;
```

Arrays of this type are constrained when they are defined by stating the type with a range constraint, as in

```
Able : Float_Array (5 .. 50);
Baker: Float_Array (-50 .. 25);
```

Unconstrained arrays are very useful in generalizing software. For example, if the solution to a problem calls for several arrays, all containing the same elementary data type but having different range constraints, a single generic type can be defined as an unconstrained array. When specific arrays of that type are defined, each may be defined with its appropriate range constraints. If these arrays must be processed by some algorithm, that algorithm may be written as one procedure,

```
procedure sort (A: in out Float_Array);
```

then the procedure uses the attributes `Float_Array'first` and `Float_Array'last` to properly access the specific array index bounds.

1.9.2 Records

1.9.2.1 Simple Record Structure

To determine whether a record is the appropriate means for representing an object, the following conditions should be addressed:

1. Is there a fixed, predetermined number of components that come together to form the structure?
2. Are the data objects, called the components, that come together to form the object heterogeneous, all different types, or possibly the same type but unrelated or independent?

The declaration of a record requires two steps of equal importance:

a. Determine the exact specification of the data types that come together to form the record structure.
b. Determine names for each component so that each name indicates the role the component plays in determining the record's value.

Once the objects are determined in step a and the component names are determined in step b, the record declaration can be created as

```
type Record_Type is
    record
        component_name: component_type;
            . . .
    end record;
```

and the system developer may proceed with the implementation of the operations on that type.

To illustrate, suppose the solution to a problem requires the representation of fractions. A fraction is a pair of integers, the numerator and the denominator of the fraction. Although fractions could be represented with arrays, because they are homogeneous, fractions lend themselves to a record representation:

```
type Fraction_Type is
    record
        Numerator  : integer;
        Denominator: integer;
    end record;
```

When a variable is a record, the components in the record are accessed using the name of the record qualified by the name of the component to be accessed. For example, if

```
P, Q: Fraction_Type;
```

then the expression forming the sum of these two fractions is formed by forming the numerator,

```
P.Numerator * Q.Denominator + Q.Numerator * P.Denominator
```

and the denominator

```
P.Denominator * Q.Denominator
```

then reducing both values, dividing them by their greatest common divisor. The complete formation of a package to support fractions is a good exercise in encapsulating an object type.

1.9.2.2 Record Discriminants

Discriminants play a role with records similar to that played by parameters with subprograms and packages. The declarations of discriminants has the same syntax as the declarations of formal parameters for subprograms and packages, including the declaration of default values. The list of discriminants appears in parentheses immediately following the record type's name:

```
type <<record_name>> ( <<discriminant list>> ) is
   record
          . . .
   end record;
```

Discriminants declare variable components within a record. There are three-ways in which discriminants are typically used to vary the structure of records and their components:

1. A component in a record could be an unconstrained array that must be constrained to form a specific instance of the record type.
2. A component in a record may be another record type which has discriminants and these discriminants must be given values to form instances of the component.

3. The record has a variant structure, it requires a value to determine which
    variant is used in a particular instance of the record. A record may have
    variants that may be determined without the use of a discriminant.
    Variant records are described in Section 1.9.2.3.

The first two instances of the use of discriminants are discussed in this section.
The use of discriminants with record variants appears in the following section.

To illustrate discriminants, consider the representation of polynomials in a
record. A polynomial is an equation of the form

$$y = a_n x^n + a_{n-1} x^{n-1} + a_{n-2} x^{n-2} + \ldots + a_3 x^3 + a_2 x^2 + a_1 x^1 + a_0.$$

A polynomial is completely determined by the degree, n, of the polynomial and
the $n + 1$ coefficients, a_i. The coefficients may be stored in an array,

```
type coef_array is array (0.. max_degree) of float;
```

if such a declaration was possible. Within the context of records with
discriminants, this may be accomplished with the declarations

```
type coef_array is array (natural range <>) of float;
type polynomial_rec (Max_degree: natural:= 25) is
   record
      degree: natural range 0..Max_degree:= 0;
      coef  : coef_array (0 .. Max_degree);
   end record;
```

In this example, the discriminant `Max_degree` constrains both the range of the
degree component and the upper range of the array `coef`. A user may declare
variables of type `polynomial_rec` either with a discriminant,

```
P, Q, R: polynomial_rec (15);
```

or without a discriminant,

```
Alpha, Beta: polynomial_rec;
```

In the first example, `P`, `Q`, and `R` may represent polynomials up to and including
degree 15. In the second example, both variables may contain polynomials up to
degree 25, the discriminant's default.

Discriminants are considered part of the record. Therefore, when records with
discriminants are passed to subprograms, the subprograms may determine the

value of the discriminant by accessing it in the same way any other record component is accessed:

```
. . . polynomial_rec.Max_degree.
```

Another result of this is that when aggregates are used to initialize the value of a record with discriminants, the discriminant values must be included in the aggregate. For example, if the polynomial

$$y = 5.0x^3 - 7.0x + 12.0$$

is placed in the record P, defined above, it could be done with the discriminant:

```
P:= (15, 3, (12.0, -7.0, 0.0, 5.0, others => 0.0));
```

1.9.2.3 Variant Records

Variant records are records where a part of the record has an alternate structure. When records have variants, the variant part must be the last part of the record. The variant part of a record is defined using a `case` structure. The `case` structure is similar to a `case` statement but with the collection of record components that associate to each variant:

```
type Example_Record is
   record
      . . .  -- non variant part

      case <<variant_selector>> is
         [when <<constant_list>> =>
               <<variant_components>>;]

      end case;
   end record;
```

The <<variant_selector>> may be either a reference to a record discriminant, a component that appears above in the record,

```
record
   . . .
   Hourly_Employee: boolean;
   . . .
   case Hourly_Employee is . . .
```

or it may define the record component as well as its use in the `case` structure:

```
case Hourly_Employee: boolean is . . .
```

The `<<constant_list>>` follows the same rules of formation as the list of constant selectors for this instance in the **case** statement, including the use of the separator '`|`' and the default selector **others**. The `<<variant_components>>` describes the components for the variant of the record. If a `<<variant_component>>` is empty, it is replaced with **null**. The braces indicate that the **case** structure may have an arbitrary number of variant components. To demonstrate a record with a variant component, consider an employee record for a company that pays some of its employees an hourly pay rate and others a fixed amount each pay period. The `employee_record` might have the following structure:

```
type Employee_Record is
   record
      . . . -- non-variant part
      case Hourly_Employee: boolean is
         when true =>
            Hourly_Rate: float;
            no_of_hours: float;
            -- other hourly related components;
         when false =>
            weekly_pay: float;
            -- other weekly related components;
      end case;
   end record;
```

An alternative would be to define the record using a discriminant to select the record variant:

```
type Employee_Record (Hourly_Employee: boolean) is
   record
      . . . -- non-variant part
      case Hourly_Employee is
         when true =>
            Hourly_Rate: float;
            No_Of_Hours: float;
            -- other hourly related components;
         when false =>
            weekly_pay: float;
            -- other weekly related components;
      end case;
   end record;
```

The wide range of possibilities of defining record structures goes far beyond this brief presentation. A good general reference to Ada 95 is Cohen's **Ada as a Second Language**. It contains a complete description of Ada 95's record structures, including the use of record structures to describe hardware specific details.

1.9.2.4 Protected Types

The primary purpose of `protected` types involves tasking, a program executing multiple threads of control. With tasking it is possible that two or more threads of control may attempt simultaneously to access the same data. As a result, the threads of control could interfere with each other. The role of `protected` types is to avoid this complication by guaranteeing that the data being protected are accessed by only one control thread at a time. A protected type is defined along with the operations that may access it:

```
protected type <class_name> is
     <visible declarations>
   private
     <protected declarations>
   end;
```

The `<visible declarations>` contains the procedures, functions, and entries that are available for this type. The `<protected declarations>` contains the specifications of the variables and actions protected by the type. For example, the declarations of a bound protected stack type of integers appears in Listing 1.6.

An `entry` is a procedure with a barrier condition. In the case of a stack, a stack may not be `popped` when it is empty. If the stack is limited in size, the `Push` operation cannot place a new object on a full stack. The body of a protected type contains the bodies of the type's procedures, functions, and entries. The body for `Protected_Int_Stack` in Listing 1.6 appears in Listing 1.7.

Listing 1.6. Example of a `protected` type

```
protected type Protected_Int_Stack is
     entry Pop  (Value:    out integer);
     entry Push (Value: in     integer);
     function Is_Empty return boolean;
     function Is_Full return boolean;
   private
     Top: natural:= 0;
     Stk: array (1..N) of integer;
   end Protected_Int_Stack;
```

Listing 1.7. Example of a `protected` body

```
protected body Protected_Int_Stack is

    entry Pop (Value:    out integer) when Top > 0 is
       begin
          Value:= Stk (Top);
          Top  := Top - 1;
       end Pop;

    entry Push (Value: in    integer) when Top # N is
       begin
          Top        := Top + 1;
          Stk (Top):= Value;
       end Push;

    function Is_Empty return boolean is
       begin
          return Top = 0;
       end Is_Empty;

    function Is_Full return boolean is
       begin
          return Top = N;
       end Is_Empty;

end Protected_Int_Stack;
```

In a tasking environment, only one thread of control at a time may be performing an operation on a protected type. As a result, threads of control cannot interfere with each other's access to the protected type. As each thread of control attempts to access a protected type, the requests are queued up by the operating system and normally service on a first–come–first–served basis. As Listing 1.7 shows, entries may have barrier conditions. For example, the `Pop` operation may perform only when `Top > 0`. If a thread of control requests the `Pop` operation and `Top = 0`, it remains queued until the barrier condition is satisfied. Meanwhile, other threads of control continue to perform.

Protected types may be used even when tasks are not being used. Protected types are access using the dotted notation. For example, if stacks are declared using the specifications in Listing 1.6,

```
My_Stack: Protected_Int_Stack;
```

access to the stack used dotted notation, as in

```
if not My_Stack.Is_Full then
    My_Stack.Push (Number);
end if;
```

```
   ...
if not My_Stack.Is_Empty then
   My_Stack.Pop (Its_Top);
end if;
```

In a nontasking environment, a user must be careful about using entries without testing the barrier condition. In such an environment, if a call is made to an entry whose barrier condition is not satisfied, the program halts or freezes the system.

It should be noted that a type cannot be both tagged and protected. However, a protected type may contain tagged components, and vice versa.

1.9.3 Compound Structures

Since the declarations that create arrays and records have no limits on the types of objects that appear in these structures, it is possible to create a great variety of structures to represent data types that naturally evolve from the analysis and design phases. The key to creating compound structures is to allow the structures to naturally evolve during the analysis and high-level design of a problem. To illustrate, consider the problem of building a software system that translates the Hindu-Arabic representation of numbers to Roman numeral representations.

One approach to solving Arabic-to-Roman translation problem, without using a computer, uses a translation table, as illustrated in Table 1.6. The table is straightforward. Given the representation of a number, like 1987, translate the number to Roman numerals by looking up the translation of each numeral in the appropriate column of the table and replacing the numeral by its equivalent Roman numeral string at that location of the table. The '1' in the thousands positions is replaced by "M"; the '9' is in the hundreds position and is replaced by the string "CM"; the '8' is replaced by "LXXX"; and the '7' by "VII".

Table 1.6. Arabic/Roman Translation Table

	Thousands	Hundreds	Tens	Units
1	M	C	X	I
2	MM	CC	XX	II
3	MMM	CCC	XXX	III
4		CD	XL	IV
5		D	L	V
6		DC	LX	VI
7		DCC	LXX	VII
8		DCCC	LXXX	VIII
9		CM	XC	IX

A software system may be written to perform the Hindu-Arabic-to-Roman translation by directly representing and using the table. The structure of the table is formed from three components; the indices that form the table's rows, the column indices, and the strings of Roman numerals at each location in the table. The sequential relation of the rows and columns is obvious. Hence the table structure naturally hints at a representation with a two-dimensional array. One possible pair of declarations for the two index ranges is

```
type Column_Type is (Units, Tens, Hundreds, Thousands);
subtype Row_Type is character range '0' .. '9';
```

However, in an array, all elements must be the same type. The objects at each position in the table are strings of at most four characters.

The objects within the conversion table may be represented with the strings

```
type Roman_String is array ( 1 .. 4 ) of character;
```

However, the strings range in size from one to four characters. Therefore, the size of the particular string also needs to be declared. This leads to the record declaration

```
type Roman_Record is
   record
      Size : natural;
      Roman: Roman_String;
   end record;
```

With the declarations defining the array ranges and the objects in the array, the array itself may be declared as

```
type Conversion_Table_Type is
        array (Row_Type, Column_Type) of Roman_Record;
```

If a table of this type is declared,

```
Table: Conversion_Table_Type;
```

and the Hindu-Arabic number is read as a string of characters,

```
type Hindu_String is array (1 .. 4) of characters;
```

the algorithm in the program in Listing 1.8 prints the Roman numeral representation of the number.

Listing 1.8. Arabic-Roman numeral conversion

```
with Text_IO;

procedure Arabic_To_Roman_Conversion is

    type Column_Type  is (Units, Tens, Hundreds, Thousands);
    subtype Row_Type  is character range '0' .. '9';

    type Roman_Record is
       record
     Size : natural:= 0;
     Roman: string (1..4);
       end record;

    type Conversion_Table_Type is
       array (Row_Type, Column_Type) of Roman_Record;

    type Hindu_String is array ( 1 .. 4) of character;

    Table: Conversion_Table_Type;

    procedure Write_Roman ( Hindu: in     Hindu_String ) is

       H_Index: positive:= 1;

       begin
       for Index in reverse Column_Type loop
     if Hindu (H_Index) in '1' .. '9' then
        Text_IO.Put (Table(Hindu(H_Index),Index).Roman
            (1..Table(Hindu(H_Index),Index).Size));
     end if;
     H_Index:= H_Index + 1;
       end loop;
       end Write_Roman;

         . . .
```

1.10 Explorations

    1. **Static Polynomials**:   Consider the issues of representing polynomials discussed in Section 1.9.2.2:
       a. Find applications that are appropriate for the static representation.
       b. Find applications for which a static representation is not appropriate.
       c. Build polynomial addition and subtraction functions.
       d. Create specifications for multiplication and division subprograms. For each of the operations:

      i. Write a paper discussing the appropriateness of implementing the operation as a procedure or as a function. This should not depend on the implementation, only on the abstraction.

      ii. Write a paper focusing on **the primary difficulty** in implementing the operation.

      iii. Write a paper describing various exceptions that might be raised in implementing the operation.

2. **Dynamic Polynomials**: Polynomials may be represented dynamically as a linked structure of record,

```
type Poly_Rec;
type Poly_Access is access to Poly_Rec;
type Poly_Rec is record
     Degree: natural;
     Next  : Poly_Access;
     Coef  : float;
   end;
```

where a static pointer of type `Poly_Access` points to a linked collection of records that represents the polynomial, as illustrated in Figure 1.5. Note that the terms of the polynomial are maintained in the linked structure in descending order of degrees.

  a. Write, test, and verify addition and subtraction subprograms.

  b. Create specifications for multiplication and division subprograms. For each of the operations:

      i. Write a paper discussing the appropriateness of implementing the operation as a procedure or as a function. This should not depend on the implementation, only on the abstraction.

      ii. Write a paper focusing on **the primary difficulty** in implementing the operation.

      iii. Write a paper describing various exceptions that might be raised in implementing the operation.

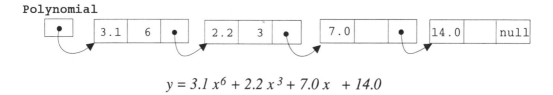

$$y = 3.1\,x^6 + 2.2\,x^3 + 7.0\,x\ + 14.0$$

Figure 1.5. A dynamic representation of a polynomial.

```
type Mixed_Rec;
type Mixed_Ptr is access Mixed_Rec;
type Mixed_Rec is record
      Back_Ptr: Mixed_Ptr;
      First   : integer;
      Second  : string (1..3);
      Third   : integer;
      Fwrd_Ptr: Mixed_Ptr;
   end record;
```

and the linked structure appearing in Figure 1.6, whose construction is based
on these declarations, determine the value of each of the following. Explain
your answers.

a. Starter
b. Starter.Second
c. Starter.all
d. Starter.Fwrd_Ptr.First
e. Starter.Fwrd_Ptr.Fwrd_Ptr.Fwrd_Ptr.Back_Ptr.First
f. Starter.Fwrd_Ptr.Fwrd_Ptr.Second
g. Starter.Second(Starter.Fwrd_Ptr.Third)
h. Starter.Fwrd_Ptr.Fwrd_Ptr.Fwrd_Ptr.Second
i. Starter.Fwrd_Ptr.Fwrd_Ptr.Back_Ptr.Back_Ptr.Back_Ptr

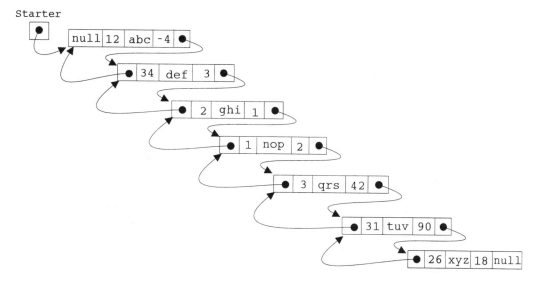

Figure 1.6. Linked example.

2

Encapsulation

2.1 Concept

An important key to software productivity is software reuse. With respect to data structures, an important key to software reuse is the encapsulation of classes of data structures in ways that encourage their reuse. The most fundamental way to encourage the reuse of data structure components is to encapsulate the representations of data structures using Ada's object-oriented programming and software packaging capabilities. Regardless of the packaging method, a client will have to construct an interface between the data structure's encapsulation and the client's application. For example, when a structure is encapsulated using Ada's object-oriented capabilities, the client constructs an interface using object-oriented type extension. A type extension example appears in Section 2.5. When a data structure is encapsulated in a generic package, a client instantiates the generic package to construct the interface between the package's data structure and the client's software. A generic instantiation example appears in Section 2.3. Both methods provide safe, reliable, efficient, and robust encapsulation.

2.2 Packaging Fundamentals

2.2.1 Initialize/Finalize

Many objects must be initialized before the representation may be used by the operations made available in the encapsulation. Some representations need no initialization at all. Some might require that certain values be placed in certain parts of the representation. Still others might require more complex initializations, including dynamic allocation.

For consistency, each encapsulation of a data structure type should include the procedures `Initialize` and `Finalize`. In some cases, these procedures might simply be null procedures. Regardless of each structure's complexity, users are encouraged to initialize each structure before they are used and to finalize each structure when it is no longer needed.

Finalization could be critical if the structure is dynamically allocated, to return the dynamically allocated records to the dynamic allocation manager when the records are no longer in use. This could be critical if a system's space requirements are close to the system's actual space availability.

A typical software development error is the failure to initialize or finalize a data structure. These processes are automated in Ada 95 with `controlled` or `limited  controlled` types, which are made visible through the `Ada .Finalization` package. `Ada.Finalization` is discussed in detail in Section 2.4.6.

2.2.2 Private Types and Safe Client/Package Interface

How does the software developer keep the data structure from being misused by the client? How does the client know whether or not the reusable software will correctly manipulate the client's objects as they are placed into and removed from the data structure? In Ada, the answer lies in the correct use of those features that describe the visibility between the client and the package. Ada's `private` types play an important role in safely interfacing between the client and the package. Understanding the roles of Ada's `private` and `limited private` types is fundamental to understanding the special needs of objects whose values are represented dynamically, or through indirection, versus those objects whose values are represented statically.

Private types describe the level of visibility between a client and a package. These declarations appear in two locations, in the instantiation parameters of generic packages and in the specifications of the package's object types. Private declarations, regular or limited, within a generic package's instantiation parameters indicate the level of visibility the package has of the client's objects. Private declarations, regular or limited, within a package's specifications indicate the client's level of visibility of the package's object types. Unfortunately, because of the restrictions on limited private types, software developers frequently use private types when limited private types would be safer, and hence more appropriate. These perceived restrictions and problems when using limited private types may be overcome if the package developer constructs the interface so that the client is required to pass along the appropriate resources along with the limited private type.

When an object type along with its attributes and operations are encapsulated within an Ada package, the object type may be made visible in the package's specification as either a private or a limited private type. The instantiation parameter of a generic package may be private or limited private. In both cases, the details of the type's representation are not visible to the other party. Private and limited private types are characterized as follows:

1. The predefined operations of assignment (":=") and equality ("=") are allowed for private types, but not for limited private types. However, "=" may be defined for a limited private type within the package that encapsulates the type.
2. The only other operations that may be applied to private and limited private types are those specified in the package defining the type and operations a user might construct, directly or indirectly, from the subprograms defined within the package.

It is important to understand where these restrictions apply. An object type is private or limited private to the client or the package but completely visible to the other party. For example, if a package has an instantiation parameter called Able_Type and makes visible a type Baker_Type, and both are private,

```
generic
   Able_Type is private;
package Example_Pack is

   Baker_Type is private;
   . . .
```

then when the client instantiates the package as

```
package My_Pack is new Example_Pack (character);
```

the client is fully aware of the attributes of the `character` type but can only define variables of type `Baker_Type`, use these variables in assignment statements, test for equality, and pass `Baker_Type` variables as parameters to the procedures specified in the package, `Example_Pack`. Similarly, within the package, the package has complete knowledge of variables of type `Baker_Type` but can only assign and test for equality variables of `Able_Type`, because the package has no knowledge of the details of the instantiating parameters.

Ada `private` types are similar to Modula-2's hidden types in that the implementation details for the type are concealed from the user. Although Modula-2's hidden types are (unnecessarily) restricted to pointers, Ada has no such restriction on `private` and `limited private` types. A closer analogy to Ada private types are the hidden types available in JPI's Modula-2 compiler. Similar capabilities are also available on Pascal systems that have UCSD Pascal-like units, and C++.

There are several issues surrounding the appropriate use of `private` and `limited private` types. `Private` and `limited private` types keep users from directly manipulating the representation of the values of objects. An obvious question, from an object-based software development and software reliability point of view, is: What should be the criterion for choosing to represent of an object type as either `private` or `limited private`?

Since both assignment and equality are available to `private` types and not available to `limited private` types, software developers should use `private` types only when the results of these operations are consistent with user expectations. Specifically, users equate the assignment operation with copying. The problem is that assignment copies only the value in a variable. Users, on the other hand, frequently think in terms of objects. The representation of the value of an object might extend beyond contents of the variable associated to the object. This is particularly true when access types are employed. The answers to the following questions help determine when a `private` type or a `limited private` type should be used as a package interface.

1. For each object of the type under consideration, is the representation of the values of objects always entirely self-contained within the variable associated with the object? If the representation of the object's value is always contained within the variable associated to the object, the

representation of objects of this type is said to be **bounded**. Otherwise the representation is **unbounded**.

2. If the representation of the value of an object type is bounded, are two representations considered equal if and only if the bit patterns representing the object are identical?

Clearly, in (1), if a representation is unbounded, then the values of objects are represented through indirection. That is, the variable contains a reference, possibly an access type, that references all or part of the value of the object associated with that variable. Part of the representation of the value is outside of the variable. Also, the equality operator looks only at the bit pattern of the contents of variables. Therefore, the entire representation of the value is not available to the operator. As a result, the equality operator does not perform as a user would expect. However, the problem with "=" may be overcome with the construction of an "=" function that performs the correct test for equality between objects.

When variables associated with objects whose representations are unbounded are manipulated with the assignment operator

        A:= B;

the assignment simply duplicates the value of the variable. The result of this duplication may produce undesirable side effects. For example, if A and B are access types, as illustrated in Figure 2.1, the result of the assignment A:= B is that A and B share the linked structure, which may represent the values of the

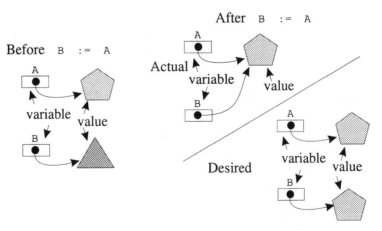

Figure 2.1. Why ":=" may be hazardous.

objects associated with A and B. As a result, any change in the value of the object associated with the variable B causes an immediate change in the value of the object associated with A. This implies that assignment is a dangerous operation for unbounded object types. Therefore, it follows that unbounded object types should be made visible with `limited private` types.

2.2.2.1 Private Types and Equality

Historically, the assignment and equality operators were thought of as manipulating variables, not objects. When the representations of the values for an object type are bounded, then assignment produces a result that is consistent with user expectations. This problem focuses on an issue associated with the decoupling of the equality and assignment operators. Boundedness guarantees that the assignment operator produces no side effects. However, boundedness does not guarantee that the equality operator produces the desired result anticipated by users. To illustrate, consider the representation of fractions:

```
type Fraction_Type is
   record
      Numerator  : integer;
      Denominator: integer;
   end record;
```

If A and B are Fraction_Types and A:= (1,2) and B:= (2,4), they are considered logically equivalent, but the equality operator

```
A = B
```

returns `false`. In this case, assignment correctly duplicates the variable, but equality, which requires identical matching of bit patterns, does not produce the expected result.

Although this decoupling can be achieved within Ada's current framework, package developers may handle this problem by overloading the "=" operator for the object:

```
function "=" ( A, B: private_type) return boolean;
```

2.2.2.2 Issues Surrounding Limited Private Types

From an object-oriented point of view, objects take on values, and in programming languages variables are associated to objects. Unfortunately, in many programming languages, including C, Fortran, COBOL, Pascal, Modula-2, and Ada, the value of an object doesn't always fit inside the variable that corresponds to the object. Specifically, when the values of objects are represented through indirection, including the use of pointers and dynamic storage allocation, the assignment operator ":=" does not produce the same result that is produced when the value of the object fits inside the variable associated to the object.

For an object type whose values fit in the variable associated with the objects, the assignment B:= A means **copy** the value of A to B. However, when the value of the object is maintained through indirection, as illustrated in Figure 2.1, the assignment B:= A results in all or part of the values of the objects associated with A and B being **shared**, which may produce undesirable side effects.

A role of Ada's limited private type is to safely represent objects whose values are represented through indirection. When a type is declared to be limited private:

1. Assignment may not be used with limited private types. This forces all attempts to create and manipulate limited private values to be performed through the subprograms made available with the encapsulated type.
2. Equality is defined for a limited private type only if it is defined in the package defining the type.
3. If a type contains a component that is limited private, then the new type must also be limited private. In particular, a limited private type may be used to instantiate a generic parameter only if the corresponding generic parameter is limited private.

At first, the inability to use assignment with limited private types appears to be too restrictive. The lack of access to the assignment operation is easily overcome by following a simple rule when creating packages that define limited private types. The rule is: When a limited private type is created, several subprograms should be provided to support the type. These subprograms may include

a. **procedure** Copy (Source: **in**   L_P_Type;
                      Target: **in out** L_P_Type);

This procedure properly duplicates the object value in Source and
assigns the duplicate to Target.

b. **procedure** Move_And_Reset (Source: **in out** L_P_Type;
                                  Target: **in out** L_P_Type);

or

procedure Swap (A, B: **in out** L_P_Type);

Sometimes duplication may be unnecessary and costly, because of either
the time or space required to duplicate the representation.
Move_And_Reset moves the value in Source to Target, then the value
of Source is set to the L_P_Type's known initialization value. In Swap,
the values of the variables, and hence the objects that correspond to those
variables, are swapped. Either procedure is usually easy to implement,
requiring just a few assignment statements to move or swap the dynamic
structure. It can be proven that the capabilities of one of these two
procedures may be derived from the other, hence they are logically
equivalent.

c. **function** "=" (Left, Right: L_P_Type) **return boolean**;

Define equality for the limited private type. If equality is
inappropriate for the type, then for the sake of consistency define it
anyway, but have the function raise an appropriate exception.

Naturally, other basic operations appropriate for the limited private types are
provided through the package. These include Initialize and Finalize,
which may be critical for safe and efficient dynamic storage allocation.

With copy and swap, along with equality, if appropriate, a client has all the
necessary support to manipulate limited private objects as if they were
private type. The only change is that where an assignment statement would be
used with a private type,

Able:= Baker;

it is replaced by the copy procedure,

Copy (Source => Baker, Target => Able);

or

```
      Copy (Baker, Able);
```

When generics contain `limited private` instantiation parameters, the three procedures described above should also be required as instantiation parameters, as in

```
      generic
         type Object_Type is limited private;
         with procedure Initialize
                                  (Source: in out Object_Type);
         with procedure Finalize (Source: in out Object_Type);
         with procedure Copy (Source: in      Object_Type;
                              Target: in out Object_Type);
         with procedure Swap (A, B: in out Object_Type);
      package Data_Structure_Lpt_Lpt is

         type Structure_Type is limited private;
            .  .  .
```

The `Swap` procedure is used to move `limited private` objects into and out of the structure being defined:

```
      procedure Object_Insertion
         (Element  : in out Object_Type;
          Structure: in out Structure_Type );
```

or

```
      procedure Object_Removal
         (Structure: in out Structure_Type;
          Element  : in out Object_Type );
```

Both would use `Swap` to transfer the value of the `Element` to and from the `Structure`. However,

```
      function Observe_Item
         (Structure: Structure_Type) return Object_Type;
```

would use `Copy` to make a duplicate of the element being observed. To guarantee that the package properly uses the client-supplied `Copy` and `Swap`, the package also requires access to `Initialize` and `Finalize`. For example, when `Swap` is used to place an object into a data structure, the object being swapped out must be initialized. When `Swap` is used to remove an object, the object swapped in must be `Finalized`.

When a `limited private` type is a parameter to a procedure, it may only be an `in` parameter or an `in out` parameter. `Limited private` types may not be `out` parameters. There is an important reason for this. Assume `out` parameters were admissible:

```
procedure Bad_Example (Source: in      L_P_Type;
                       Target:     out L_P_Type);
```

Let `L_P_Ptr` be an access associated to an object that uses dynamic storage to represent values of the object. `X` and `Y` are variables of this type,

```
X, Y: L_P_Ptr;
```

When `Bad_Example` is called,

```
Bad_Example (Source => X, Target => Y);
```

since `Y` is an `out` actual parameter, whatever value had been represented through `Y` before the call, the dynamic structure associated to `Y` before the call would be lost — it could not be recycled. However, if the parameter was `in out`,

```
procedure Good_Example (Source: in      L_P_Type;
                        Target: in out L_P_Type);
```

then in the call

```
Good_Example (Source => X, Target => Y);
```

since `Y` is `in out`, the procedure `Good_Example` has access to the value represented by the structure pointed to by `Y` before the call, and the dynamically allocated structure may be recycled before `Y` is assigned a new structure, representing a new value.

The fact that `out` parameters are not allowed for limited private types, forcing the use of `in out` parameters, does not guarantee the recycling of dynamic structures. It only provides the opportunity for recycling, which may or may not be carried out by the designers of the procedures.

2.3 Using Generic Packages

Once a client determines that a particular generic package contains the required resources, using a generic package is a two-step process. First the client

Listing 2.1. `Stack_Pt_Pt` specifications.

```
generic
   type Object_Type is private;
package Stack_Pt_Pt is

   Type Stack_Type (Max_Size: positive) is private;

   Stack_Underflow, Stack_Overflow: exception;

procedure Initialize (Stack: in out Stack_Type);

procedure Finalize (Stack: in out Stack_Type);

function Empty (Stack: in Stack_Type) return boolean;

function Top_Of (Stack: Stack_Type) return Object_Type;

procedure Pop (Stack : in out Stack_Type;
               Object:     out Object_Type);

procedure Pop (Stack: in out Stack_Type);

procedure Push (Object: in      Object_Type;
                Stack : in out Stack_Type );
private
   type Stack_Array_Type is array (positive range <>) of Object_Type;

   type Stack_Type (Max_Size: positive) is
      record
         Top    : integer:= 0;
         Actual: Stack_Array_Type (1..Max_Size);
      end record;
end Stack_Pt_Pt;
```

constructs an interface package that instantiates the generic package. Then the client uses the support that is now available through the instantiation.

To illustrate, assume a client wishes to use the stack package specifications to develop a software system that uses a stack to determine if a string of parentheses, brackets, and script brackets is properly matched (i.e., the string [[[()][{}]] is acceptable and [[]} is not). Assume the generic package Stack_Pt_Pt in Listing 2.1 satisfies the client's requirements. To use this package, the client must first instantiate the generic package. This instantiation is placed in a package that acts as an interface between the client's software and the generic package. An example of this interface appears in Listing 2.2.

The client's software system now references the package constructed by the client, Paren_Pak, and uses this instance of the generic package, Stack_Pt_Pt, in the construction of the client's software, as illustrated in Listing 2.3. In this example, the client references the package containing the instances, Paren_Pak,

Listing 2.2. Example instantiation a generic package.

```
with Stack_Pt_Pt;

package paren_pak is
   package stk is new Stack_Pt_Pt (character);

end paren_pak;
```

which contains an instance of the generic package. In this example, a `use` statement,

```
use Paren_Pak;
```

simplifies access to the instantiation in `Paren_Pak`. All references to stack resources are made to the instantiation, `stk`.

2.4 Object-Oriented Support

2.4.1 Tagged Types

Tagged types support two features that are fundamental to object-oriented programming: **type extension**, also called **polymorphism**, and **dynamic dispatch**. Type extension allows a software developer to derive a new type from an existing type by extending the declaration of an existing type. For a type to be extended, the type must first be declared as a `tagged` type. Tagged declarations are of the form

```
type identifier is [abstract] tagged
          {[limited] private|record declaration};
```

where `abstract` is described in Section 2.4.2, `private` and `limited private` have their normal implications, and the `record declaration` may be either a normal record declaration,

```
record  . . .    end record
```

or a shorthand declaration for a null record, `null`.

Listing 2.3. Software using client instantiation.

```
with paren_pak, text_io;
use paren_pak;
procedure parens is
   package tio renames text_io;
Symbol, Item: character;
Str          : string (1..200);
S_Size       : natural;
Stack        : Stk.Stack_Type (200);
OK           : boolean := true;
begin -- parens
   stk.Initialize (Stack);
   tio.Put ("Enter any string - checks for proper parenthesis matching");
   tio.New_Line;
   tio.Put ("  ([({()})((aa)]]) would be accepted, but (())) would not");
   tio.New_Line(2);
   tio.Put ("Enter Paren string: ");
   iio.Get_Line (Str, S_Size);
   tio.Put ("                    ");  Item := '(';
   for i in 1..S_Size loop
      case Str(i) is
         when '(' | '{' | '[' => Item := Str(i);
                                 stk.Push (Item, Stack); tio.Put(' ');
         when ')' => if stk.Top_Of(Stack) = '(' then
                        stk.Pop (Stack);  tio.put (' ');
                     else
                        tio.Put ("^ mismatch");    OK := false;  exit;
                     end if;
         when ']' => if stk.Top_Of(Stack) = '[' then
                        stk.Pop (Stack);  tio.put (' ');
                     else
                        tio.Put ("^ mismatch");    OK := false;  exit;
                     end if;
         when '}' => if stk.Top_Of(Stack) = '{' then
                        stk.Pop (Stack);  tio.put (' ');
                     else
                        tio.Put ("^ mismatch");
                        OK := false;  exit;
                     end if;
         when others => tio.Put (' ');
      end case;
   end loop;
   if OK then
      if stk.Empty (Stack) then
         tio.Put ("ACCEPTED"); tio.New_Line;
      else
         tio.Put("! unmatched parens"); tio.New_Line;
      end if;
   end if;
   stk.Finalize (Stack);
exception
   when stk.Stack_Underflow => tio.Put("^ Empty Stack"); tio.New_Line;
                               stk.Finalize (Stack);
end parens;
```

A tagged type declaration may be extended with type declarations of the form

```
type extended_type is new
     tagged_type with record declaration;
```

where `tagged_type` either is directly defined as a tagged type or has been derived from a tagged type. Listing 2.4 illustrates a tagged type declaration and extensions of a tagged type. The type `Figure` is declared as both tagged and abstract. `Abstract` types are discussed in Section 2.4.2. The implication of being a tagged type is that other types may be derived from a tagged type. Listing 2.4 illustrates three types derived from the `Figure` type. A derived type has all the features of the tagged type from which it was derived and the new attributes that may be added through the declaration of the new type. In the case of type `Figure`, the only attribute of `Figure` is a `Point`, a coordinate that locates, or anchors, a `Figure` in a Cartesian coordinate system. The three derived types each have additional attributes that extend the `Figure` type to include specific attributes that are needed to describe individual instances of the three derived types, `Circle`, `Rectangle`, and `Triangle`.

Each type, along with the subprograms that form the constructors and selectors for objects of that type, defines an object class. This is true for tagged types. Each tagged type, along with its subprograms, defines an object class, and each type extension defines a new collection of objects. Listing 2.4 defines four object types, `Figure`, `Circle`, `Rectangle`, and `Triangle`. The collection of a type and all the types derived from it is called the base type's `'Class`, which is discussed in Section 2.4.4.

Note that the type `Circle` is derived from `Figure` by adding a `Radius` to its attributes. The type `Triangle` adds two coordinates, `P2` and `P3`, to the original point in `Figure`. The three points define the three vertices of a triangle. The type `Rectangle` extends the type `Figure` by adding `Width` and `Height` attributes. Listing 2.5 contains the body for the package described in Listing 2.4.

Additional types may be derived from any of these types. A derived type need not add attributes. For example, one may wish to define

```
type Square is new Rectangle;
```

directly using the attributes of `Rectangle` and using other means to guarantee that the `Width` and `Height` of objects of type `Square` are equal. This is discussed in more detail in Section 2.4.5.

Listing 2.4. `Figures` **package specifications.**

```
package figures is

type Coordinate is
    record
        X, Y: float;
    end record;

type Figure is abstract tagged
    record
        Point: Coordinate;
    end record;
    function Area (F: Figure) return float is abstract;
    function Perimeter (F:Figure) return float is abstract;
    procedure Get (F: in out Figure) is abstract;
    procedure Put (F: Figure) is abstract;

type Circle is new Figure with
    record
        Radius: Float;
    end record;
    function Area (C: Circle) return float;
    function Perimeter (C: Circle) return float;
    procedure Get (C: in out Circle);
    procedure Put (C: Circle);

type Rectangle is new Figure with
    record
        Width: Float;
        Height: Float;
    end record;
    function Area (R: Rectangle) return float;
    function Perimeter (R: Rectangle) return float;
    procedure Get (R: in out Rectangle);
    procedure Put (R: Rectangle);

type Triangle is new Figure with
    record
        P2, P3: Coordinate;
    end record;
    function Area (T: Triangle) return float;
    function Perimeter (T: Triangle) return float;
    procedure Get (T: in out Triangle);
    procedure Put (T: Triangle);

end Figures;
```

2.4.2 Abstract Types

Sometime when tagged types are declared, the only purpose of the type is to be the base type from which other types are derived. If no variables of the type

Listing 2.5. Figures **package body.**

```
with Text_io, Ada.Numerics.Generic_Elementary_Functions;
package body figures is
   package fio is new text_io.float_io(float);
   package tio renames text_io;
   package math is new Ada.Numerics.Generic_Elementary_Functions (float);
   use math, Ada.Numerics;

function Almost (A, B: float; Epsilon: float:= 0.0001) return boolean is
   begin -- Almost
   if abs (A) < Epsilon then
      if abs (A-B) < Epsilon then
         return true;
       else
         return false;
      end if;
    elsif abs ((A-B)/A) < Epsilon then
      return true;
    else
      return false;
   end if;
   end Almost;
--------------------------------------------
procedure Get (C: in out Coordinate) is
   begin -- Get
      fio.Get (C.X);   fio.Get(C.Y);
   end Get;
--------------------------------------------
procedure Put (C: Coordinate) is
   begin -- Put
      tio.Put ('('); fio.Put(C.X); tio.Put(", ");
      fio.Put (C.Y); tio.Put (')');
   end Put;
--------------------------------------------
function Area (C: Circle) return float is
   begin -- Area (Circle)
      return C.radius*c.radius;
   end Area;
--------------------------------------------
function Perimeter (C: Circle) return float is
   begin -- Perimeter (Circle)
      return 2.0*pi*C.Radius;
   end Perimeter;
--------------------------------------------
procedure Get (C: in out Circle) is
   begin -- Get
      tio.Put ("Enter, x  y  r: "); Get (C.Point); fio.Get (C.Radius);
   end Get;
--------------------------------------------
procedure Put (C: Circle) is
   begin -- Put
      Put (C.Point); tio.Put(" r="); fio.Put (C.Radius); tio.Put ("  ");
   end Put;
--------------------------------------------
```

Listing 2.5. (cont.)

```
function Area (R: Rectangle) return float is
    begin -- Area
        return R.Width*R.Height;
    end Area;
--------------------------------------------
function Perimeter (R: Rectangle) return float is
    begin -- Perimeter
        return 2.0*(R.Width + R.Height);
    end Perimeter;
--------------------------------------------
procedure Get (R: in out Rectangle) is
    begin -- Get
    tio.Put ("Enter, x, y, w, h: ");
    Get (R.Point);
    fio.Get (R.Width); fio.Get (R.Height);
    end Get;
--------------------------------------------
procedure Put (R: Rectangle) is
    begin -- Put
    Put (R.Point); tio.Put(" W="); fio.Put (R.Width);
    tio.Put(" H="); fio.Put (R.Height); tio.Put ("  ");
    end Put;
--------------------------------------------
function Area (T: Triangle) return float is
    slope, Xb, Yb, Base, Height : float;
    begin -- Area
        if Almost (T.Point.x, T.P2.x) then
            Xb := T.Point.x; Yb := T.P3.y;
          elsif Almost (T.Point.y, T.P2.y) then
            Yb := T.Point.y; Xb := T.P3.x;
          else
            slope := (T.Point.y - T.P2.y) / (T.Point.x - T.P2.x);
            Xb := (T.P3.x + slope*slope*T.Point.x - slope*(T.P3.y-T.Point.y))
                    / (slope*slope + 1.0);
            Yb := slope*(Xb - T.Point.x) + T.Point.y;
        end if;
        Base := sqrt( (T.Point.x-T.P2.x)*(T.Point.x-T.P2.x)
                    + (T.Point.y-T.P2.y)*(T.Point.y-T.P2.y) );
        Height := sqrt( (Xb-T.P3.x)*(Xb-T.P3.x) + (Yb-T.P3.y)*(Yb-T.P3.y) );
        return 0.5*Base*Height;
    end Area;
--------------------------------------------
function Perimeter (T: Triangle) return float is
    DX1, DX2, DX3, DY1, DY2, DY3: float;
    begin -- Perimeter
        DX1 := (T.Point.x-T.P2.x);
        DX2 := (T.P2.X - T.P3.X);
        DX3 := (T.P3.X - T.Point.X);
        DY1 := (T.Point.Y-T.P2.Y);
        DY2 := (T.P2.Y - T.P3.Y);
        DY3 := (T.P3.Y - T.Point.Y);
        return sqrt (DX1*Dx1 + DY1*DY1) + sqrt (DX2*DX2 + DY2*DY2)
                + sqrt (DX3*DX3 + DY3*DY3);
    end Perimeter;
```

Listing 2.5. (cont.)

```
procedure Get (T: in out Triangle) is
   begin -- Get
   tio.Put ("Enter, x1  y1  x2  y2  x3  y3:");
   Get (T.Point); Get (T.P2); Get (T.P3);
   end Get;
   ------------------------------------------
procedure Put (T: Triangle) is
   begin -- Put
   Put (T.Point); Put (T.P2); Put (T.P3);
   tio.Put ("  ");
   end Put;
   ------------------------------------------
end Figures;
```

would serve a useful purpose, the developer of the type may restrict clients from declaring variables of the type by declaring the type to be abstract. For example, the type Figure, in Listing 2.4, is restricted in this fashion. With this declaration for Figure, statements like

```
      Any     : Figure;
```

would be flagged by the compiler as illegal. Simply stated, when a type is declared abstract, no variables of that type may be declared.

2.4.3 Abstract Subprograms

Sometimes a developer might create a type knowing that certain subprogram names might be dynamically dispatched, (as described in Section 2.4.5), for types derived from a particular type, but that such subprograms have no real meaning for the type itself. In this case, the software developer may declare the subprograms to be abstract. This is illustrated in Listing 2.4, where the notions of Area and Perimeter are not appropriate for the type Figure.

It should be noted that a type may be abstract and have a nonabstract subprogram. Although variables of that type may not exist, a type derived from an abstract type might dynamically dispatch the abstract type's subprogram because it may not have its own version of the subprogram and thus uses the version supplied for the abstract type.

2.4.4 'Class

For a tagged type, or types derived from tagged types, the 'Class of the type is a new type that includes the type and all types derived, implicitly or explicitly, from it. Since *type*'Class is a type, it may be utilized wherever a type may be used — to declare variables of that type, to declare formal parameters in subprograms, and so forth. In declaring formal parameters, as in,

```
procedure Analyze (F: in out Figure'Class;
                . . . );
```

any variable in Figure'Class may be passed to Analyze, a Circle, a Rectangle, or a Triangle. If the type Square is derived from type Rectangle, then the type Rectangle'Class encompasses both the types Rectangle and Square.

One may also declare access types to *type*'Class,

```
type Fig_Ptr_Type is access Figure'Class;
```

in which case the access type may point to any object in the extended class.

Variables of the extended type may be declared; however, one should consider the extended type as if it was a generic declaration. As such, additional information must be supplied to determine the particular type of object within the class when it is initialized. This is achieved by supplying an initialization in the declaration. For example, for Figure'Class, given the declarations

```
Fig_Ptr: Fig_Ptr_Type;
```

when a new dynamic Figure'Class is created, it must be given an initial value that determines the specific type within the class that is being created,

```
Fig_Ptr:= new Figure'Class'(sample);
```

where *sample* is a variable of any type within Figure'Class. Variables of type Figure'Class may be declared, but the declaration must indicate the specific type within the class that is being created. If a Figure'Class variable is declared in a procedure, it may be initialized using one of the procedure's parameters. For example, in the procedure

```
procedure Illustrate (Able : in out Fig_Ptr_Type) is
        Local_Var: Figure'Class'(Able.all);
```

```
begin -- Illustrate
  . . .
end Illustrate;
```

`Local_Var` becomes a variable of the same type being accessed by `Able`.

2.4.5 Dynamic Dispatch

Given all the types in `Figure'Class`, circles, rectangles, and triangles, each type requires unique operations to obtain the value of an object, `Get`, display the object's value, `Put`, and calculate correct values for their perimeters and areas. Suppose an access variable

```
type Fig_Ptr_Type is access Figure'Class;
  . . .

Fig_Ptr: Fig_Ptr_Type;
```

points to a variable and its area must be computed. It would be nice if the area computation was defined and the correct instance of the method `Area` is used when the computation is requested:

```
X:= Area(Fig_Ptr.all);
```

The run-time selection of the correct procedure, depending on the type of variable being passed, is referred to as **dynamic dispatch**.

Dynamic dispatch is achieved in Ada 95 in the following way: Recall that the specification for each object type is in two parts, the declaration of the type used to maintain attributes for objects of that type, followed immediately by the specification for all of the subprograms that may be dynamically dispatched for the type. Listing 2.4 illustrates the object declarations for `Figure`, `Circle`, `Rectangle`, and `Triangle`, which includes the specifications for the `Get`, `Put`, `Area`, and `Perimeter` subprograms.

As each of the types derived from `Figure` is defined, the type declaration must be followed by the specifications of the subprograms that may be dynamically dispatched with this type, as illustrated in Listing 2.4. Other derived types and their dynamically dispatched subprograms are specified similarly. These specifications may be encapsulated in separate packages or together in a single package.

Once the types are packaged along with their dynamically dispatchable subprograms, a procedure may employ these packages and call upon the dynamic dispatch of the subprograms. Listing 2.6 illustrates dynamic dispatch. Note that each time through the loop, the calls to Get, Put, Area, and Perimeter are all dynamically dispatched, depending on the type of object accessed by Point.

It should be noted that there is no requirement that each type has its own version of every dynamically dispatchable subprogram. If the run time system is to dispatch a subprogram for an object whose type does not have its own version of the subprogram, the run-time system then looks for a version of the subprogram for the type from which the given type was derived. If the run-time system finds a version of the subprogram for that type, it uses that version. Otherwise it continues searching toward the root tagged type for a usable subprogram. If none is found, a run-time exception is raised.

For example, the declaration of the object type Square might be

```
type Square is new Rectangle;
    procedure Get (S: in out Square);
```

where

```
procedure Get (S: in out Square) is
    begin -- Get
        tio.Put ("Enter, x, y, s: ");
        Get (S.Point);
        fio.Get (S.Width);
        S.Height:= S.Width;
    end Get;
```

Get for squares would obtain the anchor point and the length of a side, then place the length in both the Width and Height components. As a result, the Put, Area, and Perimeter subprograms for Rectangle would be dynamically dispatched, and produce correct results when an object of type Square is dispatched for them.

Then, if

```
S: Square
```

and

```
Point:= new Figure'Class'(S);
```

are used, then

```
Get (Point.all);
```

Listing 2.6. Example use of `Figures` package.

```
with text_io, figures, unchecked_deallocation;
use figures;
procedure uses_figures is

   package fio is new text_io.float_io(float);
   package iio is new text_io.integer_io(integer);

   type f_Ptr_Type is access figure'class;
   procedure free is new unchecked_deallocation (figure'class, f_ptr_Type);
Choice: positive;
C: Circle; R: Rectangle; T:Triangle;
Point: F_Ptr_Type;

begin -- uses_figures
text_io.Put ("Select Object type (1=Circle, 2=Rectangle, 3=Triangle): ");
iio.Get (Choice); text_io.Skip_line;
while Choice < 4 loop
   Case Choice is
      when 1 => Point:= new figure'class'(C);
      when 2 => Point:= new figure'class'(R);
      when 3 => Point:= new figure'class'(T);
      when others => raise constraint_error;
   End Case;
   Get (Point.all); -- Dyn Dispatched
   text_io.Skip_Line;
   Put (Point.all); -- Dyn Dispatched
   text_io.New_Line;
   Text_io.Put ("Perimeter ="); fio.Put (Perimeter(Point.all));
   --                                     ^^^^^^^^^ Dyn Dispatched
   Text_io.Put (",  Area ="); fio.Put (Area(Point.all));
   --                                  ^^^^ Dyn Dispatched
   Text_IO.New_Line (2);
   text_io.Put("Select Object type (1=Circle, 2=Rectangle, 3=Triangle,
Quit>3): ");
   iio.Get (Choice); text_io.Skip_line;
end loop;
end uses_figures;
```

would dispatch `Get` for `Squares`, while calls to `Put`, `Area`, and `Perimeter`
would dispatch the versions of these subprograms for `Rectangle` objects.

2.4.6 Controlled Types

The `Ada.Finalization` package supports the automatic initialization and
finalization of objects, like those whose values are represented through the use of
indirection. The package, whose specifications appear in Listing 2.7, supports
two new types, `controlled` and `limited controlled`. These types are

Listing 2.7. `Ada.Finalization` **specifications.**

```
with System.Finalization_Implementation
use System
package Ada.Finalization is

type Controlled is abstract new Finalization_Implementation.Root_Controlled
       with null record;

procedure Initialize (Object: in out Controlled);
procedure Adjust (Object: in out Controlled) is abstract;
procedure Finalize (Object: in out Controlled) is abstract;

Root_Part: Finalization_Implementation.Root_Controlled
   renames Finalization_implementation.Root_Part;

type Limited_Controlled is abstract new
       Finalization_Implementation.Root_Limited_Controlled
       with null record;

procedure Initialize (Object: in out Limited_Controlled);
procedure Finalize (Object: in out Limited_Controlled) is abstract;

end Ada.Finalization;
```

special tagged types. Software developers may create polymorphisms of these tagged types. Further, the procedures `Initialize` and `Finalize` are dynamically dispatched for extensions of these types. Also, the procedure `Adjust` is dynamically dispatched for extensions of `Controlled` type.

The procedures `Initialize` and `Finalize` are automatically invoked by the system. When Ada begins execution of a procedure in which an object is an extension of a controlled type, limited or otherwise, the `Initialize` procedure is dynamically dispatched, if declared, for that object. Use of this feature guarantees that each object is initialized and finalized.

When a procedure terminates and the procedure contains objects that are `controlled` types, the `Finalize` procedure is dynamically dispatched for each controlled object for which `Finalize` was defined. `Finalize` is critical to controlling the loss, or leakage, of dynamically allocated space. Just as `Initialize` provides an opportunity for a software developer to place an initial value in an object, when the initial value requires the creation of a dynamically allocated structure, `Finalize` provides the software developer with the opportunity to reclaim that space. With the system's automatic invocations of these two procedures, the software developer is guaranteed correct initialization of objects with initial values and an opportunity to reclaim dynamically allocated space when an object is no longer in use.

The assignment statement may be used with `controlled` types. Section 2.2.2.2 describes the problem surrounding the use of assignment with objects whose values are represented through indirection. The role of the procedure `Adjust` is to overcome that problem. Given an assignment statement involving `controlled` types,

```
A:= . . .
```

the system calls `Adjust` in the process of performing the assignment. An assignment is performed with the following five-step process:

1. The right-hand side is calculated.
2. The left-hand side is finalized.
3. The left-hand side is initialized.
4. The right-hand side result is passed to `Adjust`.
5. The result after adjusting is placed in the left-hand side.

Why is the finalization package so important? Simply stated, when using Ada 83, many software developers frequently used `private` types in an unsafe manner. For one reason or other, many software developers avoided using `limited private` types. `Limited private` types are not difficult to use as long as their needs are addressed. With Ada 95, if developers take the time to properly use the `Ada.Finalization` package by using `controlled` with `private` declarations, the `private` type will safely interact with assignment statements and be free from storage leakage and undesirable side effects.

By deriving a new `controlled` type from an existing `controlled` type and building `Initialize`, `Adjust`, and `Finalize` procedures, a client is guaranteed that the objects are correctly initialized and safely manipulated with assignment statements and that the structure is finalized without the loss of dynamically allocated storage. `Finalize` is called when a `controlled` object's value must be terminated. `Initialize` is automatically called when a procedure containing a `controlled` object is initialized. `Adjust` is called when a controlled variable is assigned to another variable. `Adjust` provides an opportunity for the software developer to adjust the variable before its value is assigned to the left-hand side.

2.5 Using Object-Oriented Packaging

As in the case of generic packaging, after determining the type of structure required to assist in solving a problem, the client uses a two-step process to interface an object-oriented, or polymorphic, package to the software under construction. First, the client constructs a package that contains the type extensions, or polymorphisms, of the tagged or controlled types supported by the base package. Next, the client uses the items provided through the base package along with the type extensions, and other support, constructed in the client's interface support package.

Consider the example polymorphic package in Listing 2.8. It is typical of the polymorphic package method used throughout this text. Note that all polymorphisms in this package are based on `controlled` types. This takes advantage of automatic initialization, finalization, and adjustment during assignment. Also, observe that two `controlled` types are made visible with this package: the data structure, `Stack_Type`, and the `Place_Holder` type that the client will extend in order to place objects into the stack.

Consider the situation described in Section 2.3, where the client needs a stack. The client creates a package to serve as the interface between the polymorphic package and the client's software. This interface package is illustrated in Listing 2.9. In this example, the client renames the polymorphic package,

```
package STK renames Stack_Polymorphic_Cntl;
```

to simplify references, as well as a type extension of `Placeholder` type, called `Paren_Type`, to assist in managing the client's objects in stacks.

The client then uses the resources available in the polymorphic package through the client's interface, as illustrated in Listing 2.10. Note the generic instantiation of the `Top_Value` function made visible as `stk`, `Stack_Polymorphic_Controlled`, in Listing 2.10. When utilizing type extensions, the client must be aware of the relationship between any type extension and the `'Class` type of the base type. An object of the extended type is a valid object of the base type's `'Class`. However, an object in the base type's `'Class` is not a valid object in the extended type. In the software in Listing 2.10, `Item` is of `Paren_Type`, a type extension of `Placeholder` and hence a valid object in `Placeholder'Class`. Consequently, `Item` may be passed to `Push` as a parameter of `Placeholder'Class` type. However, once passed, the object is a `Placeholder'Class` type object. To get the object back into a `Paren_Type`, the client must perform an explicit type conversion to move the object value from a `Placeholder'Class` object back to a `Paren_Type`. The instantiation,

Listing 2.8. Example of a polymorphic package.

```
with Ada.Finalization;    Use Ada.Finalization;
package Stack_Polymorphic_Cntl is

type Place_Holder is abstract new controlled with private;
   procedure Initialize (Source: in out Place_Holder);
   procedure Finalize (Source: in out Place_Holder);
   procedure Adjust (Source: in out Place_Holder);

type Holder_Class_Ptr is access Place_Holder'Class;
   procedure Recycle (Point: in out Holder_Class_Ptr);

type Stack_Type is new controlled with private;
   procedure Initialize (Stack: in out Stack_Type);
   procedure Finalize (Stack: in out Stack_Type);
   procedure Adjust (Stack: in out Stack_Type);

   Stack_Underflow: exception;
   Stack_Overflow : exception;

function Empty (Stack: Stack_Type) return boolean;

function Empty_Stack return Stack_Type;

generic
   type Extended_Type is new Place_Holder with private;
function Top_Value (Stack: Stack_Type) return Extended_Type;

function Top_Of (Stack: Stack_Type) return Holder_Class_Ptr;

procedure Pop (Stack : in out Stack_Type;
               Object: in out Holder_Class_Ptr);
generic
   type Extended_Type is new Place_Holder with private;
procedure Ex_Pop (Stack : in out Stack_Type;
                  Object:    out Extended_Type);
procedure Pop (Stack: in out Stack_Type);

procedure Push (Object: in     Place_Holder'Class;
                Stack : in out Stack_Type);

procedure Swap (Source: in out Stack_Type;
                Target: in out Stack_Type);
private
   type Place_Holder is abstract new controlled with
      record
         Next: Holder_Class_Ptr:= null;
      end record;
   type Stack_Type is new controlled with
      record
         Top : Holder_Class_Ptr:= null;
         Size: natural:= 0;
      end record;
end Stack_Polymorphic_Cntl;
```

Listing 2.9. Sample object-oriented client interface package.

```
with Stack_Polymorphic_Cntl;   use Stack_Polymorphic_Cntl;

package OO_paren_pak is

   package stk renames Stack_Polymorphic_Cntl;

type paren_Type is new stk.Place_Holder with
     record
        Sym: character;
     end record;

end OO_paren_pak;
```

Paren_Top, of the generic function Top_Value provides the client with a convenient function that performs the required type conversion.

The client has a second choice for retrieving objects back from the structure, which is essential when the client is placing objects of more than one type extension into a structure.   This second approach uses the type Holder_Class_Ptr. Instead of receiving the object back as a client's extended type, the client employs the access type Holder_Class_Ptr, which points to the returning object. The client may now perform a type conversion, or dynamic dispatch, to handle the returning object. This approach might change the example in Listing 2.10 as follows: First, the client would declare an access type:

```
Point: Holder_Class_Ptr;
```

This access type would be used to obtain the value at the top of the stack:

```
Point:= Top_Of (Stack);
```

This approach would replace the statement

```
if Paren_Top(Stack).Sym = '[' then
```

with

```
if Paren_Type(Top_Of(Stack)).Sym = '[' then
```

requiring the client to explicitly perform the type conversion as well as the dereference.

Listing 2.10. Example use of object-oriented packaging.

```
with OO_paren_pak, text_io;
use OO_paren_pak;
procedure OO_parens is
   package tio renames text_io;
   function Paren_Top is new stk.Top_Value (Paren_Type);

Symbol, Item: Paren_Type;
Str          : string (1..200);
S_Size       : natural;
Stack        : Stk.Stack_Type;
OK           : boolean:= true;

begin -- parens
   tio.Put ("Enter any string - checks for proper parenthesis matching");
   tio.New_Line;
   tio.Put ("   ([({()})]((aa))]) would be accepted, but ((())) would not");
   tio.New_Line(2);
   tio.Put ("Enter Paren string: ");
   tio.Get_Line (Str, S_Size);
   tio.Put ("                   ");
   Item.Sym:= '(';
   for i in 1..S_Size loop
      case Str(i) is
         when '(' | '{' | '[' => Item.Sym:= Str(i);
                                 stk.Push (Item, Stack); tio.Put(' ');
         when ')' => if Paren_Top(Stack).Sym = '(' then
                        stk.Pop (Stack);  tio.put (' ');
                     else
                        tio.Put ("^ mismatch");  OK:= false;  exit;
                     end if;
         when ']' => if Paren_Top(Stack).Sym = '[' then
                        stk.Pop (Stack);  tio.put (' ');
                     else
                        tio.Put ("^ mismatch");  OK:= false;  exit;
                     end if;
         when '}' => if Paren_Top(Stack).Sym = '{' then
                        stk.Pop (Stack);  tio.put (' ');
                     else
                        tio.Put ("^ mismatch");  OK:= false;  exit;
                     end if;
         when others => tio.Put (' ');
      end case;
   end loop;
   if OK then
      if stk.Empty (Stack) then
         tio.Put ("ACCEPTED"); tio.New_Line;
      else
         tio.Put("! unmatched parens"); tio.New_Line;
      end if;
   end if;
exception
      when stk.Stack_Underflow => tio.Put("^ Empty Stack"); tio.New_Line;
end OO_parens;
```

2.5.1 Polymorphic Versus Generic Packaging

Generics and polymorphism are two important software development tools. Polymorphism was not available in Ada 83, hence programmers with substantial Ada 83 experience tend to feel very comfortable with generics. On the other hand, polymorphism, and in particular Ada's controlled types, offers the attractive alternative of automatic initialization and finalization, as well as the use of `Adjust` during assignments. There is not a simple choice of one versus the other. Note that the polymorphic package in Listing 2.8 contains two generic functions.

Many software development decisions involve the choice between tradeoffs; so does this one. While generic packaging is easy to use, it typically requires the software developer to make available a number of generic packagings of a particular data structure in order to safely and efficiently handle the variety of representations of client objects and data structures. A key to understanding this is comprehending the choice that must be made between `private` and `limited private` visibility. To some extent, the use of `controlled` types in polymorphic packaging simplifies this choices. The automatic initialization and finalization address a number of software development concerns. Also, `Adjust` provides a safe and efficient alternative to the `private` versus `limited private` visibility issue.

2.6 A Taxonomy of Client/Package Visibility

When building a package to encapsulate a component, a software developer may wish to build many encapsulations to supply various combinations of the visibility of the client's instantiating object type with the visibility of the package's data structure type. If clients expect a certain access level of their objects by the package, then the clients should expect that their objects are manipulated in a safe, efficient manner. On the other hand, when the package makes a data structure visible in a particular way, clients should expect the structure to be safe when properly used.

There are many possible combinations of relationships between the visibility of the user's instantiating object type and the visibility of the package's object type to the user. The naming convention, `PackageObject_InstantiatingType_PackageVisibility` is used in this text to generically indicate the object types a client may use to instantiate a package, `InstantiatingType`, and the method the package uses when it makes data

structures available, *PackageVisibility*. For example, the package named
`Stack_Pt_Lpt` will be a stack package where the user's instantiating object type
is private, `Pt`, and the package makes stacks available as limited private types,
`Lpt`. The other user-package visibilities are bound, tagged, controlled, and
encapsulated, which will be indicated in the package's name with the notations
`Bnd`, `Tag`, `Cntl`, and `En`, respectively. Throughout subsequent chapters, some the
versions of packages are presented as examples, while others are left for
exploration.

2.6.1 Safe Handling of User Objects

When a user is about to select a package, what should the user look for in order
to guarantee that the package safely manages the user's objects? Users should
be aware of the complexity of their objects and what is necessary to manipulate
the objects safely. This section discusses the possible complexity of the user's
object type and its correspondence for a particular package instantiation.

2.6.1.1 `Private`

The simplest situation for a user is when the user's instantiating object type
completely contains the values of the objects represented by the type. In these
cases, the user may safely use a package where the instantiating object type is
`private`:

```
generic
    type Object_Type is private;
package Structure_Type_Private_Structure_Visibility
    .  .  .
```

Basically, as long as the representations of the values of the user's instantiating
type are completely contained within variables of that type, they may be passed
as a `private` type. As long as the representation of values is bound and does
not include the use of any indirection or dynamic allocation, `private`
instantiation is safe.

A user may wish to declare the instantiating `Object_Type` that is used to
instantiate the package with initializing attributes:

```
type Client_Object_Type is
   record
      ... := [initial value];
   end record;
```

In this way, the client ensures that when the data structure creates dynamic records that contain the object, these records will contain objects with the known initialized value.

2.6.1.2 Limited Private

When a client wishes to place unbound nonpolymorphic objects into a data structure, instantiating the package with a `limited private` object type is the safest method. But if an object type is `limited private`, the package requires that the client provide the means for the package to safely manipulate the objects, as discussed in Section 2.2.2.2. Therefore, packages that are instantiated with `limited private` types must include sufficient support for safe and efficient manipulation of objects of that type, as in

```
generic
   type Object_Type is limited private;
   with procedure Initialize
           (Source: in out Object_Type);
   with procedure Finalize (Source: in out Object_Type);
   with procedure Copy (Source: in     Object_Type;
                        Target: in out Object_Type);
   with procedure Swap (A, B: in out Object_Type);
   package Data_Structure_Lpt_Lpt is

      . . . ;
```

When it is not obvious from the actions of the package's subprograms, the specifications of the package's subprograms should indicate whether copy or swap is used to perform the action. For efficiency, the client should assume that the `Swap` procedure is used to move the client's object in and out of the structure. Objects swapped out of the package when an object value is swapped in should be `Initialized`. Also, the client should assume that the package properly `Finalizes` values of objects in records as the records are removed from the structure.

Clients should be prepared for the extra effort required when instantiating an object with a `limited private` type. This requires the client to prepare the four procedures that replace the generic subprograms `Initialize`, `Finalize`, `Copy`, and `Swap`:

```
package Client_Pak is new Data_Structure_Lpt_???
    (Object_Type => My_Type,
     Initialize  => My_Init,
     Finalize    => My_Final,
     Copy        => My_Copy,
     Swap        => My_Swap);
```

However, these four procedures should be part of the normal repertoire of subprograms provided with any `limited private` type. For example, the discussions of `limited private` encapsulation of data structures in Section 2.6.2.2 encourages that all subprograms that make a package reusable should be made available for clients. The discussion of composability of data structures in Section 2.7 states that the procedures `Initialize`, `Finalize`, `Copy`, and `Swap` must be made available when a data structure is made visible as a `limited private` in order to make the structure composable.

2.6.1.3 `Tagged`

When a `tagged` type is used to instantiate a package,

```
generic
    type Object_Type is Tagged private;
package Data_Structure_Tag_??? is
```

the package must be prepared to assist the user in handling `Object_Type'Class`. To assist in handling polymorphisms, the package should provide an access type

```
type Object_Ptr is access Object_Type'Class
```

and appropriate subprograms for inserting and removing objects. Specifically, procedures for inserting objects into the structure should handle `Object_Type'Class`:

```
procedure Insert_Object
    (Object   : in     Object_Type'Class;
     Structure: in out Structure_Type);
```

To assist the client in removing objects from the structure, it may be appropriate to provide two subprograms for each method of removing objects, one for use when the client knows the precise object type in `Object_Type'Class` that will be removed,

```
procedure Remove_Object
     (Structure: in out Structure_Type;
      Object    :     out Object_Type'Class);
```

and one for use when the client is not sure of the specific type of the object within `Object_Type'Class` that is about to be removed,

```
procedure Remove_Object
     (Structure: in out Structure_Type;
      Point     :     out Object_Ptr);
```

This approach encourages reuse by providing the client a choice, which makes it easier to use the package instead of building a new package.

2.6.1.4 Controlled

Since `controlled` types allow users to perform safe assignment on objects whose values are implemented through indirection, many users do not appreciate that although assignment is safe with `controlled` types, assignment might not be the most efficient way of carrying out the many manipulations of objects. For this reason, packages that may be instantiated with `controlled` types

```
with Ada.Finalization;   use Ada.Finalization;
generic
    type Object_Type is controlled with private;
    with procedure Swap
            (Source, Target: in out Object_Type);
package Data_Structure_Cntl_??? is
```

should require the user to supply a `Swap` procedure. This provides the user with an opportunity to furnish the package with an efficient means of moving objects. Note that the user's `controlled` type is accepted as a `private` type.

A package that would be instantiated with a `limited controlled` type would have generic parameters of the form

```
generic
    type Object_Type is limited private;
    with procedure Copy (Source: in      Object_Type;
                         Target: in out Object_Type);
    with procedure Swap
            (Source, Target: in out Object_Type);
```

```
package Data_Structure_Cntl_??? is
   . . .

end Data_Structure_Cntl_???;
```

2.6.2 Safe Encapsulation of Data Structures

2.6.2.1 `Private`

Since the assignment operation is available for unlimited `private` types, when `private` types present a package's data structure type, there is a tacit assumption that assignment may be freely used by the client. The only way a package may safely provide a data structure as an unlimited `private` type is when the structure is bound and does not use indirection. Simply stated, that implies that the value of the stack is entirely encapsulated within the variable made available to represent the structure.

There are many data structure applications where the client is aware of the maximum size of the data structure required for the system being built. In these cases, there are substantial time and space efficiencies associated with the selection of a bound representation. Bound representations usually imply that the data structure is represented with some combination of static arrays and records. Besides the obvious time advantage associated with access to static structures over access to dynamically allocated structures, the space requirements associated with dynamic storage allocation could be costly relative to the cost of static representations.

When a data structure is made available as a private type,

```
generic
   type ... ;
package data_structure_???_Pt is
   . . .
   type Structure_Type (Max_Size: positive) is private;
   . . .
```

the structure may be made with a discriminant that allows the client to state the sizes of the structure as each object is defined:

```
Small : Structure (5);
Medium: Structure (40);
Large : Structure (1000);
```

2.6.2.2 Limited Private

If a software developer cannot predetermine bounds on the sizes for a data structure type needed to solve a problem, then dynamic storage allocation must be used. When dynamic storage allocation is used, it should be encapsulated as a limited private type:

```
generic
    type ... ;
package data_structure_???_Lpt is
    . . .
    type Structure_Type is limited private;
    . . .
```

If the package makes a Structure_Type available as a limited private type, it should include sufficient resources to allow package clients to manipulate the structure. The package specifications should include Copy and Swap, as suggested in Section 2.1.3.2, and initialization and finalization procedures, as suggested in Section 2.2.1:

```
generic
    type ... ;
package data_structure_???_Lpt is

    . . .
    type Structure_Type is limited private;
    . . .

    procedure Initialize
                    (Structure: in out Structure_Type);
    procedure Finalize
                    (Structure: in out Structure_Type);
    procedure Copy (Source: in      Structure_Type;
                    Target: in out Structure_Type);
    procedure Swap (Source: in out Structure_Type;
                    Target: in out Structure_Type);
    . . .
```

These procedures allow a client to initialize, finalize, duplicate, and swap data structure objects in a safe and efficient manner. They also play an important role in safe composability of structures, as discussed in Section 2.7.

2.6.2.3 `Controlled`

Most clients find that having a data structure available as a `controlled` type is usually the most convenient form of the structure. Recall that `controlled` types provide for automatic initialization and finalization of objects and may be safely used with assignment statements. When a package makes a `controlled` type available, the package should also contain a `Swap` procedure so that the data structure might be composable, as described in Section 2.7. Also, since it is assumed that `controlled` types are automatically initialized and finalized, and may be safely assigned, the package should contain `Initialize`, `Finalize`, and `Adjust` procedures. However, these three procedures are not meant to be directly used by clients and hence should appear in the private part of the package:

```
with Ada.Finalization; Use Ada.Finalization;
generic
   type  . . .
package Data_Structure_???_Cntl is
   . . .
   type Structure_Type is controlled with private;
   . . .

   procedure Swap
             (Source, Target: in out Structure_Type);
   . . .

private
   procedure Initialize
               (Structure: in out Structure_Type);
   procedure Finalize
               (Structure: in out Structure_Type);
   procedure Adjust (Structure: in out Structure_Type);
   . . .
end Data_Structure_???_Cntl;
```

One might be tempted always to use this approach. In general, when in doubt, clients should use the safest approach available, and `controlled` types are safe. However, `controlled` types have a system overhead that may be inappropriate in certain situations, especially those with extremely limited time and space constraints.

In general, we recommend that the `controlled` type, along with the encapsulated structures described in Section 2.6.2.4, be the preferred encapsulation choice by clients when using a data structure. As clients become more aware of their problem's use of a data structure, then they should consider other encapsulations that may safely serve their problem's requirements.

2.6.2.4 Encapsulated

Perhaps the simplest, and safest, way to package a data structure is to completely hide the structure within the package. In this approach each structure is hidden within a package, one structure per package instantiation. Simply stated, if the client can't even see a structure, there is less chance that a client may inadvertently misuse it. There are several very recognizable features when a package totally encapsulates a data structure:

```
generic
   type . . . ;
package Data_Structure_???_En is
   . . .
   procedure Insertion (Object: in    Object_Type);
   . . .
   procedure Removal (Object: in out Object_Type);
   . . .
end Data_Structure_???_En;
```

First, the package does not make any data structure type declaration visible to the client. Second, none of the subprograms that manipulate the package's structure makes any reference to that structure. Finally, when a client uses a totally encapsulated structure, the client may consider the instantiations **to be** the structure:

```
package My_Str is new Data_Structure_???_En (xxx);
```

The client accesses the structure using the dotted reference notation, as in

```
My_Str.Insertion (abc);
```

There are two very real advantages for clients when they use totally encapsulated structures. First, since the structure is completely hidden, the mechanisms for using the structure are simplified. Second, encapsulated structures encourage clients to use dotted notation to manipulate the structure.

Totally encapsulated structures have several serious limitations. If the client needs access to more than one data structure object, then totally encapsulated structures may be inappropriate. Since the structure is completely hidden within the package instantiation, the structure cannot be placed into other structures. Also, total encapsulation cannot hold structures that are represented recursively, as will be discussed in Chapter 5. However, despite these limitations, total encapsulation hides data structure details and hence can be very useful in many circumstances.

2.7 Composability

From a reusability point of view, composability is an important issue. Simply stated, just as clients may use any structure they create to instantiate an appropriate client/structure visibility package of a data structure, instantiated data structures may be used to instantiate other data structures. The naming scheme used in this book makes it easy to address **composability**, the construction of a new data structure by placing one data structure within another, for example, a binary tree of lists, or a priority queue of trees. Simply stated, given two data structures, `Alpha_xxx_yyy` and `Beta_yyy_zzz`, any instantiation of the structure `Alpha` may be used to instantiate `Beta_yyy_zzz` because `Alpha` is made visible in the form indicated by `yyy` and `Beta_yyy_zzz` is instantiated by structure types of the form `yyy`. Polymorphic data structures may be composed in a similar manner.

To many clients this might seem to be a minor issue, but as clients tackle more complex problems, solutions will involve circumstances where clients create new object classes through the composition of other object classes. Several examples of this scenario are described in this book.

2.8 Child Units

When software developers package objects, they are frequently faced with the dilemma of balancing the number of subprograms in a package with the perceived readability and reusability of the package. For example, in presenting the data structures in this text, the decision was made that each package would present a pure and usable version of each data structure. Additional features that clients may find helpful appear in child packages.

The process of constructing and using child units is straightforward. However, the package developer, of both the parent unit and the child unit, must be cautious when constructing packages because of the child unit's access to the private declarations in the parent unit, as illustrated in Listing 2.11. The part of the package specification that precedes the private declarations are visible to all; the part of a package in the body of a package is visible to no one; but the private declarations are visible to a package and all its child units. In a sense, because of child units, the private declarations are no longer completely private. This means that great care must be taken when constructing parent and child units, to make sure that the child unit does not perform any actions on information made available to the child unit through the private declarations that may jeopardize the

Listing 2.11. Visibility of parent package part.

```
package Parent is

  . . .

  -- PUBLIC  Everyone see this
  . . .

private
  . . .

  -- SEMI-PRIVATE  The Parent and its children see this
  . . .

end Parent;

package body Parent is

  . . .

  -- VERY PRIVATE  Really private stuff

  . . .

end Parent;
```

integrity of the package or other child units.

With data structures, parent units are appropriate for encapsulating the fundamental resources for a data structure. Child units are an appropriate means for encapsulating additional features and resources that clients may find useful but are not typically thought of as part of the fundamental support for the structure. The encapsulation of features that go beyond the basic features of a package are best placed in child units. Generally, the basic format of the parent unit dictates the form of the child unit. A child unit's name is *parent_name.Child_name*. For example, the `Advanced` child unit for `Stack_Pt_Lpt` has the name `Stack_Pt_Lpt.Advanced`.

It is possible to have child units of a child unit, in which case the name would be *parent.child.grand_child*. When producing a child unit, the software developer may assume that the child unit has access to the parent unit's specifications. For example, while writing the body for a parent or child unit, the developer may use the resources made visible in any package, including the package's parent or the package's child, as long as the resources do not depend on the resource being constructed, causing an unresolvable interdependence.

When clients use both a child unit and its parent, there need only be a `with` statement for the child unit

```
with Stack_Pt_Lpt.Advanced;
```

to provide access to the child package and its ancestors.

There are a variety of advantages to child units. For example, from the viewpoint of developing and maintaining large systems, it is easier to maintain several smaller interrelated packages than to maintain one big package. When a child unit is modified, only those packages that depend on that unit must be recompiled. This can produce an enormous savings both in computer time and in the work effort for developers.

2.8.1 Generic Child Units

Child units of a generic unit are generic. The parent unit's instantiation parameters, as in

```
generic
   type Object_Type is private;
package Stack_Pt_Lpt is
      . . .
end Stack_Pt_Lpt;
```

are not repeated in the child unit, as in

```
generic
   -- [Additional generic parameters here]
package Stack_Pt_Lpt is
      . . .
end Stack_Pt_Lpt;
```

However, it is possible that a generic unit may have additional generic parameters, which would be declared as indicated above.

A generic child unit must be instantiated like any other generic unit. The generic parent unit must be instantiated first:

```
package Parent_Inst is new Gen_Pak (...);
```

The instantiated package includes information about the children of the original generic package. Instances of the generic children may now be created by referencing a generic child unit relative to the newly instantiated parent:

```
package Child_Inst is new Parent_Inst.Generic_Child
        (additional child instantiation parameters here);
```

For example, if support for a stack of `characters` is instantiated from `Stack_Pt_Lpt` and the `Advanced` child unit is required, then

```
package Ch_Stk is new Stack_Pt_Lpt (Character);
```

instantiated the parent package and

```
package Adv_Support is new Ch_Stk.Advanced;
```

creates an instance of the `Advanced` child, `Adv_Support`, that may be used with `Ch_Stk`.

It is possible for the generic child unit to have additional instantiation parameters. In this case, only the additional instantiation parameters are indicated in the child unit's specifications

```
generic
    Child_Pak_instantiation_parms;
package Generic_Child is
    . . .
end Generic_Child;
```

and the replacements for the child unit's additional generic instantiation parameters must appear with the instantiation of the child unit:

```
package Child_Inst is new
            Parent_Inst.Generic_Child (replacements);
```

2.9 Explorations

1. Elaborate on bounded representation issues.

2. Elaborate on bounded objects whose representations use discriminants.

3. Construct a `Polynomial` package with polynomials represented with `controlled` types.

3

Stacks

3.1 Linear Structures

This and the following two chapters describe three important **logically linear structures**: stacks, queues, and lists. Each structure is **linear** in that a linear ordering is maintained among objects within the structure. The linear relationship is **logical** in that, unlike arrays, no assumption may be made regarding any relationship between the linear ordering of the objects and their actual locations in memory. These structures are distinguished from each other by the restrictions on the ways objects are accessed with respect to each structure.

These data structures have the **linear access** property in that there is a linear time dependence on the access to objects within the structure. The time required to access the ith object in any of these structures is $T = O(i)$. For example, with a stack, the key access position is the top, which may be considered the first object in the stack. Access to the object in the ith position from the top requires time of order i, $O(i)$. This time dependence it not necessarily bad. Each structure provides a particular method of organizing data. When an application requires the organization provided by a particular structure, the structure's time-dependent access should be an acceptable cost of applying the structure safely.

There are four basic variations of dynamic linearly linked representations. The four variations are achieved through two choices associated with dynamic linearly linked structures. One choice is associated with how the last access type

	One Link	Two Links
Ground	One Way Ground Linearly Linked Structure	Two Way Ground Linearly Linked Structure
Circular	One Way Circular Linearly Linked Structure	Two Way Circular Linearly Linked Structure

Figure 3.1. Linear linking variations.

in the last record of the linearly linked structure is handled. There are two typical possibilities: Either make the access type null, or make it point to the first record in the structure. If the access type in the last record is null, the structure is said to be **grounded** and indicated with the electronic ground symbol. If the access type in the last record points to the first record in the structure, then the structure is said to be **circular**.

A second choice is to decide whether to have one or two access types per record, one pointing to the next record in the linear structure and one pointing to the previous record in the linear structure. A linearly linked structure with only one access type per record is called a **one-way linearly linked structure**. A linear structure with two access types per record is called a **two-way linearly linked structure**. Combining the ground or circular variation with the one-way and two-way variations produces the four possible variations of linearly linked structures described in Figure 3.1. The four variations are illustrated in Figure 3.2.

The most widely used variation of linearly linked structures is **one-way grounded** linearly linked structure. This chapter describes its use to represent stacks dynamically. It is also extremely useful as a means of representing lists that are processed with recursive algorithms, as described in Chapter 5.

Chapter 4 describes the use of **one-way circular** linearly linked structures to represent queues. **Two-way** linearly linked structures are used in Chapter 5 to represent lists that are processed using the positional paradigm. In general, the **one-way ground** variation of linearly linked structures handles the vast majority of programming needs for a linearly linked structure.

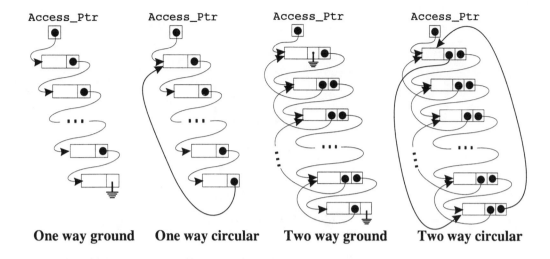

Figure 3.2. Linked list variations.

3.2 Elementary Stacks

3.2.1 Abstraction

A **stack**, also called a **pushdown stack**, is a sequential, homogeneous, variable-sized, possibly empty, collection of objects whose attributes and operations satisfy the following:

1. A stack is **empty** if it contains no objects.
2. All stack operations access one end of the stack, called the **top**. The other end of the stack is called the **bottom**.
3. Only the object at the top of the stack is accessible.
4. The **pop** operation removes the object currently at the top of the stack. The object immediately following the top object, if any, becomes the new top of the stack. If there are no other objects in the stack, the stack becomes **empty**.
5. The **push** operation places a new object on top of the stack. If the stack was not empty, the stack maintains the sequential relationship between the objects in the stack. Each object in the stack before the push operation moves one position down the stack, away from the top.

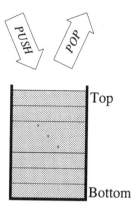

Figure 3.3. A stack.

Figure 3.3 illustrates a stack. All stack operations modify the stack by replacing the item at the top of the stack. The **push** operation places a new object on the top of the stack. The **pop** operation removes the top object. As the **push** operation places objects into the stack, the stack expands. As the **pop** operation removes objects, the stack shrinks. The order of the objects in the stack, from top to bottom, is the reverse of the order in which the objects are pushed into the stack. The term **LIFO**, last-in-first-out, is frequently used to describe the order of processing of the objects in a stack.

The description of a stack implies two constructors, Push and Pop. Examples of Push and Pop operations on a stack of integers appear in Figure 3.4, which illustrates the dynamic nature of a stack. In the example in Figure 3.4, as a new integer, 44, is Pushed into the stack, the stack expands and the new object becomes the new top of the stack. As additional objects are Pushed, 12, then 84, the stack expands each time and the newly placed object becomes the new top object. Each Pop operation removes the top object. The stack shrinks as a result of each pop operation, and the object next to the top becomes the new top object. The next Push operation places a 55 on top of the stack.

If the sequential nature of a stack may be expressed as an n-tuple. A stack containing n objects is represented by an n-tuple, $(a_1, a_2, \ldots, a_n)$. The top of the stack is a_1 and an empty stack is represented by $(\ )$, 0-tuple. If S is a stack, $(a_1, a_2, \ldots, a_n)$, and **obj** is the object being pushed into the stack, then the postcondition of the push operation is

$$S' = (obj, a_1, a_2, \ldots, a_n) = (obj, S),$$

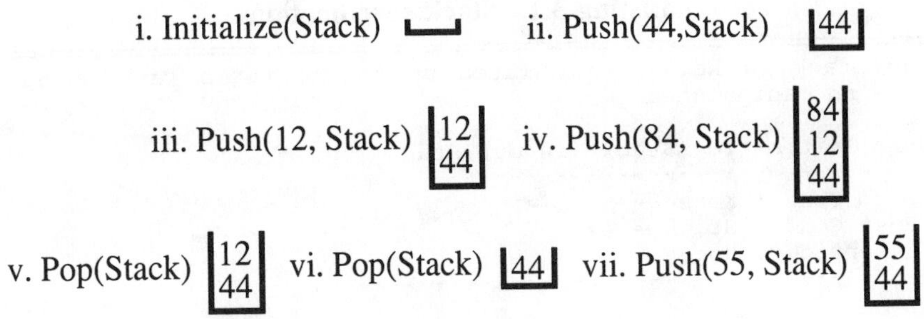

i. Initialize(Stack) ⌷   ii. Push(44,Stack) |44|

iii. Push(12, Stack) |12| iv. Push(84, Stack) |84|
                      |44| |12|
                                                  |44|

v. Pop(Stack) |12| vi. Pop(Stack) |44| vii. Push(55, Stack) |55|
               |44| |44|

Figure 3.4. Sample stack operations.

where S is a shorthand for $(a_1, a_2, \ldots , a_n)$, or equivalently,

$$(a_1' = obj) \wedge (\forall\ i \in [1..n],\ a_{i+1}' = a_i).$$

If S is a nonempty stack, then the postcondition of the pop operation is

$$S = (obj', S'),$$

or equivalently,

$$(obj' = a_1) \wedge (\forall\ i \in [1..n-1],\ a_i' = a_{i+1}).$$

Since the pop operation must be performed on a nonempty stack, an observer, Is_Empty, is provided. Is_Empty returns true when the stack is empty; otherwise the function returns false.

$$Stack = (\ ).$$

Listing 3.1 illustrates the preconditions and postconditions for the basic operations on a stack. The operations imply two additional operations, Initialize and Finalize. These operations may or may not be necessary, depending on how the structure is encapsulated. These operations are discussed in detail in the Chapter 2.

Listing 3.1. Stack specifications.

Assuming Stack is being manipulated by the operation and Object is the
object being manipulated.

```
procedure Initialize (Stack: in out Stack_Type);
-----------------------------------------------------
    -- Pre  Cond : None
    -- Post Cond : Stack = ()
    -- Exceptions: None
-----------------------------------------------------


procedure Finalize (Stack: in out Stack_Type);
-----------------------------------------------------
    -- Pre  Cond : Initialized (Stack)
    -- Post Cond : Stack' = ()
    -- Exceptions: None
-----------------------------------------------------


function Top (Stack: Stack_Type) return Object_Type;

procedure Pop (Stack : in out Stack_Type)
              Object:     out Object_Type);
-----------------------------------------------------
    -- Pre  Cond : Initialized (Stack) and Stack /= ()
    -- Post Cond : If Obj' is the object removed by the Pop
    --               operations, then Stack = (Obj', Stack')
    -- Exceptions: Stack_Is_Empty
-----------------------------------------------------
Procedure Pop (Stack: in out Stack_Type);

procedure Push (Object: in     Object_Type;
              Stack : in out Stack_Type);
-----------------------------------------------------
    -- Pre  Cond : Initialized (Stack)
    -- Post Cond : Stack' = (Object, Stack)
    -- Exceptions: Stack_Overflow
-----------------------------------------------------

function Is_Empty (Stack: in out Stack_Type) return boolean;
-----------------------------------------------------
    -- Pre  Cond : Initialized (Stack)
    -- Post Cond : Return (Stack = ())
    -- Exceptions: None
-----------------------------------------------------
```

3.2.2 Representation

3.2.2.1 Static

One static representation of stacks is obvious. The representation uses a record
that contains an array and a natural number, which keeps track of the current

Listing 3.2. Static stack declarations.

```
type Stack_Array_Type is array (positive range <>) of Object_Type;

type Stack_Type (Max_Size: positive) is
   record
      Top    : natural:= 0;
      Actual: Stack_Array_Type (1 .. Max_Size);
   end record;
```

location in the array that holds the top of the stack. Listing 3.2 illustrates the declarations for a static representation of stacks. Stack_Type represents each stack in a record. The array component, Actual, holds the objects in the stack. The natural type Top counts the number of objects in the stack and, simultaneously, the range 1..Top of locations in the array Actual that currently holds the objects in the stack. When Top is zero, the stack is empty. The user controls the initial size of the array with the generic array instantiation parameter, Stack_Size.

As stated previously, a stack is a linear structure. Note that the array indices indirectly indicate the linear relation. The objects in the stack are in array locations 1..Top, with the object at Actual(Top) being the first object in the stack, the top object. The *i*th object in the stack is at array location *Top - Position + 1*.

The stack constructor algorithms, Push and Pop, are obvious. The Push and Pop algorithms for static stacks use the component Top to access the array. The Pop algorithm in Listing 3.3 first tests Top to see if the stack is empty. If the stack is empty, the algorithm raises the Stack_Underflow exception. Otherwise, the algorithm removes the top object and decrements Top. Observe that Pop is written as a procedure, not a function. This is because the Pop parameter, Stack, is modified by the procedure and hence must be passed as an in out parameter and therefore cannot be a parameter to a function.

Listing 3.3. Static Pop algorithm.

```
function Pop (Object: in     Object_Type;
             Stack : in out Stack_Type ) is

   begin
     If Stack.Top = 0 then
        raise Stack_Underflow;
      else
         Object    := Stack.Actual (Stack.Top);
         Stack.Top:= Stack.Top - 1;
      end if;
   end Pop;
```

Listing 3.4. Static Push algorithm.

```
procedure Push (Object: in     Object_Type;
                Stack : in out Stack_Type) is
   begin
     if Stack.Top = Stack_Size then
        raise Stack_Overflow;
      else
        Stack.Top:= Stack.Top + 1;
        Stack.Actual (Stack.Top):= Object;
     end if;
   end Push;
```

The static Push algorithm in Listing 3.4 begins by comparing Top to the size of the array. If they are equal, the algorithm raises the Stack_Overflow exception. Otherwise, the algorithm increments Top and then places the new top object into the array at Stack.Actual(Stack.Top).

The code for the stack observer algorithm Is_Empty is straightforward. The Is_Empty function's value is

```
        return The_Stack.Top = 0;
```

3.2.2.2 Dynamic

Figure 3.5 contains a visualization of a dynamic stack structure. In the dynamic representation of a stack, each object in the stack is contained in a record. The records are linked and the position of the record in the linked structure indicates the position of the object in the stack. Each record contains two components, one

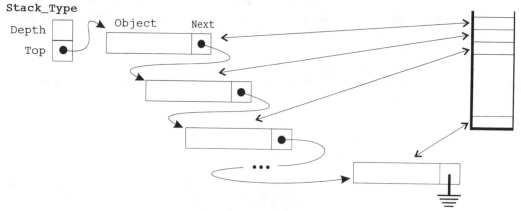

Figure 3.5. Dynamic stack representation.

contains the object and the second contains an access type. The access type links the record to the record containing the next object in the stack. Access to the stack is through a descriptor record, which contains a pointer to the linked collection of records, and a component, which contains the count of the number of objects in the stack. The first record in the linked collection contains the top object in the stack and the remaining objects appear in the linked structure in order from the top of the stack to the bottom. If the linked structure is null, the stack is empty.

Listing 3.5 contains the private declarations for the dynamic representation of stacks. The declarations Placeholder type and Stack_Type are made visible by a polymorphic stack package. The advanced stack package's child unit, described in Section 2.2.2, has access to the private declarations.

The Push and Pop algorithms add or remove, respectively, a dynamically allocated record from the linked structure and updates the Top component in the Stack_Type record. Listing 3.6 contains the Pop algorithm for dynamically allocated stacks, and Listing 3.7 contains the Push algorithm. There are two Pop procedures. The non-generic version of the Pop algorithm begins by testing for an empty stack. If the stack is empty, the algorithm raises the Stack_Is_Empty exception. Otherwise, the algorithm frees any Placeholder'Class object that may be accessed by the access type Object. Then the algorithm pops the object at the top of the stack by relinking the stack access component, Stack.Top, to the next object in the linear structure and decrements the stack's Size. The generic version of Pop calls the nongeneric Pop procedure, places the returned object in the client's Extended_type, and then frees the dynamic record.

The Push algorithm in Listing 3.7 obtains a dynamic record and places the new top object into that record. The algorithm connects the record to the beginning of the linked structure by placing the current Top pointer into the Next pointer in the new record and then resets the Top pointer to point to the new record. The stack's Size is incremented.

Listing 3.5. Private declarations for Stack_Polymorphic_Cntl.

```
private

type Place_Holder is abstract new controlled with
   record
      Next: Holder_Class_Ptr:= null;
   end record;

type Stack_Type is new controlled with
   record
      Top : Holder_Class_Ptr:= null;
      Size: natural:= 0;
   end record;
```

Listing 3.6. Dynamic Pop algorithm.

```
procedure Pop (Stack : in out Stack_Type;
               Object: in out Holder_Class_Ptr) is
   begin
      if Empty (Stack) then
         raise Stack_Underflow;
       else
         Free (Object);
         Object     := Stack.Top;
         Stack.Top := Stack.Top.Next;
         Stack.Size:= Stack.Size-1;
      end if;
   end Pop;
   -----------------------------------------------------
-- generic
--     type Extended_Type is new Place_Holder with private;
procedure Ex_Pop (Stack : in out Stack_Type;
                  Object:    out Extended_Type) is
   Obj: Holder_Class_Ptr;
   begin -- Pop
      Pop (Stack, Obj);
      Object:= Extended_Type(Obj.all);
      Free (Obj);
   end Ex_Pop;
```

The selection algorithm, Is_Empty, for dynamically allocated stacks is not complex. The Is_Empty function simply returns

```
            return Stack.Size = 0;
```

or

```
            return Stack.Top = null;
```

Listing 3.7. Dynamic Push algorithm.

```
procedure Push (Object: in      Place_Holder'Class;
                Stack : in out Stack_Type) is
   New_One: Holder_Class_Ptr:= new Place_Holder'Class'(Object);
   begin
      New_One.Next:= Stack.Top;
      Stack.Top    := New_One;
      Stack.Size   := Stack.Size+1;
   exception
      when storage_error => raise Stack_Overflow;
   end Push;
```

3.2.3 Encapsulation

3.2.3.1 `Stack_Pt_Pt`

The static representation of stacks represents the generic encapsulation of stacks that are safely instantiated with a bounded `private` type and makes stacks available as a safely assignable private representation. This encapsulation is very useful because many applications require stacks and satisfy two criteria:

1. The maximum size of the stack is determined before the stack is used.
2. The object type placed into the stack may be safely passed as a `private` type.

When these two criteria are met, the `Stack_Pt_Pt` is an appropriate choice. When a bounded representation may be used, a static representation generally has better time and memory requirements than a dynamic representation.

3.2.3.2 Dynamic Representations

The dynamic representation of stacks may be encapsulated either generically or polymorphically. For simplicity, polymorphic packaging is discussed in this section, and the specifications of the polymorphic stack package appears in Listing 3.8. This package extends `Ada.Finalization`'s `controlled` type for both the `Stack_Type` and the `Placeholder` type.

A `controlled` representation is very safe, because of its automatic initialization, finalization, and support for assignment. Along with those features comes additional run-time overhead. `Limited private` representations are safe but require the client to perform initialization and finalization, hence having less run-time overhead. For many time- and space-critical applications, clients wishing to use a representation that meets their needs, without a large overhead, may select a `limited  private` representation over a `controlled` representation. In summary, under normal software development considerations, a client will tend to use `controlled` representations, or `limited private` representations, and not some combination of both.

Listing 3.9 contains the body of the `Stack_Polymorphic_Cntl` package. The details of the `Pop` and `Push` procedures were discussed in Section 3.2.2.2. One should note the details of the `Initialize`, `Finalize`, and `Adjust` procedures. In particular, the `Finalize` procedure assists in stopping storage

Listing 3.8. `Stack_Polymorphic_Cntl` specifications.

```
with Ada.Finalization; Use Ada.Finalization;
package Stack_Polymorphic_Cntl is

type Place_Holder is abstract new controlled with private;
   procedure Initialize (Source: in out Place_Holder);
   procedure Finalize (Source: in out Place_Holder);
   procedure Adjust (Source: in out Place_Holder);

type Holder_Class_Ptr is access Place_Holder'Class;
   procedure Recycle (Point: in out Holder_Class_Ptr);

type Stack_Type is new controlled with private;
   procedure Initialize (Stack: in out Stack_Type);
   procedure Finalize (Stack: in out Stack_Type);
   procedure Adjust (Stack: in out Stack_Type);

   Stack_Underflow: exception;
   Stack_Overflow : exception;

function Empty (Stack: Stack_Type) return boolean;

function Empty_Stack return Stack_Type;

generic
   type Extended_Type is new Place_Holder with private;
function Top_Value (Stack: Stack_Type) return Extended_Type;

function Top_Of (Stack: Stack_Type) return Holder_Class_Ptr;

procedure Pop (Stack : in out Stack_Type;
               Object: in out Holder_Class_Ptr);
generic
   type Extended_Type is new Place_Holder with private;
procedure Ex_Pop (Stack : in out Stack_Type;
                  Object:    out Extended_Type);
procedure Pop (Stack : in out Stack_Type);

procedure Push (Object: in     Place_Holder'Class;
                Stack : in out Stack_Type);

procedure Swap (Source: in out Stack_Type;
                Target: in out Stack_Type);
private
   type Place_Holder is abstract new controlled with
      record
         Next: Holder_Class_Ptr:= null;
      end record;
   type Stack_Type is new controlled with
      record
         Top : Holder_Class_Ptr:= null;
         Size: natural:= 0;
      end record;
end Stack_Polymorphic_Cntl;
```

Listing 3.9. `Stack_Polymorphic_Cntl` **package body.**

```
with UnChecked_Deallocation;
package body Stack_Polymorphic_Cntl is
   procedure Free is new
         UnChecked_Deallocation (Place_Holder'Class, Holder_Class_Ptr);
   procedure Recycle (Point: in out Holder_Class_Ptr) renames Free;

procedure Initialize (Source: in out Place_Holder) is
   begin -- Initialize
      null;
   end Initialize;
   ----------------------------------------------------------
procedure Finalize (Source: in out Place_Holder) is
   begin -- Finalize
      null;
   end Finalize;
   ----------------------------------------------------------
procedure Adjust (Source: in out Place_Holder) is
   begin -- Adjust
      null;
   end Adjust;
   ----------------------------------------------------------
procedure Initialize (Stack: in out Stack_Type) is
   begin -- Initialize
      Stack.Top := null;
      Stack.Size:= 0;
   end Initialize;
   ----------------------------------------------------------
procedure Finalize (Stack: in out Stack_Type) is
   begin -- Finalize
      while not Empty (Stack) loop
         Pop (Stack);
      end loop;
   end Finalize;
   ----------------------------------------------------------
function Empty (Stack: Stack_Type) return boolean is
   begin
      return Stack.Size = 0;
   end Empty;
   ----------------------------------------------------------
function Empty_Stack return Stack_Type is
   Answer: Stack_Type;
   begin -- Empty_Stack
      return Answer;
   end Empty_Stack;
   ----------------------------------------------------------
function Top_Value (Stack: Stack_Type) return Extended_Type is
   begin
      if Empty (Stack) then
         raise Stack_Underflow;
       else
         return Extended_Type(Stack.Top.all);
      end if;
   end Top_Value;
```

Listing 3.9. (cont.)

```
function Top_Of (Stack: Stack_Type) return Holder_Class_Ptr is
   begin
      if Empty (Stack) then
         raise Stack_Underflow;
       else
         declare
           Answer:Holder_Class_Ptr:=new Place_Holder'Class'(Stack.Top.all);
         begin
            return Answer;
         end;
      end if;
   end Top_Of;
----------------------------------------------------

procedure Pop (Stack : in out Stack_Type;
               Object: in out Holder_Class_Ptr) is
   begin
      if Empty (Stack) then
         raise Stack_Underflow;
       else
         Free (Object);
         Object:= Stack.Top;
         Stack.Top := Stack.Top.Next;
         Stack.Size:= Stack.Size-1;
      end if;
   end Pop;
----------------------------------------------------
procedure Ex_Pop (Stack : in out Stack_Type;
                  Object:    out Extended_Type) is
   Obj: Holder_Class_Ptr;
   begin -- Pop
      Pop (Stack, Obj);
      Object := Extended_Type(Obj.all);
      Free (Obj);
   end Ex_Pop;
----------------------------------------------------
procedure Pop (Stack : in out Stack_Type) is
   Obj: Holder_Class_Ptr;
   begin -- Pop
      Pop (Stack, Obj);
      Free (Obj);
   end Pop;
----------------------------------------------------

procedure Push (Object: in      Place_Holder'Class;
                Stack : in out Stack_Type) is
   New_One : Holder_Class_Ptr := new Place_Holder'Class'(Object);
   begin
      New_One.Next:= Stack.Top;
      Stack.Top    := New_One;
      Stack.Size   := Stack.Size+1;
   exception
      when storage_error => raise Stack_Overflow;
   end Push;
```

Listing 3.9. (cont.)

```
procedure Adjust (Stack: in out Stack_Type) is
   Dup: Holder_Class_Ptr := Stack.Top;
   procedure Rec_Copy (Source: in out Holder_Class_Ptr) is
      begin -- Rec_Copy
         if Source /= null then
            Rec_Copy (Source.Next);
            Push (Source.all, Stack);
         end if;
      end Rec_Copy;
   ------------------------------------------------------
   begin -- Adjust
      Stack.Top := null;
      Stack.Size:= 0;
      Rec_Copy (Dup);
   end Adjust;
   ------------------------------------------------------
procedure Swap (Source: in out Stack_Type;
                Target: in out Stack_Type) is
   Temp : Holder_Class_Ptr:= Target.Top;
   Extra: natural          := Target.Size;
   begin
      Target.Top := Source.Top;
      Target.Size:= Source.Size;
      Source.Top := Temp;
      Source.Size:= Extra;
   end Swap;
   ------------------------------------------------------

end Stack_Polymorphic_Cntl;
```

leakage by returning the dynamically allocated records that remained in the stack back to the storage heap. Adjust duplicates the stack.

Recall that Adjust is used by the system as part of safely handling assignment of objects when the value of an object is unbound. Adjust places a copy of the pointer, Stack.Top, in Dup and calls the recursive copying procedure, Rec_Copy. Rec_Copy then recursively traverses to the end of the linear structure and pushes the objects into Stack as it comes out of the recursion.

The package makes Stack_Type visible as a controlled type that contains the package's stack type. Note that Initialize, Finalize, and Adjust are all private, and hence not available to clients. Also, to assist clients with efficient application of the stack type, a Swap procedure is made visible for client use.

3.2.4 Measurement

A first measurement observation should be that the `Push` and `Pop` operations for both the static and dynamic representations all execute in a constant amount of time.   None of the basic operations contains any loops.   Hence, there is no significant timing differences between the static and dynamic representations, except perhaps a slight speed advantage in favor of the static representation, array access versus dynamic allocation.

The major cost for unbound representation is the cost of access types per record that link the dynamically allocated records together.   This can be significant.   In a typical computer, the space requirements of an access type is usually four or more bytes.   If a stack of characters is being maintained, each character is represented in one byte.   Hence the actual data — characters — represent on the order of only 20 percent of the space allocated for the stack.

3.3 Advanced Features

3.3.1 Abstraction

As one works with stacks, it may become desirable to have additional support for manipulating stacks.   Occasionally, a software developer requires support for a structure that usually performs like a stack but the strict interpretation of stacks is overridden.   This support that overrides the standard support for stacks may be safely provided through a child package like `Stack_Polymorphic_Cntl.Advanced`, whose specifications appear in Listing 3.10.   The features supported by this package are

1. **Size_Of**: A function that returns the size of stacks.
2. **Peek**: A function to view objects within the stack.
3. **Poke**: A procedure to change the value of an object at any location within the stack.
4. **Insert**: Insert a new object at position i in the stack, which moves all objects from the ith object to the bottom down one.
5. **Remove**: Remove the ith object from the stack.

The availability of some of these features, like `Size_Of`, might simplify certain stack applications.   The others override the stack's structure.   `Peek` and `Poke` are very useful in two circumstances: (1) They may be useful debugging

Listing 3.10. `Stack_Polymorphic_Cntl.Advanced` **specification.**

```
package Stack_Polymorphic_Cntl.Advanced is

function Size_Of (Stack: Stack_Type) return natural;

function Peek (Stack    : Stack_Type;
              Position: positive) return Holder_Class_Ptr;

procedure Poke (Stack    : in out Stack_Type;
                Position: in      positive;
                Object  : in      Place_Holder'Class);

procedure Insert (Object  : in      Place_Holder'Class;
                  Position: in      positive;
                  Stack   : in out Stack_Type);

procedure Remove (Stack    : in out Stack_Type;
                  Position: in      positive;
                  Object  : in out Holder_Class_Ptr);

end Stack_Polymorphic_Cntl.Advanced;
```

aides; (2) they can be useful if the structure that is needed has stack-like storage characteristics and only requires an occasional override of the stack structure to see or replace an object.

The procedures `Insert` and `Remove` also prove useful when the basic structure being represented is stacklike but requires occasional support that overrides the stack structure.

3.3.2 Representation

3.3.2.1 Static

The implementation of the five advanced child unit subprograms (see Listing 3.11) for a static representation is fairly simple. The `Size_Of` function is one line that returns `Stack.Top`.

Both the `Peek` and `Poke` procedures, after testing to make sure that the `Position` parameter is within the stack's range, use the mapping relationship `Stack.Top - Position + 1` to look at, or remove, the specific object. Besides using the mapping relationship between stack objects and array locations, the `Insert` and `Remove` procedures must move the objects in the array as an object is inserted or removed. When a new object is inserted, all the objects from the top down to the location where the new object is inserted, or an object is

Listing 3.11. `Stack_Pt_Pt.Advanced` package body.

```
package body Stack_Pt_Pt.Advanced is

function Size_Of (Stack: in Stack_Type) return natural is
   begin
      return Stack.Top;
   end Size_Of;
   ------------------------------------------------------------
function Peek (Stack   : in Stack_Type;
              Position: in positive ) return Object_Type is
   My_Stack    : Stack_Type:= Stack;
   Temp_Element: Object_Type;
   begin
      if (Position > Stack.Top) then
         raise Invalid_Position;
       else
         return Stack.Actual (Stack.Top - Position + 1);
      end if;
   end Peek;
   ------------------------------------------------------------
procedure Poke (Stack   : in out Stack_Type;
                Position: in     positive;
                Object  : in     Object_Type) is
   begin
      if Position > Stack.Top then
         raise Invalid_Position;
       else
         Stack.Actual (Stack.Top - Position + 1):= Object;
      end if;
   end Poke;
   ------------------------------------------------------------
procedure Insert (Object  : in     Object_Type;
                  Position: in     positive;
                  Stack   : in out Stack_Type) is
   Low: natural;
   begin -- Insert
      if Position > Stack.Top+1 then
         raise Invalid_Position;
       elsif Position > Stack.Max_Size then
         raise Stack_Overflow;
       else
         Stack.Top:= Stack.Top + 1;
         if Position = Stack.Top then
            Low:= 1;
          else
            Low:= Stack.Top-Position+1;
         end if;
         for i in reverse Low .. Stack.Top-1 loop
            Stack.Actual(i+1):= Stack.Actual(i);
         end loop;
         Stack.Actual(Stack.Top-Position+1):= Object;
      end if;
   end Insert;
```

Listing 3.11. (cont.)

```
procedure Remove (Stack    : in out Stack_Type;
                  Position: in     positive;
                  Object  :     out Object_Type) is
   begin -- Remove
      if Position > Stack.Top then
         raise Invalid_Position;
      else
         Object := Stack.Actual(Stack.Top-Position+1);
         for i in Stack.Top-Position+1 .. Stack.Top-1 loop
            Stack.Actual(i) := Stack.Actual(i+1);
         end loop;
         Stack.Top := Stack.Top - 1;
      end if;
   end Remove;
   -------------------------------------------------------

end Stack_Pt_Pt.Advanced;
```

removed, must be shuttled one position. When an object is removed, the algorithm shuttles the objects between the top and the indicated position down one and then resets the `Stack.Top`.

If a stack contains n objects, then an insert may occur in $n + 1$ locations; the new object may become the new ith object for any i in 1..n; or it may become the new bottom object, which will be the $(i+1)$st object in the stack. The `Insert` procedure tests for potential exceptions and then determines the low index for the array shuffle. Recall that if the object becomes the new bottom object, then `Stack.Top-Position+1` becomes 0, which would raise a `constraint_error` if used as an index into the `Actual` array. Note the use of `reverse` in the `for` loop to move one object from an array location before another object is moved.

3.3.2.2 Dynamic

The implementation of the five advanced child unit subprograms for a dynamic representation is straightforward. The `Size_Of`, `Peek`, and `Poke` subprograms appear in Listing 3.12. The procedure `Size_Of` simply returns the value of the `Stack.Size` component. `Peek` uses a `for` loop to traverse down the structure to the desired object and returns an access type that points to a copy of the desired record, `new Place_Holder'Class'(Iterate.all)`. To display another search strategy, the `Poke` procedure uses a recursive subprogram to traverse down to the desired position in the linear structure and then relinks a new

Listing 3.12. `Size_Of`, `Peek`, and `Poke` **for dynamic stacks.**

```
with UnChecked_Deallocation;

package body Stack_Polymorphic_Cntl.Advanced is

   procedure Free is new
      UnChecked_Deallocation (Place_Holder'Class, Holder_Class_Ptr);

function Size_Of (Stack: Stack_Type) return natural is
   begin
      return Stack.Size;
   end Size_Of;
   ----------------------------------------------------------
function Peek (Stack   : Stack_Type;
              Position: positive ) return Holder_Class_Ptr is
   Iterate: Holder_Class_Ptr:= Stack.Top;
   begin
      if Position > Size_Of (Stack) then
         raise constraint_error;
        else
          for I in 2..Position loop
             Iterate:= Iterate.Next;
          end loop;
      end if;
      return new Place_Holder'Class'(Iterate.all);
   end Peek;
   ----------------------------------------------------------
procedure Poke (Stack   : in out Stack_Type;
               Position: in      positive;
               Object  : in      Place_Holder'Class) is
   New_One: Holder_Class_Ptr;
   procedure Rec_Poke (Anchor: in out Holder_Class_Ptr;
                       Count: in      natural) is
      begin -- Rec_Poke
        if Count = 0 then
            New_One      := new Place_Holder'Class'(Object);
            New_One.Next:= Anchor.Next;
            Free (Anchor);
            Anchor:= New_One;
          else
            Rec_Poke (Anchor.Next, Count-1);
        end if;
      end Rec_Poke;
      ----------------------------------------------------------
   begin
      if Position > Size_Of (Stack) then
         raise constraint_error;
        else
          Rec_Poke (Stack.Top, Position-1);
      end if;
   end Poke;
```

record into the structure at that position. Note that `Poke` frees the old record in the process in order to avoid storage leakage.

The remaining procedures, `Insert` and `Remove`, appear in Listing 3.13. The procedure `Insert` recursively descends until the access parameter, `Point`, is the one that must be relinked to insert the new record. The new record is inserted at that position and the size of the stack is updated. The procedure `Remove` also uses a recursive algorithm to descend down the structure until the parameter `Point`. It then frees any object pointed to by `Object`, makes `Object` point to the record being removed, and relinks the structure around the removed record.

3.3.3 Encapsulation

The advanced stack capabilities are encapsulated in `.Advanced` child units, which are illustrated in Listing 3.14. The bodies of these subprograms appear in Listings 3.12 and 3.13. Recall that these subprograms all have access to the private declarations in the parent unit, `Stack_Polymorphic_Cntl`.

On the other hand, both the parent unit, `Stack_Pt_Pt`, and the child unit, `Stack_Pt_Pt.Advanced`, are generic units. The parent unit must be instantiated first, then the child unit is instantiated, creating a child unit of the instantiation, as illustrated in Listing 3.18.

3.3.4 Measurement

The timing for the subprograms in the advanced child unit vary. The `Size_Of` subprogram executes in constant time. The dynamic versions of the remaining operations are all bound by the size of the stack, `O(Size_Of(Stack))`, since all of them require linear processing of at least part of the stack.

Similar observations may be made for the timing of subprograms for the static representations, except for the static versions of `Peek` and `Poke`, which can use the `Position` variable to directly access the stack location that contains the object being processed:

```
return Stack.Actual (Stack.Top - Position + 1); -- in peek
```

and

```
Stack.Actual (Stack.Top - Position + 1):= Object;
```

Both perform in constant time.

Listing 3.13. Insert **and** Remove **algorithms for polymorphic stacks.**

```
procedure Insert (Object   : in       Place_Holder'Class;
                  Position: in       positive;
                  Stack    : in out Stack_Type) is
   New_One: Holder_Class_Ptr;
   procedure Rec_Insert (Point: in out Holder_Class_Ptr;
                         Count: in       natural) is
      begin -- Rec_Insert
      if Count = Position then
         New_One:= new Place_Holder'Class'(Object);
         if Point = null then
            New_One.Next:= null;
          else
            New_One.Next:= Point.Next;
         end if;
         Point:= New_One;
         Stack.Size:= Stack.Size + 1;
       else
         Rec_Insert(Point.Next, Count+1);
      end if;
      end Rec_Insert;
      --------------------------------------------------
   begin -- Insert
   if Position > Stack.Size+1 then
      raise constraint_error;
    else
      Rec_Insert (Stack.Top, 1);
   end if;
   end Insert;
   --------------------------------------------------
procedure Remove (Stack    : in out Stack_Type;
                  Position: in       positive;
                  Object   : in out Holder_Class_Ptr) is
   procedure Rec_Remove (Point: in out Holder_Class_Ptr;
                         Count: in       positive) is
      begin -- Rec_Remove
      if Count = Position then
         Free (Object);           Object:= Point;
         Point:= Point.Next;  Stack.Size:= Stack.Size-1;
       else
         Rec_Remove (Point.Next, Count+1);
      end if;
      end Rec_Remove;
      --------------------------------------------------
   begin -- Remove
   if Position > Stack.Size then
      raise constraint_error;
    else
      Rec_Remove (Stack.Top, 1);
   end if;
   end Remove;
   --------------------------------------------------

end Stack_Polymorphic_Cntl.Advanced;
```

Listing 3.14. `Stack_Pt_Cntl.Advanced` **body.**

```
package body Stack_Pt_Cntl.Advanced is

function Size_Of (Stack: Stack_Type) return natural is
   begin
      return adv_PPS.Size_Of (Stack.Stack);
   end Size_Of;
   --------------------------------------------------------
function Equal (Stack_1, Stack_2: Stack_Type;
               EQ              : EQ_Type) return boolean is
   begin
      return adv_PPS.Equal (Stack_1.Stack, Stack_2.Stack, EQ);
   end Equal;
   --------------------------------------------------------
function Peek (Stack   : Stack_Type;
              Position: positive ) return Object_Type is
   begin
      return adv_PPS.Peek(Stack.Stack, Position);
   end Peek;
   --------------------------------------------------------
procedure Poke (Stack   : in out Stack_Type;
               Position: in     positive;
               Object  : in     Object_Type) is
   Obj: Object_Type:= Object;
   begin
      adv_PPS.Poke (Stack.Stack, Position, Obj);
   end Poke;
   --------------------------------------------------------
procedure Insert (Object  : in     Object_Type;
                 Position: in     positive;
                 Stack   : in out Stack_Type) is
   Obj: Object_Type:= Object;
   begin -- Insert
      adv_PPS.Insert (Obj, Position, Stack.Stack);
   end Insert;
   --------------------------------------------------------
procedure Remove (Stack   : in out Stack_Type;
                 Position: in     positive;
                 Object  :     out Object_Type) is
   Obj: Object_Type;
   begin -- Remove
      adv_PPS.Remove (Stack.Stack, Position, Obj);
      Object:= Obj;
   end Remove;
   --------------------------------------------------------
end Stack_Pt_Cntl.Advanced;
```

3.4 Iterators

An **incomplete algorithm**, or **partial algorithm**, is an algorithmic template that becomes a complete algorithm when subprograms are added to the template at specified locations. An **iterator** is a partial algorithm that visits each object in a homogeneous data structure in a predetermined order one or more times in such a way that one or more subprograms must be added to the iterator to make it a complete algorithm.

There are three obvious iterators for stacks:

1. **Top_Down**: Visits each object in the stack starting with the object at the top and traversing down the stack to the object at the bottom, performing the same subprogram at each object.
2. **Bottom_Up**: Visits each object in the stack starting with the object at the bottom and traversing up the stack to the object at the top, performing the same subprogram at each object.
3. **Round_Trip**: Visits each object in the stack twice by first performing **Top_Down**, executing a subprogram at each object, then performing **Bottom_Up** with a second subprogram at each node.

Since **Round_Trip** is a combination of **Top_Down** and **Bottom_Up**, only **Top_Down** and **Bottom_Up** are discussed in this section.

3.4.1 Abstraction

The iterators may be viewed as incomplete algorithms that are completed with other procedures. This may be accomplished in two-ways in Ada 95: as generic procedures that are instantiated with the procedure that is performed at each node, as illustrated in Listing 3.15; or as a procedure that accepts another procedure as a parameter, as illustrated in Listing 3.16. Note the use of a boolean parameter, Continue. The role of this parameter is to allow the user to terminate the iteration by setting the parameter to false. In this text, iterators are constructed

Listing 3.15. Stack iterator as a generic procedure.

```
generic
   with procedure Process (Object  : in out Object_Type;
                           Continue: in out boolean);
procedure Top_Down (Stack: in out Stack_Type);
```

Listing 3.16. Stack iterator specifications.

```
package Stack_Polymorphic_Cntl.Iterators is

type Process_Type is access
   procedure (Object  : in out Place_Holder'Class;
              Continue: in out boolean  );

procedure Top_Down (Stack  : in out Stack_Type;
                    Process:          Process_Type);

procedure Bottom_Up (Stack  : in out Stack_Type;
                     Process:          Process_Type);

end Stack_Polymorphic_Cntl.Iterators;
```

by passing the completing algorithm, or algorithms as procedure parameters, as in Listing 3.16.

To illustrate one use of an iterator, consider building a system that recognizes strings of the form xcx^r, where x is any string of symbols that does not contain the symbol 'c', and x^r is the reversal of that string. Recognizing strings of this form can be done with a stack by pushing symbols into the stack until the 'c' is encountered. Then as each symbol after the 'c' is read, it is matched against a symbol popped from the top of the stack. The string is recognized, or accepted, only if all matches are successful and when the end of the string occurs, just as the stack becomes empty. As the system processes the string, we would like to demonstrate how the contents of the stack change.

Listing 3.17 contains both the specifications and the body of a client's interface package that sits between the Stack_Pt_Pt.Iterator package and the client's program, as illustrated in Listing 3.18. The iterator is used to display the contents of the stack when the first 'c' is encountered in the input string. Observe how both the stack package and the iterator are instantiated:

```
package stk is new stack_pt_pt (character);
package stk_it is new stk.iterators;
```

The iterator is applied in the procedure Show_Stack. Show_Stack displays an image of the top of the stack, then applies the iterator, which uses Print_Obj to display each object in the stack, and then displays the bottom of the stack. For

Listing 3.17. xcx^r support package.

```
with text_io, Stack_Pt_Pt.Iterators;
package xcx_Pak is
   package stk is new stack_pt_pt (character);
   package stk_it is new stk.iterators;
procedure Print_Obj (Obj      : in out character;
                      Continue: in out boolean  );
end xcx_Pak;


                           <<Body>>

package body xcx_Pak is
   procedure Print_Obj (Obj      : in out character;
                         Continue: in out boolean) is
      begin -- Print_Obj
         Text_IO.Put ('|' & Obj & '|'); Text_IO.new_line;
      end Print_Obj;
   --------------------------------------------------------
end xcx_Pak;
```

example, if the string was **0010c0100**, upon reading the 'c', Show_Stack would
print

```
            |0|
            |1|
            |0|
            |0|
            +-+
```

3.4.2 Representation

3.4.2.1 Static

Listing 3.19 illustrates the Top_Down and Bottom_Up stack iterators. Since the
stack objects are in an array, each iterator sequentially processes the array in the
indicated order, top-down or bottom-up, until the entire stack is processed, or the
user procedure sets Continue to false.

Listing 3.18. xcx^r program with stack display.

```
with text_io, xcx_Pak;
use  xcx_Pak;
procedure xcxrev is
   package tio renames text_io;
   Buffer: string (1..255);
   B_Size: natural;

procedure Show_Stack (Stack: in out stk.Stack_Type) is
   begin -- Show_Stack
      tio.Put("| |");  tio.new_line;
      stk_it.Top_Down (Stack, Print_Obj'Access);
      tio.Put("+-+");  tio.new_line;  tio.Skip_Line;
   end Show_Stack;
   ------------------------------------------------------------
procedure Acceptor (Input:in out string) is
   Symbol, Popped: character;
   Stack: stk.Stack_Type (100);
   Index: natural:= Input'First;
   OK_String: boolean:= true;
   begin -- Acceptor
      stk.Initialize (Stack);
      while (Index /= Input'Last) and then (Input(Index) /= 'c') loop
         tio.Put(Input(Index));            tio.new_line;
         stk.Push (Input(Index), Stack);  Index:= Index + 1;
      end loop;
      tio.Put(Input(Index)); tio.new_line;  Show_Stack (Stack);
      if Input(Index) /= 'c' then
         tio.New_Line; tio.Put ("Not Accepted"); tio.New_Line;
        else
         Index:= Index + 1;
         while OK_String and then (not stk.Empty (Stack))
               and then (Index <= Input'Last) loop
            tio.Put(Input(Index)); tio.new_line;   stk.Pop(Stack, Popped);
            if Popped /= Input(Index) then
               OK_String:= false;
              else
               Index:= Index + 1;
            end if;
         end loop;
         if OK_String and stk.Empty (Stack) and (Index > Input'Last) then
            tio.New_Line; tio.Put ("Accepted"); tio.New_Line;
           else
            tio.New_Line; tio.Put ("Not Accepted"); tio.New_Line;
         end if;
      end if;
      stk.Finalize (Stack);
   end Acceptor;
   ------------------------------------------------------------
begin -- xcxrev
   tio.Put ("Enter your string"); tio.New_Line;
   tio.Get_Line (Buffer, B_Size);
   while B_Size > 0 loop
      Acceptor (Buffer(1..B_Size));   tio.Put ("Enter your string");
      tio.New_Line;                   tio.Get_Line (Buffer, B_Size);
   end loop;
end xcxrev;
```

Listing 3.19. Static stack iterators.

```
procedure Top_Down (Stack   : in out Stack_Type;
                    Process:          Process_Type) is
   Continue: boolean:= true;
   begin
      for i in reverse 1..Stack.Top loop
         Process (Stack.Actual(i), Continue);
         exit when not Continue;
      end loop;
   end Top_Down;
-----------------------------------------------------
procedure Bottom_Up (Stack   : in out Stack_Type;
                     Process:          Process_Type) is
   Continue: boolean:= true;
   begin
      for i in 1..Stack.Top loop
         Process (Stack.Actual(i), Continue);
         exit when not Continue;
      end loop;
   end Bottom_Up;
```

3.4.2.2 Dynamic

Stack iterators for the dynamic representation present an interesting challenge when compared to the static stack iterators described in Section 2.3.2.1. Both iterators in Listing 3.20 recursively process the list. The recursive Top_Down iterator makes an initial call to a recursive procedure, Rec_Top_Down, that calls Process, and then recursively calls itself with a pointer to the record containing the next object as long as Continue is true.

In a sense, there are two sides to recursion, the recursive descent and the recursive ascent. The recursive Top_Down iterator uses recursive descent to process the objects in the stack from the top object down to the bottom object. The Bottom_Up iterator for the dynamic representation recursively calls itself to get to the bottom of the stack Then on the recursive ascent it calls Process, starting with the bottom object and working its way back up to the top object until either it processes the top object, or Process sets Continue to false.

Listing 3.20. Dynamic stack iterators.

```
procedure Top_Down (Stack    : in out Stack_Type;
                     Process:          Process_Type) is
   Continue: boolean:= true;
   Procedure Rec_Top_Down (Current : in       Stack_Ptr;
                           Continue: in out boolean) is
      begin -- Rec_Top_Down
         if Current /= null then
            Process (Current.Object, Continue);
            if Continue then
               Rec_Top_Down (Current.Next, Continue);
            end if;
         end if;
      end Rec_Top_Down;
      ------------------------------------------------
   begin
      Rec_Top_Down (Stack.Top, Continue);
   end Top_Down;
   ------------------------------------------------------
procedure Bottom_Up (Stack    : in out Stack_Type;
                     Process:          Process_Type) is
   Continue: boolean:= true;
   Procedure Rec_Bottom_Up (Current : in       Stack_Ptr;
                            Continue: in out boolean) is
      begin -- Rec_Bottom_Up
         if Current /= null then
            Rec_Bottom_Up (Current.Next, Continue);
            if Continue then
               Process (Current.Object, Continue);
            end if;
         end if;
      end Rec_Bottom_Up;
      ------------------------------------------------
   begin
      Rec_Bottom_Up (Stack.Top, Continue);
   end Bottom_Up;
```

3.4.3 Encapsulation

Both the bounded and polymorphic encapsulations of the iterator child units are performed in a manner similar to the advanced child units. Both implementations use procedure parameters to pass the client's completion of the iterator.

3.4.4 Measurement

The timing for all iterators, both static and dynamic, is bound by O(Size_Of(Stack)). However, if a program has real-time speed considerations, or limited space requirements, then every attempt should be made to use a static representation instead of a dynamic representation. When it comes to time requirements, although both the static and dynamic iterators have timings that are bound linearly to the size of the stack, the actual timing for the static implementation will be faster.

3.5 Explorations

1. Rewrite the `Peek` function in `Stack_Polymorphic_Cntl.Advanced` using a recursive subprogram instead of the `for` loop.
2. Rewrite the `Insert` and `Remove` subprograms in `Stack_Pt_Pt.Advanced` using a recursive algorithm instead of the `for` loop.
3. Rewrite the `Top_Down` iterator in `Stack_Polymorphic_Cntl.Iterator` as a while loop instead of the recursive subprogram.
4. Rewrite the `Top_Down` and `Bottom_Up` iterators in `Stack_Pt_Pt.Iterator` with recursive subprograms replacing the `for` loops.
5. Assume the stack objects do not contain a `.Size` component. Write the `Size_Of` function in `Stack_Polymorphic_Cntl`, which determines the size by counting the number of records:

    a. Do it with a loop.
    b. Do it recursively.

4

Queues

4.1 Elementary Queues

4.1.1 Abstraction

A **queue** is a sequential, homogeneous, variable-sized, possibly empty collection of objects whose attributes and operations satisfy the following:

1. A queue is said to be **empty** when it contains no objects.
2. A queue has two ends, called the **front** and the **rear**.
3. The only object in a queue that is visible is the object at the front of the queue.
4. The **Dequeue** operation removes the object currently at the **front** of the queue. All remaining objects in the queue, if any, move one position forward toward the front of the queue. The object immediately following the front object becomes the new front of the queue. If there are no other objects in the queue, the queue becomes **empty**.
5. The **Enqueue** operation inserts new objects at the **rear** of the queue. If the queue was empty, the enqueued object becomes the front object in the queue. At any time, new objects may be enqueued. When an object is enqueued, it becomes the rear object in the queue.

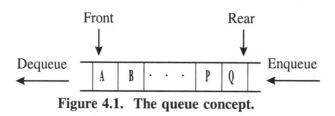

Figure 4.1. The queue concept.

Figure 4.1 illustrates a queue. The queue constructors modify the queue
either by removing the object at the front of the queue or by adding new objects
to the rear of the queue. The Enqueue operation places a new object at the rear
of the queue. The Dequeue operation removes the front object. As the Enqueue
operation places an object into the queue, the queue expands. As the Dequeue
operation removes objects, the queue shrinks. The order of the objects in the
queue, from front to rear, is the order in which the objects were Enqueued. The
term **FIFO**, first-in-first-out, describes the order of processing of the objects in
a queue.

The description of a queue implies two constructors, Enqueue and Dequeue.
Examples of Enqueue and Dequeue operations on a queue of integers appear in
Figure 4.2, which illustrates the dynamic nature of a queue. As integers 14, 12,
and 84 are Enqueued, the queue expands and each object lines up behind the
object that immediately precedes it in the queue. Each Dequeue operation
removes the front object, first 14, then 12, and so forth. The queue shrinks in
size, as a result of each dequeue operation, and the object next to the front
becomes the new front object. Subsequent dequeue operations place additional
objects at the rear of the queue.

The sequential nature of a queue may be represented with an n-tuple. A
queue that contains n objects is represented by an n-tuple, $(a_1, a_2, \ldots, a_n)$.
The front of the queue is a_1 and an empty queue is represented by $(\ )$, an empty

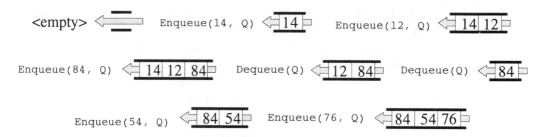

Figure 4.2. Sample queue operations.

n-tuple. If Q is a queue, $(a_1, a_2, \ldots, a_n)$ and obj is the object being enqueued onto the queue, then the postcondition of the enqueue operation is

$$Q' = (a_1, a_2, \ldots, a_n, obj) = (Q, obj),$$

where Q is a shorthand for $(a_1, a_2, \ldots, a_n)$, or equivalently,

$$(a'_{n+1} = obj) \wedge (\forall \ i \in [1..n], \ a'_i = a_i).$$

If Q is a nonempty stack, then the postcondition of the Dequeue operation is

$$Q = (obj', Q'),$$

or equivalently,

$$(obj' = a_1) \wedge (\forall \ i \in [2..n], \ a'_i = a_{i+1}).$$

Since the Dequeue operation must be performed on a nonempty queue, an observer, Is_Empty, is helpful. Is_Empty returns true when the queue is empty, otherwise the function returns false. Similarly, the Front_Of function provides visibility to the only object visible in a queue, the object at the front. Note that two versions of Dequeue are provided, one that simply dequeues the front object, and a second version that dequeues the front object and returns it. Some clients find it more convenient to use Front_Of and the version of Dequeue that does not return the front object. Others may find it more convenient to use only the version of Dequeue that dequeues and returns the front object:

$$Queue = (\ ).$$

Listing 4.1 illustrates the preconditions and postconditions for the basic operations on a queue. The operations imply two additional operations, Initialize and Finalize. These operations may or may not be necessary, depending on how the structure is encapsulated.

Listing 4.1. Basic queue specifications.

```
package Queue_??_?? is
   type Queue_Type is . . . ;

   Queue_Underflow: exception;
   Queue_Overflow : exception;

procedure Initialize (Queue: in out Queue_Type);

procedure Finalize (Queue: in out Queue_Type);

function Is_Empty (Queue: Queue_Type) return boolean;

function Front_Of (Queue: Queue_Type) return Object_Type;

procedure Dequeue (Queue : in out Queue_Type;
                   Object: in out Object_Type);

procedure Dequeue (Queue: in out Queue_Type);

procedure Enqueue (Object: in out Object_Type;
                   Queue : in out Queue_Type);

end Queue_??_??;
```

4.1.2 Representation

4.1.2.1 Static: First Thoughts

A first attempt at a static representation for queues might be made by deriving one from the static representation for stacks. This would suggest that the objects in the queue are kept in an array with either the front or rear of the queue at the first location of the array and that a variable is used as an index to keep track of the index to the other end of the queue in the array. Listing 4.2 contains the declarations for a representation with the front of the queue kept at the first location of the array. However, this is a poor choice for the representation. To see this, consider the implementation of the Dequeue operation. Every time an object is dequeued, all of the remaining objects must be moved one position forward. As a result, the timing of the Dequeue operation could be problematic because the time to dequeue an object depends on the current size of the queue, which might be large. It is desirable to keep the timings of the basic operations as small as possible, preferably a constant amount of time, and certainly not dependent on the size of the structure.

It is always important that software be time and memory efficient. It is even more important that a reusable package be efficient. If a package is not efficient,

Listing 4.2. Poor choice for static queue representation.

```
private
   subtype Array_Range is natural range 1 .. Max_Queue_Size;
   type Object_Array   is array (Array_Range) of Object_Type;
   type Queue_Type is
      record
         Rear  : natural:= 0;
         Object: Object_Array;
      end record;
```

the lack of efficiency is frequently magnified in the software that uses the package. For this reason, it is desirable that the constructors and observers exported by every package be as efficient as possible. Therefore, it is desirable that both the Enqueue and Dequeue operations not contain unnecessary looping processes.

4.1.2.2 Static: Wraparound

A potential inefficiency in the queue constructor algorithms based on the algorithm in Section 4.1.2.1 is the need to move objects from one location in the array to another to maintain the queue representation. Figure 4.3 suggests a method that avoids the need to move objects once they are placed in the array. The contents of the queue are not moved as objects are enqueued and dequeued. Instead, two indices are used, one to keep track of the location of the front of the

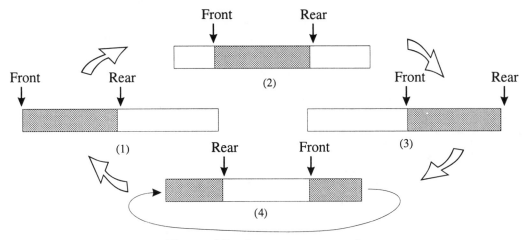

Figure 4.3. Array wraparound.

queue and one to locate the rear of the queue. As objects are inserted, the index to the rear of the queue is incremented. As objects are removed, the index to the front is incremented. As either index is about to exceed the size of the array, the index is reset to the front of the array. It is a relatively simple task to build a function to support the "wraparound" incrementation using modular arithmetic.

This approach, called **array wraparound**, logically maintains the sequential structure of the array. Listing 4.3 contains declarations for the wraparound representation of queues. Initially, the two indices are set to the same value, which indicates that the queue is empty. As objects are enqueued, the `Rear` index is incremented and used to place new objects. When objects are removed, the `Front` index is incremented and then the object is removed. With this approach, the `Front` index actually points to the position **just before** the first object. The private declarations also contain two procedures, `Incr` and `Decr`, that assist in manipulating the `.Front` and `.Rear` indices and maintaining array wraparound.

Each queue corresponds to a record. Besides the array that contains the objects in the queue, the record also contains two components, `Front` and `Rear`, that keep track of the location of the queue in the array. Note that a `Length` component is unnecessary because the length of the queue may be determined from the values of `Front` and `Rear`:

```
if Front <=Rear then
   Length:= Rear - Front;
  else
   Length:= Max_Size-Front+Rear-1;
end if;
```

Listing 4.4 illustrates the `Enqueue` algorithm for the static implementation of queues. The algorithm first checks to see if the array is full. If it is, the algorithm raises the `Queue_Overflow` exception. Otherwise, the `Rear` index is incremented using modular arithmetic,

Listing 4.3. **Static queue representation.**

```
private
   function Incr (Index, Max: natural) return natural;
   function Decr (Index, Max: natural) return natural;
   type Queue_Array_Type is array (natural range <>) of Object_Type;
   type Queue_Type (Max_Size: positive:= 32) is
      record
         Front : natural:= 0;
         Rear  : natural:= 0;
         Actual: Queue_Array_Type (0 .. Max_Size);
      end record;
```

Listing 4.4. Static Enqueue **and** Dequeue.

```
procedure Enqueue (Queue  : in out Queue_Type;
                   Element: in     Object_Type) is
   begin -- Enqueue
      if Incr (Queue.Rear, Queue.Max_Size) = Queue.Front then
         raise Queue_Overflow;
      else
         Queue.Rear:= Incr (Queue.Rear, Queue.Max_Size);
         Queue.Actual (Queue.Rear):= Element;
      end if;
   end Enqueue;
   ------------------------------------------------------
procedure Dequeue (Element:    out Object_Type;
                   Queue  : in out Queue_Type) is
   begin -- Dequeue
      If Queue.Rear = Queue.Front then
         raise Queue_Underflow;
      else
         Element     := Queue.Actual (Queue.Front);
         Queue.Front:= Incr (Queue.Front, Queue.Max_Size);
      end if;
   end Dequeue;
```

```
The_Queue.Rear:= (The_Queue.Rear + 1) mod Max_Queue_Size;
```

to handle wraparound, the object is inserted into the array, and the queue length is updated.

Listing 4.4 contains the Dequeue algorithm for static queues. The algorithm first tests to see if the queue is empty. If it is, the algorithm raises the Queue_Underflow exception. Otherwise, the Front index is incremented, using modular arithmetic, the length is updated, and the object that was at the front of the queue is returned as the Object parameter.

4.1.2.3 Dynamic: Two-Pointer Queues

After seeing the dynamic representation of a stack, it is natural to consider a linked structure to maintain the order of objects in the queue. However, the representation of a queue needs access to both ends of the queue. Because of the linear nature of a queue, it is natural to consider representing a queue as a linearly linked structure, but with two access variables, one pointing to the front and one pointing to the rear. Figure 4.4 illustrates a visualization of a queue maintained with two pointers.

Listing 4.5 contains declarations for a two-pointer queue representation. The access component Front points to the record containing the first object in the

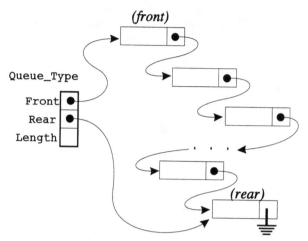

Figure 4.4. Two pointer queue.

linked structure. As in the case of the dynamic stack structures, each record
contains an access component that links each record to the record containing the
next object in the queue. The pointer in the record that contains the rear object
is null, indicating that there are no additional objects in the queue. Access to the
rear of the queue is required to make the Enqueue operation efficient. If the
component Rear was not included, the timing for the Enqueue operation would
depend on the length of the queue.

Listing 4.6 illustrates the enqueuing and algorithm for a dynamic queue that
uses two pointers, one pointing to the front and one pointing to the rear of the

Listing 4.5. Two pointer queue specifications.

```
private
   type Object_Holder;
   type Queue_Ptr is access Object_Holder;
   type Object_Holder is
      record
         Object: Object_Type; -- Generic data type
         Next   : Queue_Ptr;
      end record;
   type Queue_Type is
      record
         Front: Queue_Ptr;
         Rear : Queue_Ptr;
         Size : natural;
      end record;

end Queue_??_Lpt;
```

Listing 4.6. `Enqueue` **algorithm for a two-pointer queue.**

```
procedure Enqueue (Object: in out Object_Holder'Class;
                   Queue : in out Queue_Type) is
  New_One: Queue_Ptr := new Get_Holder;
  begin
     New_One.Object:= new Object_Holder'Class'(Object);
     If Queue.Size = 0 then
        Queue.Front:= New_One;
       else
        Queue.Rear.Next:= New_One;
     end if;
     Queue.Rear:= New_One;
     Queue.Size:= Queue.Size+1;
  exception
     when storage_error => raise Queue_Overflow;
  end Enqueue;
```

linked sequence of objects. When called, the algorithm obtains a new holder for the object being placed into the queue. The object is placed into the holder. If the queue had been empty, the `Front` pointer is resent; otherwise, it is linked into the existing sequence of records by having the access component `Next` point to the new record. The `Rear` pointer and queue length are then updated. Note that the exception `storage_error` might be raised if the system runs out of space. This exception is handled by raising the `Queue_Overflow` exception.

Listing 4.7 illustrates the `Dequeue` algorithm for queues kept with two pointers. If the queue was empty, the `Queue_Underflow` exception is raised. Otherwise, the object is copied from the record at the front of the queue and is

Listing 4.7. `Dequeue` **algorithm for a two-pointer queue.**

```
procedure Dequeue (Queue : in out QueueType;
                   Object: in out Holder_Class_Ptr) is
    begin
    if Queue.Size = 0 then
       raise Queue_Is_Empty;
      else
       Free (Object);
       Object:= Queue.Rear.Next;
       Queue.Rear.Next:= Object.Next;
       If Old_One = Queue.Rear then
           Queue.Front:= null;
           Queue.Rear := null;
         else
           Queue.Front:= Object.Next;
       end if;
       Queue:= (Queue.Rear, Queue.Size-1);
    end if;
    end Dequeue;
```

returned in the Object parameter. The record is removed from the linked structure if the length of the queue had been greater than one. If the length of the queue had been one, both the Front and Rear pointers are set to null, indicating that the queue is now empty. Finally, the length of the queue is updated and the record removed from the linked structure is recycled.

4.1.2.4 Dynamic: One-Pointer Queues

At first glance it might appear as if the two pointers Front and Rear are necessary for the dynamic representation of a queue. Compare the illustration in Figure 4.4 with that in Figure 4.5. The Next link in the record containing the rear object in Figure 4.4 is null, while the Next link in the record containing the rear object in Figure 4.5 points to the record containing the front object. By making this link, the Rear pointer now has constant time access to both the front and rear objects.

Listing 4.8 contains the private declarations for a queue representation that requires only one access type to access the structure. This listing also illustrates the structure of the declarations for a polymorphic representation. The specifications for a dynamic queue representation that requires only a single access type is similar to the declarations in Listing 4.7 but with the Front access

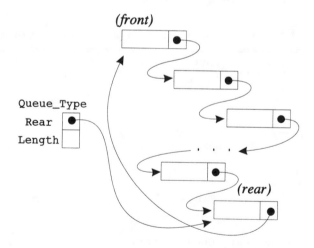

Figure 4.5. One pointer representation.

Listing 4.8. One-pointer queue specifications.

```
private
   type Place_Holder is abstract new controlled with
      record
         Next: Holder_Class_Ptr:= null;
      end record;
   type Queue_Type is new controlled with
      record
         Rear: Holder_Class_Ptr:= null;
         Size: natural:= 0;
      end record;

end Queue_Polymorphic_Cntl;
```

component removed. This approach maintains the queue representation as a circular linked structure by having the Next component in the record containing the rear object point to the record containing the front object. The .Rear component in Queue_Type directly accesses the rear of the queue and the .Next component in the first record provides access to the front.

Listing 4.9 contains the enqueing algorithm for the specifications in Listing 4.8. Compare the algorithm with the Enqueue algorithm in Listing 4.6. They are essentially the same except for the need in Listing 4.6 to maintain the link from the record containing the rear object to the record containing the front object. To see how this link is maintained, note how the Next component is manipulated. If the queue had been empty, then the Next component is set to point to itself,

```
New_One.Next:= New_One
```

Listing 4.9. One-pointer Enqueue algorithm.

```
procedure Enqueue (Object: in      Place_Holder'Class;
                   Queue : in out Queue_Type) is
   New_One: Holder_Class_Ptr:= new Place_Holder'Class'(Object);
   begin
      If Queue.Size = 0 then
         New_One.Next:= New_One;
        else
         New_One.Next    := Queue.Rear.Next;
         Queue.Rear.Next:= New_One;
      end if;
      Queue.Rear:= New_One;
      Queue.Size:= Queue.Size+1;
   exception
      when storage_error => raise Queue_Overflow;
   end Enqueue;
```

Listing 4.10. One-pointer Dequeue algorithm.

```
procedure Dequeue (Queue : in out Queue_Type;
                      Object: in out Holder_Class_Ptr) is
   begin
      if Queue.Size = 0 then
         raise Queue_Underflow;
      else
         Free (Object);
         Object:= Queue.Rear.Next;
         If Object = Queue.Rear then
             Queue.Rear:= null;
           else
             Queue.Rear.Next:= Object.Next;
         end if;
         Queue.Size:= Queue.Size-1;
    end if;
   end Dequeue;
----------------------------------------------------
procedure Dequeue (Queue: in out Queue_Type) is
   Obj: Holder_Class_Ptr;
   begin -- Dequeue
      Dequeue (Queue, Obj);
      Free (Obj);
   end Dequeue;
----------------------------------------------------
--generic
--   type Extended_Type is new Placeholder with private;
procedure Dequeue (Queue : in out Queue_Type;
                      Object: in out Extended_Type) is
   Obj: Holder_Class_Ptr;
   begin -- Dequeue
      Dequeue (Queue, Obj);
      Object:= Extended_Type(Obj.all);
      Free (Obj);
   end Dequeue;
```

since there are no other objects in the queue. Otherwise, the pointer in the rear component is copied to it,

```
New_One.Next:= Queue.Rear.Next;
```

so that it points to the front object in the queue. Then the pointer in what had been the rear object is set to point to the new rear, with the statement

```
Queue.Rear:= New_One;
Queue.Size:= Queue.Size+1;
```

In either case, the Rear pointer is set to point to the new object, and Rear.Next in the rear record points to the front object.

The algorithm in Listing 4.10 illustrates the dequeing algorithm for the queue specifications in Listing 4.8. For `Queue_Polymorphic_Cntl`, there are three implementations of the dequeing procedures, including a generic procedure that may be instantiated with the client's type extensions of `Placeholder`. The algorithm raises the `Queue_Underflow` exception if the queue was empty. Otherwise, the object at the front is accessed, by using the `Next` pointer in the record containing the rear object:

```
Queue.Rear.Next;
```

Once the object at the front is obtained, if the queue had contained only one object, then the `Rear` pointer is set to null. Otherwise, the record containing the front object is removed, but the `Next` pointer in that record locates the new front object:

```
Queue.Rear.Next:= Queue.Rear.Next.Next;  -- = Object.Next
```

Algorithms for the queue observers with a one-pointer representation, a rear pointer, are very similar to those for queues represented with two pointers, a `Front` and a `Rear` pointer.

4.1.3 Encapsulation

The static representation of the queue is encapsulated in a generic package, `Queue_Pt_Pt`, which handles queues in a bounded representation and may be safely instantiated by clients with bounded object types. The dynamic representation uses a circularly linked structure to represents queues and may be safely encapsulated using `controlled` types in `Queue_Polymorphic_Cntl`.

Listing 4.11 contains the `Initialize`, `Finalize`, and `Adjust` procedures for the `controlled` dynamic queue representation. Note how the `Adjust` procedure copies the size and pointer to the circular structure into two variables and then traverses the structure and forms a duplicate using the `Enqueue` procedure.

The `Front_Value` and `Front_Of` functions, in Listing 4.12, provide access to the object at the front of the queue. `Front_Value` is a generic function that may be instantiated by the client to return the value of the client's extended type in `Placeholder'Class`. The `Empty` function simply returns true when the

Listing 4.11. Finalization procedures for `Queue_Polymorphic_Cntl.`

```
procedure Initialize (Queue: in out Queue_Type) is
   begin -- Initialize
      Queue.Rear:= null;
      Queue.Size:= 0;
   end Initialize;
----------------------------------------------------
procedure Finalize (Queue: in out Queue_Type) is
   begin
      While Queue.Size /= 0 loop
         Dequeue (Queue);
      end loop;
   end Finalize;
----------------------------------------------------
procedure Adjust (Queue: in out Queue_Type) is
   Dup  : Holder_Class_Ptr:= Queue.Rear;
   Count: natural          := Queue.Size;
   begin -- Adjust
      Queue.Rear:= null;
      Queue.Size:= 0;
      for I in 1 .. Count loop
         Enqueue (Dup.all, Queue);
         Dup:= Dup.Next;
      end loop;
   end Adjust;
```

queue is empty. The `Empty_Queue` function is provided as a simple method for clients to empty a queue using assignment

```
        My_Queue:= Empty_Queue;
```

Finally, there is a `Swap` procedure. This procedure may provide an efficient alternative to the use of assignment. `Swap` simply moves the values of the access types that point to the lined structures. The statements

```
        Temp     := Other;
        Other    := Original;
        Original:= Temp;
        Temp     := Empty_Queue;
```

are obviously more time-consuming than

```
        Swap (Other, Original);
```

Listing 4.12. Other dynamic queue subprograms.

```
-- generic
--    type Extended_Type is new controlled with private;
function Front_Value (Queue: Queue_Type) return Extended_Type is
   begin -- Front_Value
      if Empty (Queue) then
         raise Queue_Underflow;
       else
         return Extended_Type(Queue.Rear.Next.all);
      end if;
   end Front_Value;
   ----------------------------------------------------

function Front_Of (Queue: Queue_Type) return Holder_Class_Ptr is
   begin -- Front_Of
      if Empty (Queue) then
         raise Queue_Underflow;
       else
         declare
           Answer: Holder_Class_Ptr:=
                   new Place_Holder'Class'(Queue.Rear.Next.all);
         begin
           return Answer;
         end;
      end if;
   end Front_Of;
   ----------------------------------------------------

function Empty (Queue: Queue_Type) return boolean is
   begin
      return Queue.Size = 0;
   end Empty;
   ----------------------------------------------------

function Empty_Queue return Queue_Type is
   Answer: Queue_Type;
   begin -- Empty_Queue
      return Answer;
   end Empty_Queue;
   ----------------------------------------------------
procedure Swap (Source: in out Queue_Type;
                Target: in out Queue_Type) is
   Temp     : Holder_Class_Ptr:= Target.Rear;
   Temp_Size: natural          := Target.Size;
   begin
      Target.Rear:= Source.Rear;
      Target.Size:= Source.Size;
      Source.Rear:= Temp;
      Source.Size:= Temp_Size;
   end Swap;
```

4.2 Advanced Features

4.2.1 Abstraction

The features that are desirable for advanced queue support parallel the features described for advanced stack support. For example, rather than dequeing from the front of the queue, one might wish simply to view the front. The desirable advanced support features are as follows:

1. Size_Of: A function that returns the size of queues.
2. Peek: A function to view objects within the queue.
3. Poke: A procedure to change the value of an object at any location within the queue.
4. Insert: A procedure to insert a new object at position i in the queue, which moves all objects from the ith object to the bottom object down one.
5. Remove: A procedure to remove the ith object from the queue.

Listing 4.13 contains the specifications of these features. These features override the pure definition of a queue, but some clients might require these procedures because their application needs a structure that is similar to a queue, but not purely like a queue.

Listing 4.13. Specifications for advanced features.

```
package Queue_Polymorphic_Cntl.Advanced is

function Size (Queue: Queue_Type) return natural;

procedure Insert (Object  : in      Place_Holder'Class;
                  Position: in      positive;
                  Queue   : in out Queue_Type);

procedure Remove (Queue   : in out Queue_Type;
                  Position: in      positive;
                  Object  : in out Holder_Class_Ptr);

function Peek (Queue   : in      Queue_Type;
              Position: in      positive) return Holder_Class_Ptr;

procedure Poke (Queue   : in out Queue_Type;
                Position: in      positive;
                Object  : in      Place_Holder'Class);

end Queue_Polymorphic_Cntl.Advanced;
```

The five operations provided in the advanced queue package are direct analogies to the five operations discussed for stacks. Listing 4.13 illustrates the specifications for the `Stack_Polymorphic_Cntl` package. The same procedures would be declared for any other possible encapsulation of stacks, including `Stack_Pt_Pt`.

4.2.2 Representation

Although two static and two dynamic representations were discussed in Section 4.1.2, only the static wraparound and one-pointer dynamic representations are pursued here.

4.2.2.1 Static Wraparound

The implementation of the five advanced child unit subprograms for a static wraparound representation is fairly simple. Listing 4.14 contains the algorithms for the `Size`, `Insert`, and `Remove` subprograms and Listing 4.15 illustrates `Peek` and `Poke`.

The `Size` procedure simply reports the value of `Queue.Size`. The `Insert` and `Remove` procedures use the wraparound calculation to locate where the insertion or removal is to take place. Then the procedure must adjust the locations of the rest of the objects in the queue because of the insertion or removal.

4.2.2.2 Dynamic: One-Pointer Queues

The algorithms in the advanced package in Listing 4.15 for a dynamically allocated queue are analogous to the corresponding algorithms for a dynamically allocated stack that appear in the previous chapter. The fundamental difference is that where the access type in `Stack_Type` pointed directly to the first object, `Stack.Top`, the access type in `Queue_Type` points to the rear; hence `Queue.Rear.Next` points to the front. Other than that, the procedures in `Queue_Polymorphic_ Cntl.Advanced` are practically a direct rewrite of the corresponding procedures in `Stack_Polymorphic_Cntl.Advanced`.

The `Size` function returns the value of the `Queue.Size` component. The `Insert` and `Remove` procedures both use recursive subprograms to locate the

Listing 4.14. `Queue_Pt_Pt.Advanced` **body.**

```
package body queue_pt_pt.Advanced is
function Size_Of (Queue: in Queue_Type) return natural is
   begin
      if Queue.Rear > Queue.Front then
         return Queue.Rear - Queue.Front;
       else
         return Queue.Max_Size - Queue.Front + Queue.Rear + 1;
      end if;
   end Size_Of;
   -----------------------------------------------------------
procedure Insert (Object  : in out Object_Type;
                  Position: in      positive;
                  Queue   : in out Queue_Type) is
   Low: natural;
   From_Ix, To_Ix: natural;
   begin -- Insert
   if Position > (Size_Of(Queue)+1) then
      raise constraint_error;
    elsif Incr(Queue.Rear,Queue.Max_Size) = Queue.Front then
      raise Queue_Overflow;
    else
      Queue.Rear:= Incr (Queue.Rear, Queue.Max_Size);
      Low       := (Queue.Front + Position) mod (Queue.Max_Size+1);
      To_Ix     := Queue.Rear;
      From_Ix   := Decr(To_Ix, Queue.Max_Size);
      While From_Ix /= Low loop
         Queue.Actual(To_Ix):= Queue.Actual(From_Ix);
         To_Ix:= From_Ix;  From_Ix:= Decr(From_Ix, Queue.Max_Size);
      end loop;
      Queue.Actual(Low):= Object;
   end if;
   end Insert;
   -----------------------------------------------------------
procedure Remove (Queue   : in out Queue_Type;
                  Position: in      positive;
                  Object  : in out Object_Type) is
   Pos, Pos_Next: natural;
   begin -- Remove
   if Position > Size_Of(Queue) then
      raise constraint_error;
    else
      Pos     := (Queue.Front+Position) mod (Queue.Max_Size+1);
      Object  := Queue.Actual(Pos);
      Pos_Next:= Incr(Pos, Queue.Max_Size);
      while Pos /= Queue.Rear loop
         Queue.Actual(Pos):= Queue.Actual(Pos_Next);
         Pos               := Pos_Next;
         Pos_Next          := Incr(Pos_Next, Queue.Max_Size);
      end loop;
      Queue.Rear:= Decr(Queue.Rear, Queue.Max_Size);
   end if;
   end Remove;
```

Listing 4.14. (cont.)

```
function Peek (Queue    : Queue_Type;
               Position: positive ) return Object_Type is
   Real_Index: natural;
   begin
      if (Position > Size_Of(Queue)) then
         raise constraint_error;
       else
         return
            Queue.Actual((Queue.Front+Position)mod(Queue.Max_Size+1));
      end if;
   end Peek;
  ---------------------------------------------------------------
procedure Poke (Queue    : in out Queue_Type;
                Position: in      positive;
                Object   : in out Object_Type) is
   Real_Index: natural;
   begin
      if Position > Size_Of (Queue) then
         raise constraint_error;
       else
         Queue.Actual ((Queue.Front+Position)mod(Queue.Max_Size+1))
             := Object;
      end if;
   end Poke;
  ---------------------------------------------------------------

end  queue_pt_pt.Advanced;
```

position of the insertion or removal. Note how each procedure handles the
special case when the adjustment involves changing the object at the front or rear
of the queue. The Insert procedure handles this by simply calling the enqueing
procedure. The removal procedure handles this by directly changing the pointer
to the rear, Queue.Rear.

4.3 Iterators

4.3.1 Abstraction

The collection of possible iterators for queues parallels the stack iterators. The
three obvious queue iterators are

1. Front_To_Rear: Visits each object in the queue starting with the object at
    the front and traversing through to the object at the rear, performing the same
    subprogram at each object.

Listing 4.15. `Queue_Polymorphic_Cntl.Advanced` **body.**

```
with Unchecked_Deallocation;
package body Queue_Polymorphic_Cntl.Advanced is
   procedure Free is new Unchecked_Deallocation
         (Place_Holder'Class, Holder_Class_Ptr);
function Size (Queue: Queue_Type) return natural is
   begin
      return Queue.Size;
   end Size;
   ------------------------------------------------------
procedure Insert (Object  : in      Place_Holder'Class;
                  Position: in      positive;
                  Queue   : in out Queue_Type) is
   New_One: Holder_Class_Ptr;
   procedure Rec_Insert (Point: in out Holder_Class_Ptr;
                         Count: in      natural) is
      begin -- Rec_Insert
         if Count = Position then
            New_One:= new Place_Holder'Class'(Object);
            New_One.Next:= Point.Next;    Point:= New_One;
         else
            Rec_Insert (Point.Next, Count+1);
         end if;
      end Rec_Insert;
      ---------------------------------------------
   begin -- Insert
   if Position = (Queue.Size + 1) then
      Enqueue (Object, Queue);
     elsif Position > (Queue.Size + 1) then
      raise constraint_error;
     else
      Rec_Insert (Queue.Rear.Next, 1);
      Queue.Size:= Queue.Size + 1;
   end if;
   end Insert;
   ------------------------------------------------------
function Peek (Queue   : in      Queue_Type;
              Position: in      positive) return Holder_Class_Ptr is
   function Rec_Peek (Point: Holder_Class_Ptr;
                      Count: natural) return Holder_Class_Ptr is
      begin -- Rec_Peek
         if Count = Position then
            return new Place_Holder'Class'(Point.all);
          else
            return Rec_Peek (Point.Next, Count+1);
          end if;
      end Rec_Peek;
      ------------------------------------------------------
   begin
      if Position > Size (Queue) then  raise constraint_error;
       else  return Rec_Peek (Queue.Rear.Next, 1);
      end if;
   end Peek;
```

Listing 4.15. (cont.)

```
procedure Remove (Queue    : in out Queue_Type;
                  Position: in      positive;
                  Object   : in out Holder_Class_Ptr) is
   procedure Rec_Remove (Point: in out Holder_Class_Ptr;
                         Count: in       natural) is
      begin -- Rec_Remove
         if Count = Position then
            Free (Object);
            Object:= Point;
            Point := Point.Next;
          else
            if Position = (Count+1)
               and then position = Queue.Size then
                Queue.Rear:= Point;
            end if;
            Rec_Remove (Point.Next, Count+1);
         end if;
      end Rec_Remove;
      ----------------------------------------------
   begin -- Remove
   if Position = 1 then
      Dequeue (Queue, Object);
     elsif Position > Queue.Size then
       raise constraint_error;
     else
       Rec_Remove (Queue.Rear.Next, 1);
   end if;
   end Remove;
   -------------------------------------------------------

procedure Poke (Queue    : in out Queue_Type;
                Position: in      positive;
                Object   : in      Place_Holder'Class) is
   New_One: Holder_Class_Ptr;
   procedure Rec_Poke (Point: in out Holder_Class_Ptr;
                       Count: in       natural) is
      begin -- Rec_Poke
         if Count = Position then
            New_One      := new Place_Holder'Class'(Object);
            New_One.Next:= Point.Next;
            Free(Point);
            Point        :=New_One;
          else
            Rec_Poke (Point.Next, Count+1);
         end if;
      end Rec_Poke;
      ----------------------------------------------------
   begin
      if Position > Size (Queue) then  raise constraint_error;
        else  Rec_Poke (Queue.Rear.Next, 1);
      end if;
   end Poke;

end Queue_Polymorphic_Cntl.Advanced;
```

2. `Rear_To_Front`: Visits each object in the queue starting with the object at the rear and traversing to the object at the front, performing the same subprogram at each object.

3. `Round_Trip`: Visits each object in the queue twice by first performing `Front_To_Rear`, executing a subprogram at each object, and then performing `Rear_To_Front` with a second subprogram at each node.

Since `Round_Trip` is a combination of `Front_To_Rear` and `Rear_To_Front`, only `Front_To_Rear` and `Rear_To_Front` are provided in the iterator package. The specifications for `Queue_Pt_Pt.Iterators` appear in Listing 4.16.

Listing 4.16. `Queue_Pt_Pt.Iterators` specifications.

```
generic
package Queue_Pt_Pt.Iterators is

type Process_Type is access
   procedure (Object  : in out Object_Type;
              Continue: in out boolean);

procedure Front_To_Rear (Queue   : in out Queue_Type;
                         Process:           Process_Type);
procedure Rear_To_Front (Queue   : in out Queue_Type;
                         Process:           Process_Type);
end Queue_Pt_Pt.Iterators;
```

4.3.2 Representation

4.3.2.1 Static

Listing 4.17 illustrates iterators over the static wraparound representation of queues. The queue traversals are handled by starting at the indicated end of the queue and using either the `Incr` or `Decr` function in the parent unit to handle array wraparound correctly. Note that the procedure `Front_To_Rear` initializes `Index`,

```
Index:= Incr(Queue.Front, Queue.Max_Size);
```

to point directly to the front object in the queue. After calling the client procedure, `Process`, each iterator checks to see if the client wishes to terminate the iteration by setting the `Continue` parameter to `false`.

Listing 4.17. Queue iterators, static implementation.

```
package body queue_pt_pt.Iterators is

procedure Front_To_Rear (Queue   : in out Queue_Type;
                         Process:          Process_Type) is
   Index: natural;
   Continue: boolean:= true;
      begin -- Front_To_Rear
      If Queue.Front /= Queue.Rear then
         Index:= Incr(Queue.Front, Queue.Max_Size);
         loop
            Process (Queue.Actual(Index), Continue);
            exit when (not Continue) or (Index = Queue.Rear);
            Index:= Incr(Index, Queue.Max_Size);
         end loop;
      end if;
   end Front_To_Rear;
-------------------------------------------------
procedure Rear_To_Front (Queue   : in out Queue_Type;
                         Process:          Process_Type) is
   Index: natural;
   Continue: boolean:= true;
   begin -- Rear_To_Front
      if Queue.Front /= Queue.Rear then
         Index:= Queue.Rear;
         loop
            Process (Queue.Actual(Index), Continue);
            Index:= Decr(Index, Queue.Max_Size);
            exit when (not Continue) or (Index = Queue.Front);
         end loop;
      end if;
   end Rear_To_Front;
-------------------------------------------------

end queue_pt_pt.Iterators;
```

4.3.2.2 Dynamic

Both iterators could be implemented recursively, as illustrated in Listing 4.18. However, the `Front_To_Rear` iterator may be implemented as a looping process that traverses down the linked structure, passing the objects to `Process`.

4.3.3 Measurement

All version of iterators have the same timing characteristic, $O(\#(Queue))*$ $O(Process)$, regardless of whether the representation is static or dynamic or of whether the algorithms are recursive or nonrecursive.

Listing 4.18. `Queue_Polymorphic_Cntl.Iterator` **body.**

```
package body Queue_Polymorphic_Cntl.Iterators is

procedure Front_To_Rear (Queue  : in out Queue_Type;
                         Process:        Process_Type) is
   Continue: boolean:= true;
   procedure rec_F_R (Point: in out Holder_Class_Ptr) is
      begin -- Rec_F_R
         Process (Point, Continue);
         if Continue and (Point /= Queue.Rear.Next) then
            Rec_F_R (Point.Next);
         end if;
      end Rec_F_R;
   -----------------------------------------------------
   begin
      if Queue.Rear /= null then
         Rec_F_R (Queue.Rear.Next);
      end if;
   end Front_To_Rear;
-----------------------------------------------------
procedure Rear_To_Front (Queue  : in out Queue_Type;
                         Process:        Process_Type) is
   Continue: boolean      := true;
   Iterate : Holder_Class_Ptr:= Queue.Rear;
   procedure Rev_Rec (Point   : in out Holder_Class_Ptr;
                      Continue: in out boolean) is
      begin -- Rev_Rec
         if Point.Next /= Queue.Rear.Next then
            Rev_Rec (Point.Next, Continue);
         end if;
         if Continue then
            Process (Point, Continue);
         end if;
      end Rev_Rec;
   -----------------------------------------------------
   begin
      if Queue.Rear /= null then
         Rev_Rec (Queue.Rear.Next, Continue);
      end if;
   end Rear_To_Front;
-----------------------------------------------------

end Queue_Polymorphic_Cntl.Iterators;
```

4.4 Explorations

1. Implement the `Round_Trip` iterator for `Queue_Pt_Pt`.

2. Implement the `Round_Trip` iterator for `Queue_Polymorphic_Cntl`.

5

Lists

Queues and stacks are sequential abstract data types with their specified access limits. All stack access is limited to one end of the stack, the top. With queues, objects enter the structure from one end, called the rear, and leave from the other end, called the front. Access to an arbitrary object in a structure is said to be **independent**, **immediate**, or **random** if the time required to access the object does not depend on either the location of the object within the structure or which object within the structure had been previously accessed. A structure has **independent access** if every object in the structure may be accessed within a constant period of time. Independent access is frequently referred to as **random access**. Arrays are the classical example of structures with independent, or random, access. Access to any object in an array does not depend on access to any other object in the array.

Lists are logical structures with the **sequential, or linear, access limit**. Recall that for a structure to be sequential, there is a one-on-one mapping between the natural numbers and the order of the objects within the structure, $o_1, o_2, \ldots$, o_n. This chapter presents two paradigms for list structures. The first, and the more elegant, is the **recursive paradigm**. In this paradigm, lists may be viewed either as being empty or as an ordered pair *(head, tail)*, where head is an object and tail is a list. This paradigm leads to many refined recursive algorithms for processing lists.

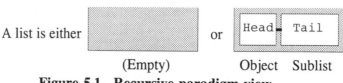

Figure 5.1. Recursive paradigm view.

A second paradigm is the **positional paradigm**. In this paradigm, lists may be viewed as an $(n+1)$-tuple, $(k, a_1, a_2, \ldots, a_n)$, where k, $k \in [0..n]$, is called the viewing position. The tuple, (0), indicates an empty list. The positional paradigm is discussed in Section 5.2.

5.1 Recursive Paradigm

Figure 5.1 illustrates the recursive list paradigm. In the recursive paradigm, a list is either empty or a pair of objects *(head, tail)*, an object called the *head* of the list and a sublist called the *tail* of the list. As the name implies, the recursive paradigm encourages the design of recursive processes to manipulate lists. Specifically, a list is processed recursively by writing algorithms so that they observe that the current list is empty, or perform the desired process on the head of the current list, or recursively reapply the process to the tail of the list. Listing 5.1 describes the specifications for the `List_Polymorphic_Cntl` package, whose implementation is discussed in Section 5.1.2.2.

5.1.1 Abstraction

The specifications in Listing 5.1 contain the procedures `Initialize`, `Finalize`, `Adjust`, and `Swap`. Recall that `Initialize` and `Finalize` are usually necessary to prepare an object for use and to terminate its use. `Adjust` supports assignment of `controlled` types, and `Swap` in many cases is an efficient alternative to multiple uses of assignment statements. For purposes of discussing the various list operations in Listing 5.1, assume *List* = *(head, tail)*, where *head* is an object and *tail* is a list.

All operations on a list may be viewed as an operation that maps a list onto a list. For example, the operation `Insert (Object, List)` has as its postcondition *List'* = *(head, tail)*, that is, the new list is composed of the `Object` as head and the old list as its tail. As a complement of this, if *List'* = *(head, tail)* is a precondition of `Remove_Head`, then the postcondition of `Remove_Head` is

Listing 5.1. Recursive list specifications.

```ada
with Ada.Finalization; Use Ada.Finalization;
package List_Polymorphic_Cntl is

type Place_Holder is abstract new controlled with private;
   procedure Initialize (Object: in out Place_Holder);
   procedure Finalize (Object: in out Place_Holder);
   procedure Adjust (Object: in out Place_Holder);
type Holder_Class_Ptr is access Place_Holder'Class;
   procedure Recycle (Point: in out Holder_Class_Ptr);
type List_Type is new controlled with private;
   procedure Initialize (List: in out List_Type);
   procedure Finalize (List: in out List_Type);
   procedure Adjust (List: in out List_Type);

   List_Underflow: exception;
   List_Overflow : exception;

function Tail_Of (List: List_Type) return List_Type;

generic
   type Extended_Type is new Place_Holder with private;
function Head_Value (List: List_Type) return Extended_Type;

function Head_Of (List: List_Type) return Holder_Class_Ptr;

function Empty (List: in     List_Type) return boolean;

function Empty_List return List_Type;

procedure New_Head (Object: in     Place_Holder'Class;
                    List  : in     List_Type);
generic
   type Ext_Type is new Place_Holder with private;
procedure Remove_Ext_Head (List  : in     List_Type;
                           Object: in out Ext_Type);
procedure Remove_Head (List  : in     List_Type;
                       Object: in out Place_Holder'Class);
procedure Remove_Head (List  : in     List_Type;
                       Object: in out Holder_Class_Ptr);
procedure Swap_Tail (Source: in     List_Type;
                     Target: in     List_Type);
procedure Append (List    : in     List_Type;
                  New_Tail: in out List_Type);
procedure Append (List    : in     List_Type;
                  New_Tail: in     Place_Holder'Class);

procedure Update_Head (List  : in     List_Type;
                       Object: in     Place_Holder'Class);
procedure Swap (Source: in out List_Type;
                Target: in out List_Type);
private
   . . .
end List_Polymorphic_Cntl;
```

List' = *tail*. If *List* = (*head, tail*), then the functions `Head_Of` (`List`) and `Tail_Of` (`List`) return the *head* and *tail*, respectively.

If *Source* = (*shead, stail*) and *Target* = (*thead, ttail*) are preconditions of `Swap_Tail`, then the postcondition is

$$Source' = (shead, ttail) \land Target' = (thead, stail).$$

However, if either *Source* or *Target* is empty, then its corresponding tail is empty and the postcondition for the corresponding list, *Source'* or *Target'*, would be *ttail* or *stail*, respectively, *Source'* = *ttail* or *Target'* = *stail*.

The two append operations append the second operand to the first. In the case of the operation that appends a list to a list, `Append` (`List, Sublist`), only is the value of the sublist appended to the list, the postcondition of the operation for the sublist is that it is empty. `Process_Head` and `Update_Head` either perform a process on the head of a list, which might modify the value of the head, or update the value of the head.

The abstraction for lists, described in Listing 5.1, might best be appreciated through a simple application. Consider using a list to sort an unbound collection of numbers. The client's interface package, which appears in Listing 5.2, connects the `List_Polymorphic_Cntl` package with the client's program that appears in Listing 5.3. The client's software sorts an unbound collection of numbers. First, note that since the list is implemented as a `controlled` type the initialization and finalization are performed automatically by the system. Both the sort, `Sort_In`, and listing, `Print`, algorithms are recursive. Observe the use of just a few resources, `New_Head`, `Head`, and `Tail_Of`, from `List_Polymorphic_Cntl`, to accomplish the task. This is because of the elegant match between the abstraction, the encapsulation, and the representation of lists as a recursively defined and dynamically allocated structure.

Listing 5.2. Client's `List_Sort` interface.

```
with List_Polymorphic_cntl, Text_IO;   use List_Polymorphic_cntl;

package List_Sort_Pak is
   package tio renames Text_IO;
   package iio is new Text_IO.integer_io(integer);
   package lst renames List_Polymorphic_Cntl;

type Int_Obj is new Place_Holder with
   record
      Data: integer;
   end record;

end List_Sort_Pak;
```

Listing 5.3. `List_Sort` **program.**

```
with List_Sort_Pak;   use List_Sort_Pak;
procedure List_Sort is
   function Head is new lst.Head_Value (Int_Obj);
List: lst.List_Type;
Item: integer;

procedure Print (List: in      lst.List_Type) is
   begin -- Print
   if not lst.Empty (List) then
      iio.Put (Head(List).Data, 8);
      Print (lst.Tail_Of(List));
   end if;
   end Print;
----------------------------------------------------------
procedure Get_And_Sort (List: in out lst.List_Type;
                        str : in      string) is
   In_File: tio.File_Type;
   Number : Int_Obj;
   procedure Sort_In (Number: in      Int_Obj;
                      List  : in      lst.List_Type) is
      begin -- Sort_In
         if lst.Empty (List) then
            lst.New_Head (Number, List);
          elsif Number.Data < Head(List).Data then
            lst.New_Head (Number, List);
           else
            Sort_In (Number, lst.Tail_Of (List));
         end if;
      end Sort_In;
   -----------------------------------------------
   begin -- Get_And_Sort
      tio.Open (In_File, tio.in_file, str);
      while not tio.End_Of_File (In_File) loop
         iio.Get (In_File, Number.Data);         tio.Skip_Line (In_File);
         Sort_In (Number, List);
      end loop;
      tio.Close (In_File);
   end Get_And_Sort;
----------------------------------------------------------
begin -- List_Sort
   Get_And_Sort (List, "random.dat");    tio.New_Line;
   Print (List);    tio.New_Line;
end List_Sort;
```

A careful study of the `Sort_In` reveals the classical structure of recursive algorithms. Recursive algorithms are typically if-else or case structures that contain one or more alternatives that terminate the recursion and one or more alternatives that make a direct or indirect recursive call. In the case of `Sort_In`, there are two terminating alternatives, when the list is empty, and when the value

Listing 5.4. Private declarations for a static `List_Type`.

```
private
   type List_Rec is
      record
         Object: Object_Type;
         Index : natural;
      end record;
   type Array_Type is array (natural range <>) of List_Rec;

   type List_Type (Max_Size: positive) is
      record
         Start    : natural;
         Available: natural;
         Item     : (1..Max_Size);
      end record;
```

of the number that is being inserted is less than the value of the object at the head of the list. Otherwise, the procedure recursively calls itself and passes the tail of the current list to the recursive call. By passing the tail to the recursive call, the original list is processed one object at a time until the proper location for the new object is found.

Note the simplicity of the `Print` procedure; it too is written recursively. The head of the list is printed and the tail of the list is passed on to the recursive call to print the rest of the list. Typical of most recursive procedures, there is a surprisingly small amount of code, when compared to most nonrecursive procedures that perform the same process.

5.1.2 Representation

5.1.2.1 Static

A frequently overlooked representation of lists is a static representation. A list may be stored as an array of records, each record containing an `Object_Type` and an index. The index indicates the array location that contains the next record in the linear structure. Listing 5.4 illustrates one possible set of declarations leading to `List_Type`.

The static representation encapsulates many of the challenges that must be addressed with dynamic representations, including memory management. For example, the `Initialize` procedure sets `Start` to zero, to indicate the list is empty, and uses `Available` to create a linked structure of records. This is accomplished with the loop in Listing 5.5, along with making `List.Available`

Listing 5.5. Static `Initialize`.

```
procedure Initialize (List: in out List_Type) is
   begin -- Initialize
      List.Start    := 0;
      List.Available:= 1;
      for i in 1..Max_Size-1 loop
         List.Item(i).Index:= i+1;
      end loop;
      List.Item (Max_Size).Index:= 0;
   end Initialize;
```

point to the first available record and placing a zero in `List.Item(Max_Size)`, to indicate that no record follows this one.

Now, as records are inserted and removed from the list, not only must the record be added to the list structure, which is pointed to by `List.Start`, but a record must be removed from the linked collection of available records, pointed to by `List.Available`. For example, consider `Insert`, illustrated in Listing 5.6. This procedure must remove array records from the linked structure indicated by `List.Available` and place it on the list.

Listing 5.6. Static `Insert`.

```
procedure Insert (Object: in      Object_Type;
                  List  : in out List_Type) is
   begin -- Insert
      if List.Available = 0 then
         raise List_Overflow;
       else
         Hold:= List.Item(List.Available).Next;
         List.Item(List.Available).Next:= List.Start;
         List.Start:= List.Available;
         List.Available:= Hold;
         List.Item(List.Start).Object:= Object;
      end if;
   end Insert;
```

5.1.2.2 Dynamic

Perhaps the most important dynamic representation of a homogeneous structure is the dynamic representation of lists. Not only does it form the basis of the representation of many linear structures, but the basic recursive algorithmic structure described here becomes the foundation for the algorithmic structures for the most important nonlinear structure, trees. The structure may be built upon the private declarations that appear in Listing 5.7. A visualization of that structure appears in Figure 5.2.

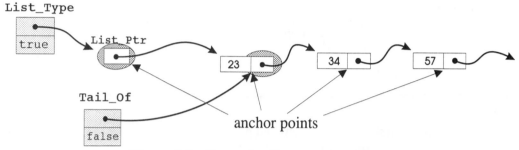

Figure 5.2. Recursive list representation.

An important key to the simplicity of the implementation is the use of **aliasing**. An `aliased` declaration means that the aliased object may be accessed with an alias, another name. Aliasing may be dangerous because a statement could change the value of an `aliased` variable without referencing the variable's, or component's, original name. However, here `aliased` declarations only appear in the private declarations, where they are not accessible by package clients. The combination of the `aliased` component within each record with the `access all` declaration of `List_Ptr` provides the features needed to support clean recursive processing of recursively defined structures. Having the access types within each record `aliased` supports the formation of the address of the

Listing 5.7. Private declarations for `List_Polymorphic_Cntl`.

```
       . . .
private

type Place_Holder is abstract new controlled with
    record
        Next: aliased Holder_Class_Ptr:= null;
    end record;
----------------------------------------
type List_Anchor is access all Holder_Class_Ptr;

type List_Type is new controlled with
    record
        Actual: List_Anchor:= null;
        Base  : boolean     := true;
    end record;

end List_Polymorphic_Cntl;
```

component through the 'Access attribute. The access all clause in the List_Anchor declaration permits an aliased access to be placed in a List_Anchor. Aliased components permit lists to be processed recursively in an efficient manner with direct access to each record's access component, which simplifies the code and passing the address of the sublist anchor point, which is the Next component in the record containing the head of the list.

Listing 5.8 contains the body for List_Polymorphic_ Cntl and contains Initialize and Finalize, which are automatically dispatched by the system each time a new List_Type is created and terminated. Initialize prepares a List_Type for use by allocating a List_Anchor and setting it to null. The role of Finalize is to recycle all dynamically allocated space that has been allocated to the list. This is accomplished by using Cur_Ptr and Nxt_Ptr to deallocate the linear structure.

Head_Of returns a copy of the front object, List.all.Object. Tail_Of returns a new List_Type that contains access to the tail of the current list, list.all.next'Access, which is itself a list. Since Tail_Of is a function, and during recursive processing this value is passed as a parameter, it must be passed as an in-only parameter. This is why the List_Type parameters in most of the subprograms in this package are in-only parameters. Note that Tail_Of sets Answer.Base to false. This is used by the Finalize procedure to distinguish between the List_Type that points to the anchor point of the entire list, and other List_Type objects that point only to the anchor points of sublists. Hence, the part of the list they anchor should not be finalized.

Since List_Types are passed as in-only parameters, how can lists be modified? The answer requires a careful look at Figure 5.2. Note that the List_Anchor in List_Type points to an access type. The List_Anchor is not modified, but the contents of the location it accesses may be modified.

Listing 5.8 contains the bodies of the procedures Swap_Tail, New_Head, and Remove_Head. The procedure New_Head takes a list and adds a new head to the list. The old head becomes part of the tail of the list. This is accomplished by allocating a new record, linking the pointer to the original head into the Next component, placing the new head object into that record, and then resetting the list pointer to point to the new record.

There are two head removal procedures, Remove_Head, which returns a pointer to the removed object at the head of the list, and the generic procedure Remove_Ext_Head, which may be instantiated to directly receive the client's object that is being removed from the list. Remove_Head complements New_Head, in that it removes the head of a list and replaces the head by the first object in the tail, the head of the tail sublist. The list head is removed by

Listing 5.8. `List_Polymorphic_Cntl` **body.**

```
with Unchecked_Deallocation;
package body List_Polymorphic_Cntl is
   procedure Free is new
      Unchecked_Deallocation (Place_Holder'Class, Holder_Class_Ptr);
   procedure Free is new
      Unchecked_Deallocation (Holder_Class_Ptr, List_Anchor);
   procedure Recycle (Point: in out Holder_Class_Ptr) renames Free;

procedure Initialize (Object: in out Place_Holder) is
   begin -- Initialize
      null;
   end Initialize;
-------------------------------------------------------
procedure Finalize (Object: in out Place_Holder) is
   begin -- Finalize
      null;
   end Finalize;
-------------------------------------------------------
procedure Adjust (Object: in out Place_Holder) is
   begin -- Adjust
      null;
   end Adjust;
-------------------------------------------------------
procedure Initialize (List: in out List_Type) is
   begin -- Initialize
      List.Actual:= new Holder_Class_Ptr;
      List.Base  := true;
   end Initialize;
-------------------------------------------------------
function Tail_Of (List: List_Type) return List_Type is
   Answer: List_Type;
   begin -- Tail_Of
      if List.Actual = null then
         raise List_Underflow;
       else
         Answer.Actual:= list.Actual.all.next'Access;
         Answer.Base  := false;
         return Answer;
      end if;
   end Tail_Of;
-------------------------------------------------------
procedure Finalize (List: in out List_Type) is
   Cur_Ptr: Holder_Class_Ptr;
   begin -- Finalize
      if List.Base then
         while List.Actual.all /= null loop
            Remove_Head (List, Cur_Ptr);
         end loop;
            Finalize (Cur_Ptr.all);
            Free (Cur_Ptr);
            Free (List.Actual);
      end if;
   end Finalize;
```

Listing 5.8. (cont.)

```
function Head_Value (List: List_Type) return Extended_Type is
   begin -- Head_Value
      if List.Actual.all = null then
         raise List_Underflow;
       else
         declare
            Ans_Ptr: Holder_Class_Ptr := Head_Of(List);
            Answer : Extended_Type := Extended_Type(Ans_Ptr.all);
         begin
            Free (Ans_Ptr);
            return Answer;
         end;
      end if;
   end Head_Value;
----------------------------------------------------
function Head_Of (List: List_Type) return Holder_Class_Ptr is
   begin -- Head_Of
      if List.Actual.all = null then
         raise List_Underflow;
       else
         declare
            Answer: Holder_Class_Ptr
                   := new Place_Holder'Class'(List.Actual.all.all);
         begin
            Answer.Next := null;
            return Answer;
         end;
      end if;
   end Head_Of;
----------------------------------------------------
function Empty (List: List_Type) return boolean is
   begin -- Empty
      return List.Actual.all = null;
   end Empty;
----------------------------------------------------
procedure New_Head (Object: in      Place_Holder'Class;
                    List   : in      List_Type) is
   New_Elem: Holder_Class_Ptr;
   begin -- New_Head
      New_Elem:= new Place_Holder'Class'(Object);
      New_Elem.Next  := List.Actual.all;
      List.Actual.all:= New_Elem;
   end New_Head;
----------------------------------------------------
procedure Remove_Ext_Head (List  : in      List_Type;
                           Object: in out Ext_Type) is
   Old_One: Holder_Class_Ptr;
   begin -- Remove_Ext_Head
      Remove_Head (List, Old_One);
      Object := Ext_Type(Old_One.all);
      Free (Old_One);
   end Remove_Ext_Head;
```

Listing 5.8. (cont.)

```
function Empty_List return List_Type is
    Answer: List_Type;
    begin -- Empty_List
        return Answer;
    end Empty_List;
--------------------------------------------------
procedure Remove_Head (List  : in      List_Type;
                       Object: in out Holder_Class_Ptr) is
    begin -- Remove_Head
        if List.Actual.all = null then
            raise List_Underflow;
          else
            if Object /= null then
                Finalize (Object.all);    Free (Object);
            end if;
            Object          := List.Actual.all;
            List.Actual.all:= Object.Next;
            Object.Next     := null;
        end if;
    end Remove_Head;
--------------------------------------------------
procedure Append (List    : in     List_Type;
                  New_Tail: in out List_Type) is
    procedure Rec_app (Point: in out Holder_Class_Ptr) is
        begin -- Rec_app
            if Point = null then
                Point:= New_Tail.Actual.all;
                New_Tail.Actual.all:= null;
              else
                Rec_App (Point.Next);
            end if;
        end Rec_app;
    --------------------------------------------------
    begin -- Append
        if New_Tail.Actual.all = List.Actual.all then
            raise constraint_error;
          elsif New_Tail.Actual.all /= null then
            Rec_App (List.Actual.all);
        end if;
    end Append;
--------------------------------------------------
procedure Update_Head (List  : in     List_Type;
                       Object: in     Place_Holder'Class) is
    Holder_Ptr: Holder_Class_Ptr;
    begin -- Update_Head
        if List.Actual.all /= null then
            Remove_Head (List, Holder_Ptr);    Free (Holder_Ptr);
            New_Head (Object, List);
          else
            raise List_Underflow;
        end if;
    end Update_Head;
```

Listing 5.8. (cont.)

```
procedure Append (List    : in      List_Type;
                  New_Tail: in      Place_Holder'Class) is
   Temp: List_Type;
   begin -- Append
      New_Head (New_Tail, Temp);   Append (List, Temp);
   end Append;
-------------------------------------------------------
procedure Adjust (List: in out List_Type) is
   Original: Holder_Class_Ptr;
   procedure Clone (Source, Target: in out Holder_Class_Ptr) is
      begin -- Clone
         if Source /= null then
            Target     := new Place_Holder'Class'(Source.all);
            Target.all := Source.all;   Target.Next:= null;
            Clone (Source.Next, Target.Next);
         end if;
      end Clone;
   -------------------------------------------------------
   begin
      Original:= List.Actual.all;   List.Actual.all:= null;
      Clone (Original, List.Actual.all);
   end Adjust;
-------------------------------------------------------
procedure Swap (Source: in out List_Type;
                Target: in out List_Type) is
   Temp: Holder_Class_Ptr;
   begin -- Swap
      Temp := Target.Actual.all;   Target.Actual.all:= Source.Actual.all;
      Source.Actual.all:= Temp;
   end Swap;
-------------------------------------------------------
procedure Swap_Tail (Source: in      List_Type;
                     Target: in      List_Type) is
   Tail_S, Tail_T: Holder_Class_Ptr;
   begin -- Swap_Tail
      if Source.Actual.all = Target.Actual.all then raise constraint_error;
         else
            if Target.Actual.all = null then Tail_T:= null;
              else
                 Tail_T:=Target.Actual.all.Next; Target.Actual.all.Next:= null;
            end if;
            if Source.Actual.all = null then
                 Tail_S := null; Source.Actual.all:= Tail_T;
               else
                 Tail_S:=Source.Actual.all.Next;Source.Actual.all.Next:=Tail_T;
            end if;
            if Target.Actual.all = null then Target.Actual.all:= Tail_S;
               else                                Target.Actual.all.Next:= Tail_S;
            end if;
      end if;
   end Swap_Tail;
end List_Polymorphic_Cntl;
```

replacing the contents of the list's anchor point with access to the dynamic record immediately following the original head.

Swap_Tail is one of the more complex algorithms in this package because it must consider the possibility that one, or both, of the Source and Target lists are empty. As a result, it must go through a series of if-else structures to handle these possibilities. The first if-else structure finds the tail of Target, or a null pointer to indicate an empty tail. The second if-else structure does the same for Source, but as it finds the tail of Source, it properly attaches Tail_T as either the tail of Source, or the entire value of Source, if it had been empty. Finally, in the third if-else structure, Source's original tail is properly attached to Target.

Listing 5.8 contains a variety of useful subprograms, Process_Head, Update_Head, and two versions of Append. The procedure Update_Head simply changes the value of the head of the list. Process_Head allows a client to perform a procedure on the head of a list without the need to copy the object from the list, perform the process, and then update the head with the value returned by the process. This is accomplished by passing the procedure as a parameter to Process_Head, which in turn performs that process on the head of the list.

Two versions of Append are provided, one that appends an object to a list, and a second that appends a list to the tail of a list. The version of Append that concatenates one list onto the end of another uses a recursive subprogram to recursively process down to the end of the list. When it finds the end of the list, the New_Tail is attached and set to null, to indicate that it is now empty.

The version of Append that attaches a single object makes use of the version that appends a list, by creating a new list, Temp, initializes it, inserts the object into the new list, calls the other version of Append, and then finalizes the temporary list.

Finally, Listing 5.8 contains Adjust and Swap. Adjust is dispatched by the system during assignment of List_Types to duplicate the list structure:

```
A:= B;
```

Swap is made available as an alternative to using assignment if the values of objects need only be swapped. Recall that when unbounded object types are copied,

```
temp:= A;      -- time dependent on object size
A    := B;      -- time dependent on object size
B    := temp;   -- time dependent on object size
```

the time required to perform this depends on the sizes of objects. However, swapping may frequently be achieved by simply exchanging pointers to structures. Swap is essential if List_Type becomes the base object type upon which other objects are constructed. For many data structures to be safely and efficiently manipulated, safe assignment and swap are both essential. Duplication can be expensive, in terms of both timing and memory. Sometimes the data structure package need only swap object values in lieu of duplicating data structures. Swapping is both time and memory efficient.

The Adjust procedure contains a recursive subprocedure, Clone, that recursively traverses both the list to be copied and the copy being made to duplicate the original list. On the other hand, Swap is a very quick procedure that uses a temporary variable to assist in swapping the values of the two lists.

5.1.3 Encapsulation

The list representation was described along with its encapsulation in the List_Polymorphic_Cntl package. This is only one of many potential encapsulations of list structures.

5.1.4 Advanced Support

Listing 5.9 contains the specification for the List_Polymorphic_Cntl. Advanced child unit. It contains the usual assortment of advanced support procedures for linear structures, Size_Of, Peek, Poke, Insert, and Remove subprograms. The bodies of some of these procedures take maximum advantage of the recursive nature of the list.

For example, the Size function, which appears in Listing 5.10, uses recursion to traverse down the list and counts the number of objects in the list. Recursion is not always the most efficient way to solve a problem. The Size function could have been written iteratively to traverse the loop. This is left as an exercise for the reader.

Peek and Poke, in Listing 5.10, are written recursively. Peek traverses the list recursively until it locates the head of the list containing the desired object and then produces the result:

```
return Head_Of(Sublist);
```

Listing 5.9. `List_Polymorphic_Cntl.Advanced` **specifications.**

```
package List_Polymorphic_Cntl.Advanced is

function Size (List: List_Type) return integer;

procedure Insert (Object  : in      Place_Holder'Class;
                  Position: in      positive;
                  List    : in      List_Type);

procedure Remove (List    : in      List_Type;
                  Position: in      positive;
                  Object  : in out Holder_Class_Ptr);

function Peek (List : List_Type;
              Index: positive) return Holder_Class_Ptr;

procedure Poke (List  : in      List_Type;
                Index : in      positive;
                Object: in      Place_Holder'Class);

end List_Polymorphic_Cntl.Advanced;
```

Similarly, `Poke` uses recursion to traverse to the sublist whose head is to be replaced, and performs

```
Update_Head (Sublist, Object);
```

Finally, the procedures `Insert` and `Remove`, which appear in Listing 5.10, algorithmically are somewhat like the `Poke` procedure in that they recursively traverse to the head of the sublist where the insertion or removal is to take place. Once the position is found, the `Insert` procedures performs

```
New_Head (Object, Sublist);
```

to insert the new object, and `Remove` performs

```
Remove_Head (Sublist, Object);
```

to remove the object.

5.1.5 Iterators

The child unit `List_Polymorphic_Cntl.Iterators` contains three list iterators, as indicated by its specifications in Listing 5.11. Two of the iterators traverse the list in the directions indicated by their names, passing the objects in the list, one at a time, to the user-supplied `Process`. Note also the type

Listing 5.10. `List_Polymorphic_Cntl.Advanced` **body.**

```
package body List_Polymorphic_Cntl.Advanced is

function Size (List: List_Type) return integer is
   function Rec_Size (Point: Holder_Class_Ptr) return integer is
      begin -- Rec_Size
         if Point = null then return 0;
            else return 1+Rec_Size (Point.Next);
         end if;
      end Rec_Size;
   -------------------------------------------------
   begin -- Size
      return Rec_Size (List.Actual.all);
   end Size;
   -------------------------------------------------
procedure Poke (List  : in      List_Type;
                Index : in      positive;
                Object: in      Place_Holder'Class) is
   procedure Rec_Poke (Sublist: in    List_Type; Count: in     natural) is
      begin -- Rec_Poke
         if Count = Index then Update_Head (Sublist, Object);
            else Rec_Poke (Tail_Of(Sublist), Count+1);
         end if;
      end Rec_Poke;
   -------------------------------------------------
   begin -- Poke
      if Empty(List) then
         raise List_Underflow;
       elsif Index > Size (List) then
         raise constraint_error;
       else
         Rec_Poke (List, 1);
      end if;
   end Poke;
   -------------------------------------------------
function Peek (List: List_Type;
              Index  : positive) return Holder_Class_Ptr is
   function Rec_Peek (Sublist: in     List_Type;
                      Count  : in      natural) return Holder_Class_Ptr is
      begin -- Rec_Peek
         if Count = Index then
            return Head_Of(Sublist);
          else
            return Rec_Peek (Tail_Of(Sublist), Count+1);
         end if;
      end Rec_Peek;
   -------------------------------------------------
   begin -- Peek
      if Empty(List) then
         raise List_Underflow;
       elsif Index > Size (List) then raise constraint_error;
       else return Rec_Peek(List, 1);
      end if;
   end Peek;
```

Listing 5.10. (cont.)

```
procedure Insert (Object   : in      Place_Holder'Class;
                  Position: in      positive;
                  List     : in      List_Type) is
    procedure Rec_Insert (Sublist: in     List_Type;
                          Count  : in     natural) is
        begin -- Rec_Insert
            if Count = Position then New_Head (Object, Sublist);
                else         Rec_Insert (Tail_Of(Sublist), Count+1);
            end if;
        end Rec_Insert;
        ------------------------------------------------
    begin -- Insert
    if Position > (Size (List)+1) then raise List_Underflow;
       elsif Position = (Size (List)+1) then Append (List, Object);
       else  Rec_Insert (List, 1);
    end if;
    end Insert;
    ------------------------------------------------
procedure Remove (List     : in      List_Type;
                  Position: in      positive;
                  Object   : in out Holder_Class_Ptr) is
    procedure Rec_Remove (Sublist: in     List_Type;
                          Count  : in     natural) is
        begin -- Rec_Remove
            if Count = Position then Remove_Head (Sublist, Object);
                else             Rec_Remove (Tail_Of(Sublist), Count+1);
            end if;
        end Rec_Remove;
        ------------------------------------------------
    begin -- Remove
    if Position > Size(List) then raise constraint_error;
       else                          Rec_Remove (List, 1);
    end if;
    end Remove;

end List_Polymorphic_Cntl.Advanced;
```

declaration for the specifications of the procedure type that is passed to the iterators. As with other iterators, procedures passed to this iterator have an additional parameter that may be used to terminate the iteration. The third iterator makes a round trip, first processing down the list calling one procedure, then processing up the list calling a second procedure.

Listing 5.12 contains the bodies of the three recursive list iterators. Each procedure contains a recursive subprocedure. The Front_To_Rear iterator calls the Round_Trip iterator with the client's process as Down_Proc. Rear_To_Front calls Round_Trip with the client's process as the Up_Proc. As a result, there is only one algorithm, Round_Trip, that recursively traverses

Listing 5.11. `List_Polymorphic_Cntl.Iterators` **specifications.**

```
package List_Polymorphic_Cntl.Iterators is

type Process_Type is access
   procedure (Object  : in out Holder_Class_Ptr;
              Continue: in out Boolean);

procedure Front_To_Rear (List    : in      List_Type;
                         Process:          Process_Type);

procedure Rear_To_Front (List    : in      List_Type;
                         Process:          Process_Type);

procedure Round_Trip (List      : in      List_Type;
                      Down_Proc,
                      Up_Proc   :         Process_Type);

end List_Polymorphic_Cntl.Iterators;
```

down the list calling `Down_Proc` and then recursively ascends calling `Up_Proc`.

5.1.6 Measurement

The time requirements that correspond to the various procedures in the parent unit `List_Polymorphic_Cntl` are all bound by a constant or linear time. The `Peek`, `Poke`, `Insert`, and `Remove` procedures in `List_Polymorphic_Cntl.Advanced` all contain loops. In each case, the number of loops is bound by the number of objects in the list, which is not an unreasonable bound. If a procedure is recursive, it has a space requirement, $S(n)$, that is a linear function of the number of recursive calls n, $S(n) = O(n)$.

The two iterators in `List_Polymorphic_Cntl.Iterators` use recursion to process the list. Obviously, the time for each of these procedures is bound by the sum of the timings of each call to the user-defined process. If P is the upper bound on the time of one call to the user-defined process, then the time required to perform an iterator that uses the process is bound by $T \le nP$. Since the iterators are recursive, the space requirements for each iterator are bound by $O(n)$, where n is the number of objects in the list being processed.

Listing 5.12. `List_Polymorphic_Cntl.Iterators` **body.**

```
package body List_Polymorphic_Cntl.Iterators is

procedure Null_Proc (Object  : in out Holder_Class_Ptr;
                     Continue: in out boolean) is
   begin -- Null_Proc
      null;
   end Null_Proc;
   -------------------------------------------------
procedure Front_To_Rear (List    : in    List_Type;
                         Process:            Process_Type) is
   begin -- Front_To_Rear
      Round_Trip (List, Process, Null_Proc'Access);
   end Front_To_Rear;
   -------------------------------------------------
procedure Rear_To_Front (List    : in    List_Type;
                         Process:            Process_Type) is
   begin -- Rear_To_Front
      Round_Trip (List, Null_Proc'Access, Process);
   end Rear_To_Front;
   -------------------------------------------------
procedure Round_Trip (List     : in    List_Type;
                      Down_Proc,
                      Up_Proc  :        Process_Type) is
   Continue: boolean:= true;
   procedure Rec_Iter (Point: in out Holder_Class_Ptr) is
      begin -- Rec_Iter
         if Point /= null then
            Down_Proc (Point, Continue);
            if Continue then
               Rec_Iter (Point.Next);
               if Continue then
                  Up_Proc (Point, Continue);
               end if;
            end if;
         end if;
      end Rec_Iter;
      -------------------------------------------------
   begin -- Round_Trip
      Rec_Iter (List.Actual.all);
   end Round_Trip;
   -------------------------------------------------
end List_Polymorphic_Cntl.Iterators;
```

5.2 Positional Paradigm

Another view of lists is with the positional paradigm, which is illustrated in Figure 5.3. This paradigm views the contents of a list by navigating a current position indicator across the list in a linear way from object to object. In the positional paradigm, the current viewing position is moved an object at a time

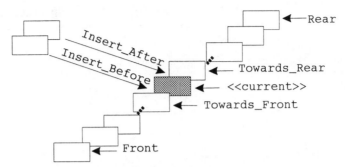

Figure 5.3. Positional paradigm view.

from the current viewing position to either the object that precedes it, the object that follows it, or two special positions, the beginning of the list or the end of the list.

5.2.1 Abstraction

The positional paradigm requires more support than the recursive paradigm. Where the recursive paradigm has one navigation procedure, `Tail_Of`, the positional paradigm has four, `Move_To_Front`, `Move_To_Rear`, `Move_Towards_Front`, and `Move_Towards_Rear`. The recursive paradigm has one insertion procedure, `Insert_Head`; the positional paradigm has two, `Insert_Before` and `Insert_After`. Listing 5.13 contains the specifications for the positional paradigm.

The positional paradigm may be viewed formally as an $(n+1)$-tuple, $L = (i, a_1, \ldots, a_n)$, where i is a natural number, $i \in [0..n]$, and n is the number of objects in the list. An empty list is represented in this formalism with the 1-tuple, (0). The $(n+1)$ tuple, $L = (0, a_1, a_2, \ldots, a_n)$, indicates a list where the current viewing position is undefined. This formalism provides an easy way to describe the preconditions and postconditions of the subprograms in the package's specifications. For example, if the list L is specified as $L = (i, a_1, a_2, \ldots, a_n)$, then the postconditions of the navigation procedures may be specified as

$$L' = (i-1, a_1, a_2, \ldots, a_n) \text{ if } i \notin \{0,1\}$$

Listing 5.13. `List_Pos_Polymorphic_Cntl` **specifications.**

```
   with Ada.Finalization; use Ada.Finalization;
package List_Pos_Polymorphic_Cntl is
   type Place_Holder is abstract new controlled with private;
      procedure Initialize (Object: in out Place_Holder);
      procedure Finalize (Object: in out Place_Holder);
      procedure Adjust (Object: in out Place_Holder);
   type Holder_Class_Ptr is access Place_Holder'Class;
      procedure Recycle (Point: in out Holder_Class_Ptr);
   type List_Type is new controlled with private;
      procedure Initialize (List: in out List_Type);
      procedure Finalize (List: in out List_Type);
      procedure Adjust (List: in out List_Type);

   List_Underflow, List_Overflow, Undefined_position: exception;
   Invalid_Remove, Invalid_Share: exception;

procedure Move_To_Front (List: in out List_Type);
procedure Move_To_Rear (List: in out List_Type);
procedure Move_Towards_Front (List: in out List_Type);
procedure Move_Towards_Rear (List: in out List_Type);

function Current_Object (List: List_Type) return Holder_Class_Ptr;
function Current_Defined (List: List_Type) return boolean;
function Empty (List: List_Type) return boolean;
function At_Rear (List : List_Type) return boolean;
function At_Front (List: List_Type) return boolean;
procedure Append (List    : in out List_Type;
                  New_Tail: in out List_Type);
procedure Append (List    : in out List_Type;
                  New_Tail: in out Place_Holder'Class);
procedure Insert_Before (Object: in out Place_Holder'Class;
                         List  : in out List_Type);
procedure Insert_Before (Objects: in out List_Type;
                         List   : in out List_Type);
procedure Insert_After (Object: in out Place_Holder'Class;
                        List  : in out List_Type  );
procedure Insert_After (Objects: in out List_Type;
                        List   : in out List_Type);
   type In_Place_Process_Type is access
       procedure (Object: in out Holder_Class_Ptr);
procedure Process_Current (List   : in out List_Type;
                           Process:         In_Place_Process_Type);
procedure Remove_Current (List  : in out List_Type;
                          Object: in out Holder_Class_Ptr);
procedure Update_Current (List  : in out List_Type;
                          Object: in out Place_Holder'Class);
procedure Slice_Tail (Source: in out List_Type;
                      Target: in out List_Type);
procedure Swap (Source: in out List_Type;
                Target: in out List_Type);
private
   ...
end List_Pos_Polymorphic_Cntl;
```

for `Move_Towards_Front`;

$$L' = ((i+1) \bmod (n+1), a_1, a_2, \ldots, a_n) \text{ if } i \notin \{0, n\}$$

for `Move_Towards_Rear`;

$$L' = (1, a_1, a_2, \ldots, a_n) \text{ if } n \neq 0$$

for `Move_To_Front`; and

$$L' = (n, a_1, a_2, \ldots, a_n) \text{ if } n \neq 0$$

for `Move_To_Rear`.

`Insert_Before` inserts an object into the list before the currently viewed object. If $L = (i, a_1, a_2, \ldots, a_n)$, then

$$L' = (i+1, a_1, \ldots, a_{i-1}, Object, a_i, \ldots, a_n)$$

is the postcondition for `Insert_Before`. Note that the object a_i is in the $(i+1)$-st position. The postcondition for `Insert_After` is

$$L' = (i, a_1, \ldots, a_i, Object, a_{i+1}, \ldots, a_n).$$

Given a list, $L = (i, a_1, a_2, \ldots, a_n)$, if $i \neq n$, the postcondition for the procedure `Remove_Current` is $L' = (i, a_1, \ldots, a_{i-1}, a_{i+1}, \ldots, a_n)$, where a_{i+1} is in the ith position in the list. When $i = n$, the postcondition is

$$L' = (n-1, a_1, a_2, \ldots, a_{n-1}).$$

5.2.2 Representation

Figure 5.4 illustrates one implementation of the positional paradigm. This representation includes structures that are required to handle additional features that will be presented in the `.Advanced` package. The `Current` component in

`List_Type` points to the record that contains the currently viewed objects. The `Actual` component points to the list descriptor record, `List_Descriptor` type, which contains the pointers, `First` and `Last`, that point to the two ends of the linked structure.   The reason for the existence of both `List_Type` and `List_Desc` is to assist in the implementation of list sharing, where lists may share a part of their representations.

The dynamic representation contains two subprograms, `Size` and `Insert_First`, that are used by other subprograms.   The bodies of these procedures appear in Listing 5.14. `Size` establishes a `List_Ptr`, `Temp`, that is set to the first object in the list and counts the number of objects in the list until `Temp` becomes `null`.

`Insert_First` is used by both `Insert_Before` and `Insert_After` to place the first object in the linked structure when they detect that the structure is empty.   `Insert_First` allocates a new `List_Descriptor`, as well as an `Object_Holder`, points the `First` and `Last` components to the newly allocated

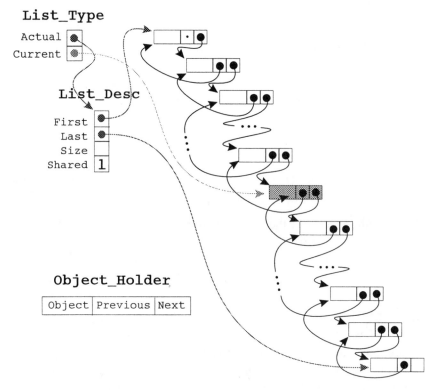

Figure 5.4. Two way positional list representation.

Listing 5.14. `List_Pos_Polymorphic_Cntl` **body.**

```
with Unchecked_Deallocation;
package body List_Pos_Polymorphic_Cntl is
   procedure Free is new
           Unchecked_Deallocation (Place_Holder'Class, Holder_Class_Ptr);
procedure Free is new Unchecked_Deallocation (List_Descriptor, Desc_Ptr);
procedure Recycle (Point: in out Holder_Class_Ptr) renames Free;

procedure Initialize (Object: in out Place_Holder) is
   begin -- Initialize
      null;
   end Initialize;
----------------------------------------------------------
procedure Finalize (Object: in out Place_Holder) is
   begin -- Finalize
      null;
   end Finalize;
----------------------------------------------------------
procedure Adjust (Object: in out Place_Holder) is
   begin -- Adjust
      null;
   end Adjust;
----------------------------------------------------------
procedure Initialize (List: in out List_Type) is
   begin -- Initialize
   List.Current:= null;
   List.Actual := null;
   end Initialize;
----------------------------------------------------------
procedure Finalize (List: in out List_Type) is
   Ignore: Holder_Class_Ptr;
   begin
      if List.Actual.Shared > 1 then
         List.Actual.Shared:= List.Actual.Shared - 1;
         List.Current:= null;
         List.Actual := null;
        else -- if List.Actual /= null then
         Move_To_Front (List);
         while List.Current /= null loop
            Remove_Current (List, Ignore);
            Finalize (Ignore.all);
            Free (Ignore);
         end loop;
      end if;
   end Finalize;
----------------------------------------------------------
function Empty (List: List_Type) return boolean is
   begin
      if List.Actual = null then
         return true;
        else
         return false;
      end if;
   end Empty;
```

Listing 5.14. (cont.)

```
procedure Adjust (List: in out List_Type) is
   Old_Actual: Desc_Ptr:= List.Actual;
   Old_Current: Holder_Class_Ptr:= List.Current;
   procedure Rec_Clone (Source: in      Holder_Class_Ptr;
                         Target: in out Holder_Class_Ptr) is
      begin -- Rec_Clone
         if Source /= null then
            Target := new Place_Holder'Class'(Source.all);
            if Source = Old_Current then   List.Current := Target;
            end if;
            if Source = Old_Actual.Last then   List.Actual.Last := Target;
            end if;
            Rec_Clone (Source.Next, Target.Next);
            if Target.Next /= null then   Target.Next.Previous := Target;
            end if;
         end if;
      end Rec_Clone;
      -----------------------------------------------------------------
   begin -- Adjust
      if Old_Actual /= null then
         List.Actual := new List_Descriptor;
         Rec_Clone (Old_Actual.First, List.Actual.First);
         List.Actual.Size := Old_Actual.Size;
      end if;
   end Adjust;
   -----------------------------------------------------------------
function Size (List: List_Type) return natural is
   Answer : natural := 0;      Temp : Holder_Class_Ptr;
   begin -- Size
      if List.Actual /= null then
         Temp := List.Actual.First;
         while Temp /= null loop
            Answer := Answer + 1;  Temp := Temp.Next;
         end loop;
      end if;
   return Answer;
   end Size;
   ---------------------------------------------------------------
procedure Insert_First (Object: in out Place_Holder'Class;
                        List   : in out List_Type ) is
   New_Elem: Holder_Class_Ptr:= new Place_Holder'Class'(Object);
   begin
      if List.Actual = null then
         List.Actual           := new List_Descriptor;
         List.Actual.First := New_Elem;  List.Actual.Last   := New_Elem;
         List.Actual.Size  := 1;         List.Actual.Shared:= 1;
         New_Elem.Next     := null;      New_Elem.Previous := null;
         List.Current      := New_Elem;
       else
         Free (New_Elem);   raise Undefined_Position;
      end if;
   end Insert_First;
```

Listing 5.14. (cont.)

```
function Current_Defined (List: List_Type) return boolean is
   begin -- Current_Defined
      return not (List.Current = null);
   end Current_Defined;
-------------------------------------------------------------------
function At_Rear (List: List_Type) return boolean is
   begin
      if List.Actual = null or List.Current = null then
         return false;
       elsif List.Current = List.Actual.Last then
         return true;
       else
         return false;
      end if;
   end At_Rear;
-------------------------------------------------------------------
function At_Front (List: List_Type) return boolean is
   begin
      if List.Actual = null or List.Current = null then
         return false;
       elsif List.Current = List.Actual.First then
         return true;
       else
         return false;
      end if;
   end At_Front;
-------------------------------------------------------------------

procedure Move_To_Front (List: in out List_Type) is
   begin
      if List.Actual = null then
         raise List_Underflow;
       else
         List.Current:= List.Actual.First;
      end if;
   end Move_To_Front;
-------------------------------------------------------------------
procedure Move_To_Rear (List: in out List_Type) is
   begin
      if List.Actual = null then
         raise List_Underflow;
       else
         List.Current:= List.Actual.Last;
      end if;
   end Move_To_Rear;
-------------------------------------------------------------------
procedure Move_Towards_Front (List: in out List_Type) is
   begin
      if List.Actual = null then
          raise List_Underflow;
       elsif List.Current = null then
         raise Undefined_Position;
       else
         List.Current:= List.Current.Previous;
      end if;
   end Move_Towards_Front;
```

Listing 5.14. (cont.)

```
procedure Move_Towards_Rear (List: in out List_Type) is
   begin
      if List.Actual = null then              raise List_Underflow;
        elsif List.Current = null then      raise Undefined_Position;
        else                              List.Current:= List.Current.Next;
      end if;
   end Move_Towards_Rear;
------------------------------------------------------------------
procedure Insert_Before (Object: in out Place_Holder'Class;
                         List  : in out List_Type) is
   New_Elem: Holder_Class_Ptr:= new Place_Holder'Class'(Object);
   begin
      if List.Actual = null then
         Insert_First (Object, List);
        elsif List.Current = null then
         Free (New_Elem);   raise Undefined_Position;
        else                       -- The list is not empty
         New_Elem.Previous      := List.Current.Previous;
         List.Current.Previous := New_Elem;
         New_Elem.Next          := List.Current;
         if New_Elem.Previous = null then -- front
            List.Actual.First := New_Elem;
           else
            New_Elem.Previous.Next := New_Elem;
         end if;
         List.Actual.Size := List.Actual.Size + 1;
      end if;
   end Insert_Before;
------------------------------------------------------------------
procedure Insert_Before (Objects: in out List_Type;
                         List   : in out List_Type) is
   begin
      if Objects.Actual = null then          null;
        elsif Objects.Actual = List.Actual then
         raise Undefined_Position;
        elsif List.Actual = null then
         List := Objects;
         Objects.Current := null;  Objects.Actual  := null;
        elsif List.Current = null then        raise Undefined_Position;
        else
         Objects.Actual.First.Previous := List.Current.Previous;
         List.Current.Previous         := Objects.Actual.Last;
         Objects.Actual.Last.Next      := List.Current;
         if Objects.Actual.First.Previous = null then -- new front
            List.Actual.First := Objects.Actual.First;
           else
            Objects.Actual.First.Previous.Next:= Objects.Actual.First;
         end if;
         List.Actual.Size:= List.Actual.Size + Objects.Actual.Size;
         Free (Objects.Actual);   Objects.Current := null;
      end if;
   end Insert_Before;
```

Listing 5.14. (cont.)

```
procedure Append (List    : in out List_Type;
                  New_Tail: in out List_Type) is
   begin
      if New_Tail.Actual = List.Actual then  raise Undefined_Position;
         elsif New_Tail.Actual.Shared > 1 then  raise Invalid_Share;
         elsif not Empty (New_Tail) then
            If Empty (List) then
               List := New_Tail;
               New_Tail.Current := null;   New_Tail.Actual  := null;
             else
               List.Actual.Last.Next := New_Tail.Actual.First;
               New_Tail.Actual.First.Previous := List.Actual.Last;
               List.Actual.Last := New_Tail.Actual.Last;
               List.Actual.Size := List.Actual.Size + New_Tail.Actual.Size;
               Free (New_Tail.Actual);
               New_Tail.Current:= null;
            end if;
      end if;
   end Append;
------------------------------------------------------------------
procedure Append (List    : in out List_Type;
                  New_Tail: in out Place_Holder'Class) is
   Clone: List_Type:= List;
   begin -- Append
      If Empty (List) then                        raise List_Underflow;
         else
            Move_To_Rear (List);       Insert_After (New_Tail, List);
            if Clone.Current /= null then  List.Current := Clone.Current;
            end if;
      end if;
   end Append;
------------------------------------------------------------------
procedure Insert_After (Object: in out Place_Holder'Class;
                        List  : in out List_Type ) is
   New_Elem: Holder_Class_Ptr:= new Place_Holder'Class'(Object);
   begin
      if List.Actual = null then
         Insert_First (Object, List);
         elsif List.Current = null then
            Free (New_Elem);       raise Undefined_Position;
         else                        -- The list is not empty
            New_Elem.Next          := List.Current.Next;
            New_Elem.Previous       := List.Current;
            New_Elem.Previous.Next:= New_Elem;
            if New_Elem.Next = null then
               List.Actual.Last:= New_Elem;
             else
               New_Elem.Next.Previous:= New_Elem;
            end if;
            List.Actual.Size:= List.Actual.Size + 1;
      end if;
   end Insert_After;
```

Listing 5.14. (Cont.)

```
procedure Insert_After (Objects: in out List_Type;
                        List    : in out List_Type) is
   begin
      if Objects.Actual = List.Actual then
         raise Undefined_Position;
       elsif List.Actual = null then
         List := Objects;
         Objects.Current := null;
         Free (Objects.Actual);
       elsif List.Current = null then
         raise Undefined_Position;
       else
         Objects.Actual.First.Previous    := List.Current;
         Objects.Actual.Last.Next         := List.Current.Next;
         List.Current.Next            := Objects.Actual.First;
         if Objects.Actual.Last.Next = null then
            List.Actual.Last:= Objects.Actual.Last;
          else
            Objects.Actual.Last.Next.Previous:= Objects.Actual.Last;
         end if;
         List.Actual.Size:= List.Actual.Size + Objects.Actual.Size;
         Free (Objects.Actual);
      end if;
   end Insert_After;
-----------------------------------------------------------------
function Current_Object (List: List_Type) return Holder_Class_Ptr is
   Answer: Holder_Class_Ptr;
   begin
      if List.Current /= null then
         --Copy (List.Current.Object, Answer);
         Answer := new Place_Holder'Class'(List.Current.all);
         return Answer;
       else            raise Undefined_Position;
      end if;
   end Current_Object;
-----------------------------------------------------------------
procedure Process_Current (List    : in out List_Type;
                           Process:       In_Place_Process_Type) is
   begin
      if List.Current /= null then
         Process (List.Current);
       else
         raise Undefined_Position;
      end if;
   end Process_Current;
-----------------------------------------------------------------
procedure Swap (Source: in out List_Type;
                Target: in out List_Type) is
   Temp: List_Type := Target;
   begin -- Swap
      Target:= Source;    Source:= Temp;
   end Swap;
```

Listing 5.14. (cont.)

```
procedure Update_Current (List   : in out List_Type;
                          Object: in out Place_Holder'Class) is
   New_One: Holder_Class_Ptr := new Place_Holder'Class'(Object);
   begin
      if List.Current /= null then
         if List.Current.Previous /= null then
            New_One.Previous       := List.Current.Previous;
            New_One.Previous.Next:= New_One;
         end if;
         if List.Current.Next /= null then
            New_One.Next           := List.Current.Next;
            New_One.Next.Previous:= New_One;
         end if;
         free (List.Current);
         List.Current := New_One;
      else
         free (New_One);
         raise Undefined_Position;
      end if;
   end Update_Current;
-----------------------------------------------------------
procedure Remove_Current (List   : in out List_Type;
                          Object : in out Holder_Class_Ptr) is
   Posit: Holder_Class_Ptr := List.Current;
   begin
      if List.Actual.Shared > 1 then
         raise Invalid_Remove;
      elsif List.Current = null then
         raise Undefined_Position;
      else
         if List.Actual.Size = 1 then
            Free (List.Actual);
            List.Current:= null;
         else
            if Posit.Previous = null then -- front removed
               List.Actual.First  := Posit.Next;
            else
               Posit.Previous.Next := Posit.Next;
            end if;
            if Posit.Next = null then -- rear removed
               List.Actual.Last:= Posit.Previous;
               List.Current      := List.Actual.Last;
            else
               Posit.Next.Previous := Posit.Previous;
               List.Current:= Posit.Next;
            end if;
            List.Actual.Size:= List.Actual.Size - 1;
         end if;
         Free (Object);
         Object:= Posit;
      end if;
   end Remove_Current;
```

Listing 5.14. (cont.)

```
procedure Slice_Tail (Source: in out List_Type;
                      Target: in out List_Type) is
   begin -- Slice_Tail
      if Source.Actual = Target.Actual then
          raise Undefined_Position;
         elsif (Source.Actual = null) or (Target.Actual = null) then
          raise Undefined_Position;
         elsif (Target.Actual.Shared > 1) or (Source.Actual.Shared > 1) then
          raise Invalid_Share;
         elsif Source.Current /= null then
          Finalize (Target);
          Initialize (Target);
          If Source.Current /= Source.Actual.Last then
             Target.actual          := new List_Descriptor;
             Target.actual.all    := Source.actual.all;
             Target.Actual.First:= Source.Current.Next;
             Source.Actual.Last := Source.Current;
             Target.Current        := Source.Current.Next;
             Target.Actual.Size:= Size (Target);
             Source.Actual.Size:= Size (Source);
             Source.Actual.Last.Next       := null;
             Target.Actual.First.Previous:= null;
          end if;
      end if;
   end Slice_Tail;

end List_Pos_Polymorphic_Cntl;
```

Object_Holder, places the Object in the holder, and places null values in the Previous and Next components in the Object_Holder.

There are two versions of the Insert_Before and Insert_After procedures. The versions that attach a single object appear in Listing 5.13. Note that both procedures call the procedure Insert_First if the list is empty. If the list is not empty, both procedures raise an exception if the current position is undefined. The current position may become undefined through illegal navigation, moving forward off the front of the list, or moving backwards off the rear. Since the structure has bidirectional linking, four links must be made to place the new record between the current record and the record immediately in front of it, in the case of Insert_Before, or immediately after it, in the case of Insert_After. In the process of linking the new record into the proper position, Insert_Before checks to see if the current position had been at the front of the list, which would require the procedure to reset the pointer to the front. Similarly, Insert_After must address the possibility of resetting the pointer to the rear of the list when the new object is placed at the rear.

The other versions of `Insert_Before` and `Insert_After` attach a complete list either before or after the current viewing position. Listing 5.14 illustrates the `Insert_Before` procedure inserting a sublist into a list. Observe the parallels between the two versions of `Insert_Before` in Listing 5.13 and Listing 5.14. Where the version in Listing 5.13 calls a special procedure, `Insert_First`, to insert the first object into the list, the version in Listing 5.14 simply replaces the `List` with the new structure of `Objects`, which is a list, and resets `Objects` to the representation of an empty list. Otherwise, the sublist, `Objects`, is linked in before the current position and addresses the possibility of having to reset the pointer to the front of the `List`. The sublist linking a `Insert_After` functions in an analogous fashion.

Navigating a list using the recursive paradigm requires only two support subprograms, `Empty` and `Tail_Of`. The positional paradigm has seven support subprograms, the four navigational procedures and three subprograms for obtaining information about the current viewing position. The four navigation procedures appear in Listing 5.14.

`Move_To_Front` and `Move_To_Rear` first test the list to make sure that it is not empty and then use the `List.Actual.First` and `List.Actual.Last`, respectively, to reset the current viewing position to the front or rear of the list. Note that these two procedures, `Move_To_Front` and `Move_To_Rear`, reset the current viewing position, even if the position had been previously undefined. The other two navigation procedures, `Move_Towards_Front` and `Move_Towards_Rear`, require that the current viewing position be defined.

`Move_Towards_Front` and `Move_Towards_Rear` support linear access as they move from object to object along the linearly linked structure. Both functions test to verify that the list is not empty and then move the current viewing position in the indicated direction. `Move_Towards_Front` resets the `Current` component to `List.Current.Previous` to effect the move of the viewing position. `Move_Towards_Rear` resets the `Current` component to `List.Current.Next`.

The bodies of the three positional paradigm query functions, `At_Front`, `At_Rear`, and `Current_Defined`, appear in Listing 5.14. The three query functions provide a means of testing for three circumstances that surround the current viewing position: If it is at the front of the list, `List.Current = List.Actual.First`; if it is at the rear, List.Current = List.Actual.Last; and if it is defined, `List.Current /= null`.

Although there are four navigational procedures and three positional testing procedures, traversing the list normally requires the combined use of three of these subprograms. This usually requires statement sequences like

```
Move_To_Front (List);
while Current_Defined (List) loop
   . . . -- processing at the current node
   Move_Towards_Rear (List);
end loop;
```

or

```
Move_To_Front (List);
loop
   . . . -- processing at the current node
   exit when At_Rear (List);
   Move_Towards_Rear (List);
end loop;
```

to process the structure from front to rear, or similar looping constructs when processing a list from rear to front.

5.3 Explorations

1. Construct the `List_Pos_Polymorphic_Cntl.Advanced` child package specifications.

2. Construct the `List_Pos_Polymorphic_Cntl.Advanced` child package body.

3. Construct the `List_Pos_Polymorphic_Cntl.Iterators` child package specifications. Include in the specifications iterators that traverse from the current position to the front of the list and from the current position to the rear of the list.

4. Construct the `List_Pos_Polymorphic_Cntl.Iterators` child package body.

5. Construct a `Bounded_Generic_List` package. This package would represent a list in an array with

```
type List_Rec is
   record
      Previous, Next: natural;
      Object: Object_Type;
   end record;
type List_Array is array (natural range <>) of List_Rec;
type Bounded_List(Max_Size: positive) is
   record
      Front, Rear, Avail: natural;
      Space: List_Array (1..Max_Size);
   end record;
```

whose specifications are based on the positional paradigm. *The package specifications should be based on the positional paradigm.* Included in the construction of this package is the need to construct subprograms to manage the array as objects are inserted and removed from the list structure. The role of the record component, Avail, is to act as an index to the first available record, which, in turn, will contain the index to the next available record, and so forth. An index of zero is used to play the analogous role of a null pointer. In a sense, the array contains two lists, the client's list and the list of available records.

6. Investigate the possibilities of constructing a bound list based on the recursive paradigm.

6

Trees

6.1 Nonlinear Structures

When dynamically linked structures contain only one access type per record, they must be linearly linked. With two or more access types per record, the links between records may logically form nonlinear structures. The next four chapters describe various tree structures, tree applications, graphs, directed graphs, and sets.

Trees are a fundamental nonlinear data structure. They play a central role in information organization and access. Formally, trees are a special type of digraph. A complete discussion of digraphs and graphs appears in Chapter 8. The fundamental definitions and terminology of digraphs appear in this chapter to facilitate the discussion of trees.

A **directed graph**, also called a **digraph**, is an ordered pair of sets, (N, A), called the set of **nodes**, N, and the set of **arcs**, A. Each arc in A is itself an ordered pair, (n_a, n_b), of nodes, n_a, n_b in N. An example digraph appears in Figure 6.1. The set

$$\{A, B, C, D, E, F\}$$

is the set of nodes for this digraph. The arrows connecting the nodes represent the arcs in the graph. Each arc implies a direction. The arc (A, B), read as the

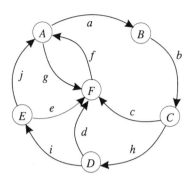

Figure 6.1. A digraph.

arc from node *A* to node *B*, **connects** node *A* to node *B*. The arc *(A, B)* is said
to leave *A* and **enter** *B*. The arrow on the arc indicates the **direction** of the arc,
which points to the second node in the ordered pair. Labels have been placed on
the arcs for reference.

A sequence of arcs,

$$a_1, a_2, \ldots, a_k$$

is called a **path** between two nodes, N_0 and N_k, if there exists nodes N_1, N_2, . . .
N_k, N_{k-1}, and for each *i*,

$$a_i = (N_{i-1}, N_i).$$

The sequence of arcs, *b*, *g*, and *f* in Figure 6.1 forms a path from node *B* to node
A, *b* = (*B*, *C*), *c* = (*C*, *F*), and *f* = (*F*, *A*) form an example of a path. There may
be more than one path between two nodes. This is not the only path from *B* to
A.

The **length** of a path is the number of arcs in the path. For a path with *k*
arcs, $a_i = (N_{i-1}, N_i)$ for *i* in *[1..k]*, the path **traverses** the nodes, N_i, for *i* in *[0..k]*.
A path is **simple** if no node appears twice in the path. A path is a **cycle** if
$A_0 = A_k$.

A **tree** is a digraph with the following properties:

1. There is a special node, called the **root**. No arcs enter the root.
2. For each node in the tree, there is one and only one path from the root
    to the node.

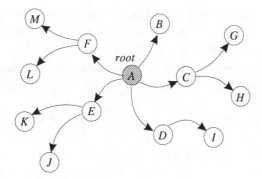

Figure 6.2. Example of a tree.

The **level** of a node in a tree is the length of the path from the root to the node.
For each node, the path from the root to the node is unique. An example of a
tree appears in Figure 6.2. Because of the unique relationship between the root
and the other nodes in the tree, trees are normally drawn with the root at the top
of the figure and the other nodes appearing below. Nodes at the same level
appear at the same horizontal level in the figure, if possible. Figure 6.3 illustrates
the tree from Figure 6.2 drawn in the preferred fashion.

For every node in a tree, the nodes that are reached with a path of length one
are called its **children** nodes, and the node is referred to as the **parent** node of
its children nodes. Two nodes are **siblings** if they have the same parent. Nodes
with no children are called **leaf** nodes, or **terminal** nodes. In Figure 6.3, J and
K are siblings, the children of node E, and, in turn, E is the parent of J and K.
Nodes B, G, H, I, J, K, L, and M are leaf nodes.

Observe that trees may be constructed from directed graphs in the following
manner. Build a tree by first selecting a node. This node becomes the root of
the tree formed as follows: Add to the tree a node and arc if the node is not
already in the tree and the arc attaches this node to a node already in the tree.

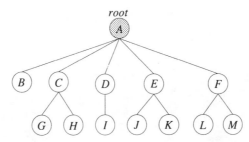

Figure 6.3. Tree, normal representation.

Continue this process until no additional nodes may be added. If the original digraph was connected, all nodes will be included in the tree. The resulting tree is called a **spanning tree** of the digraph.

Each node in a tree may be viewed as the root of a tree containing that node and all nodes that may be reached from that node. Such a tree is called a **subtree** of the original tree. Using the notion of subtrees, one may define trees recursively as follows: Either a tree is empty, or it contains a node, called its root. If a tree contains a root, the root may have an arbitrary number, including zero, of subtrees. Consider the tree in Figure 6.3. The tree whose root is A has five subtrees, whose roots are B, C, D, E, and F. The tree whose root is B has no subtrees, while the tree whose root is D has one subtree. The subtrees with roots C, E, and F all have two subtrees.

For many applications there is a limit on the maximum number of child nodes per node. A **binary tree** is a tree where each node has at most two children. An **n-ary tree** is a tree that has at most n children per node. It will be demonstrated later in this chapter that binary trees are sufficient for all tree applications. For that reason, we concentrate on the specifications and representation of binary trees.

Access to the nodes in a tree is limited. The root of a tree may always be immediately accessed. Access to other nodes is restricted in that a node may be accessed only after its parent or one of its child nodes is accessed. Tree specifications are based on one of two paradigms that describe these access limits. The two paradigms are analogous to the two list paradigms and are referred to by the same names, the **positional paradigm** and the **recursive paradigm**.

The recursive paradigm for binary trees is illustrated in Figure 6.4. In the recursive paradigm, either the binary tree is empty or it contains an object, called the **root of the tree**, and two subtrees, called the **left subtree** and the **right subtree**. Although the two paradigms appear radically different, they are logically equivalent. Both paradigms address the access limits associated to trees, but they address them in different ways. These differences show up in the ways the paradigms affect the design of algorithms. It should be noted that recursive algorithms may be constructed using the positional paradigm. That is not to say

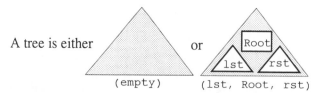

Figure 6.4. Binary tree, recursive paradigm.

that recursive algorithms may be defined using the positional paradigm. However, when recursive algorithms are designed using the positional paradigm, the programmer must address the navigation of the current viewing position. The recursive paradigm handles navigation in conjunction with recursive processing.

The positional paradigm is illustrated in Figure 6.5. In the illustration, <<current>> indicates the node currently being viewed. The next node that may be viewed is the parent, or one of the children, of the <<current>> node, or the current viewing position may be reset to the root.

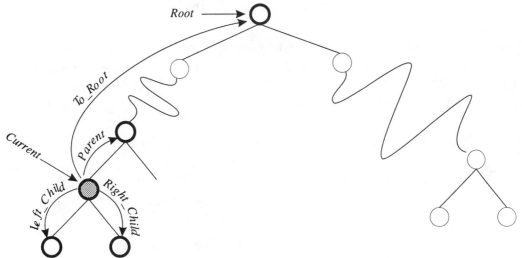

Figure 6.5. Binary tree, positional paradigm.

6.2 Binary Trees, Positional Paradigm

6.2.1 Abstraction

A binary tree may be viewed abstractly as an ordered pair *(i, S)* where *i* is a natural number and *S* is an infinite sequence $s_1, s_2, \ldots, s_k, \ldots$ of objects, representing the nodes in the tree, where only a finite number of objects in the sequence are not empty. The object s_1 represents the root of the tree. For each object s_i, its left child is the object s_{2i} and its right child is the object s_{2i+1}, as illustrated in Figure 6.6. Correspondingly, for each object s_i, except the root, its parent is $s_{[i/2]}$, where *[i/2]* is the quotient of the integer division of *i* by 2. Further, if s_i is empty, then s_{2*i} and s_{2*i+1} are also empty. Frequently, a tree *(i, S)*

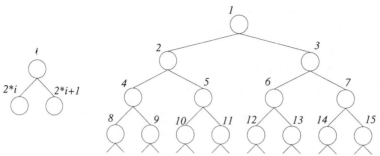

Figure 6.6. Complete tree.

is written as $(i, s_1, s_2, \ldots, s_k)$, where s_k is the last term in the sequence that represents a nonempty node in the tree. The 1-tuple (i) represents an empty tree.

The node s_j is a descendent of s_i if and only if $i = [j/2^m]$ for some $m > 1$. A node s_i and its descendents form a subtree with s_i as its root. Given the trees represented with the formalism $\boldsymbol{S} = (i, S)$ and $\boldsymbol{T} = (j, T)$, if s_i is empty, then T may be grafted onto $\boldsymbol{S}$ at location i, written as $S' = S \cup T_j$, means that $s_i = t_1$ and the other objects in T are placed into S so as to maintain their descendency relationships, t_2 into s_{2*i}, t_3 into s_{2*i+1}, and so forth. Given a tree $S = (i, S)$, pruning the subtree whose root is s_i, $S \backslash T_{s_i}$, removes the node s_i and all its descendents from S, $\boldsymbol{S} = (i, S \backslash T_{s_i})$.

This formalism helps describe the preconditions and postconditions of the subprograms that support the positional paradigm. For example, given the tree $\boldsymbol{S} = (i, S)$, the results of the various positional navigation procedures are described as $\boldsymbol{S}' = (1, S)$ for the `Move_To_Root`, $\boldsymbol{S}' = ([i/2], S)$ for `Move_To_Parent`, $\boldsymbol{S}' = (2*i, S)$ for `Move_To_Left_Child`, and $\boldsymbol{S}' = (2*i+1, S)$ for `Move_To_Right_Child`. The various reporter functions may be formalized with simple tests. For example, a tree is empty if and only if $s_1 = \{\}$. The current position, i, is null if and only if $s_i = \{\}$.

The binary search tree is a classical application of binary trees. Objects placed in a binary search tree must satisfy a linear ordering. Nodes are attached to a binary search tree using the following algorithm: If the root of the tree is empty, attach the value in the root; otherwise, compare the new item to the value at the root. If the new object is less than the root, recursively execute this process on the left subtree; otherwise, recursively execute this process on the right subtree (see Figure 6.7).

Listing 6.1. Binary tree, positional specifications.

```
with Ada.Finalization; use Ada.Finalization;
package Tree_Binary_Pos_Polymorphic_Cntl is

type Place_Holder is abstract new controlled with private;
   procedure Initialize (Object: in out Place_Holder);
   procedure Finalize (Object: in out Place_Holder);
   procedure Adjust (Object: in out Place_Holder);

type Holder_Class_Ptr is access Place_Holder'Class;
   procedure Recycle (Point: in out Holder_Class_Ptr);

type Tree_Type is new controlled with private;
   procedure Initialize (Tree: in out Tree_Type);
   procedure Finalize (Tree: in out Tree_Type);
   procedure Adjust (Tree: in out Tree_Type);

   Invalid_Position, Empty_Tree, Invalid_Graft,
   Tree_Overflow, No_Parent_Of_Root, Root_Exists,
   Invalid_Prune, Invalid_Share, Recursive_Only: exception;

procedure Graft (Object: in out Place_Holder'Class;
                 Tree   : in out Tree_Type );
procedure Graft (Subtree: in out Tree_Type;
                 Tree    : in out Tree_Type);
procedure Prune (Tree    : in out Tree_Type;
                 Subtree: in out Tree_Type);

procedure Move_To_Root (Tree: in out Tree_Type);
procedure Move_To_Parent (Tree: in out Tree_Type);
procedure Move_To_Left_Child (Tree: in out Tree_Type);
procedure Move_To_Right_Child (Tree: in out Tree_Type);

procedure Swap (Source: in out Tree_Type;
                Target: in out Tree_Type);

type In_Place_Process_Type is access
   procedure (Object: in out Place_Holder'Class);
procedure Process_Current (Tree   : in     Tree_Type;
                           Process:        In_Place_Process_Type);
procedure Update_Current (Tree   : in     Tree_Type;
                          Object: in     Place_Holder'Class);
function Empty (Tree: Tree_Type) return boolean;
function Current_Null (Tree: Tree_Type) return boolean;

function At_Root (Tree: Tree_Type) return boolean;
function Level (Tree: Tree_Type) return integer;

function Current_Object (Tree: Tree_Type) return Holder_Class_Ptr;
```

Listing 6.2 contains the interface a client might use when constructing a binary search tree based on the positional paradigm illustrated in Listing 6.1. A binary tree search procedure that uses the interface appears in Listing 6.3. The

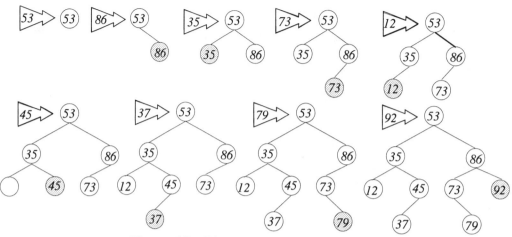

Figure 6.7. Binary search tree example.

procedure begins by moving the current position to the root of the binary tree, which may be empty. It performs the looping process until the current position is null. Within the loop a comparison is made between the number being placed into the tree and the Current_Object in the tree. If the number is less than the current object, the current position navigates to the left child of the current node; otherwise, the current object navigates to right child of the current node. Looping continues in this fashion until the current node is null. At that point the looping process is terminated and the number is grafted to that null position in the tree.

Listing 6.2. Client binary search tree interface.

```
with Tree_Binary_Pos_Polymorphic_Cntl;

package BS_Pos_Tree_Pak is
   package tre renames Tree_Binary_Pos_Polymorphic_Cntl;

   type Number_Type is new tre.Place_Holder with
      record
         Value: integer;
      end record;

end BS_Pos_Tree_Pak;
```

Listing 6.3. Binary search tree procedure using the positional paradigm.

```
procedure BS_Insert (No  : in out Number_Type;
                     Tree: in out tre.Tree_Type) is
   begin -- BS_Insert
      tre.Move_To_Root (Tree);
      while not tre.Current_Null(Tree) loop
         if No.Value < Node_Value(Tree) then
             tre.Move_To_Left_Child (Tree);
           else
             tre.Move_To_Right_Child (Tree);
         end if;
      end loop;
      tre.Graft (No, Tree);
      tre.Move_To_Root (Tree);
   end BS_Insert;
```

6.2.2 Representation

A direct representation of the abstraction illustrated in Figure 6.6 implies the use
of an array. However, a binary tree does not normally have every possible node
at every level. Hence, an array implementation might waste much space. Instead,
the nodes of the tree are dynamically allocated and linked. Besides containing
the value at the node, each record also contains the anchor points for the left and
right subtrees of the node, and the address of the anchor of the parent node of the
given node. The private declarations appear in Listing 6.4. Note that the
Left_Node and Right_Node components are aliased, to assist in navigating and
manipulating the subtrees. Specifically, these locations are aliased to allow
these anchor points to be conveniently accessed for the grafting and pruning
operations.

The Tree_Descriptor separates the variable Tree_Type from the tree
representation in anticipation of the implementation of sharing in the Advanced
child unit of the package. The Tree_Descriptor supports the safe sharing of
tree representations among Tree_Types while allowing each Tree_Type to have
a separate current position indicator. A Tree_Type contains three components:
Actual points to the Tree_Descriptor record that anchors the tree
representation; Current contains the address of the anchor point of the current
position in the tree; and Nul_Parent contains the address of the anchor point of
the parent node of the current position when the current position is null.
Nul_Parent is necessary to assist in implementing the Move_To_Parent
navigation when the current node position is empty. Hence, it does not have a
Node_Record, and an alternate means of returning to the parent node must be

Listing 6.4. Positional paradigm binary tree, `private` declarations.

```
private
   type Ptr_Addr is access all Holder_Class_Ptr;
   type Place_Holder is new controlled with
      record
         Parent_Node: Ptr_Addr:= null;
         Left_Node   : aliased Holder_Class_Ptr:= null;
         Right_Node  : aliased Holder_Class_Ptr:= null;
      end record;
         -----------------------------------------------------
   type Tree_Descriptor is
      record
         Root   : aliased Holder_Class_Ptr:= null;
         Shared: positive                  := 1;
      end record;
   type Desc_Ptr is access Tree_Descriptor;
         -----------------------------------------------------
   type Tree_Type is new controlled with
      record
         Actual     : Desc_Ptr:= null;
         Current    : Ptr_Addr;
         Nul_Parent: Ptr_Addr;
      end record;
         -----------------------------------------------------
end Tree_Binary_Pos_Polymorphic_Cntl;
```

provided. Note that the `Parent_Node` component points to the anchor point of the parent node. Figure 6.8 illustrates this representation.

Listing 6.5 contains the beginning of the `Tree_Binary_Pos_Polymorphic_Cntl` package body. The tree navigation procedures appear in Listing 6.6. The navigational procedures place the address of the appropriate anchor point into `Tree.Current`. In the case of `Move_To_Root`, the address of the anchor point for the entire tree, `Tree.Current:= Tree.Actual.Root'Access`, is placed in the `Current` component. `Move_To_Root` also places a `null` value in the `Nul_Parent` component in case the tree is empty.

All of the remaining navigation procedures must address the possibility of raising an exception when an inappropriate navigation is requested. In addition, the `Move_To_Parent` procedure must address navigating to the parent node of a null, or empty, tree node. Since the node is empty, its anchor point contains a `null` address; hence, there is no corresponding `Node_Record`. When the current position is empty, the address of the parent anchor is obtained from `Nul_Parent`; otherwise, the address of the parent anchor is in the `Parent_Node` component, `Tree.Current:= Tree.Current.all. Parent_Node`.

The `Move_To_Left_Child` and `Move_To_Right_Child` procedures are similar. Both procedures perform tests to avoid improper navigation of an empty

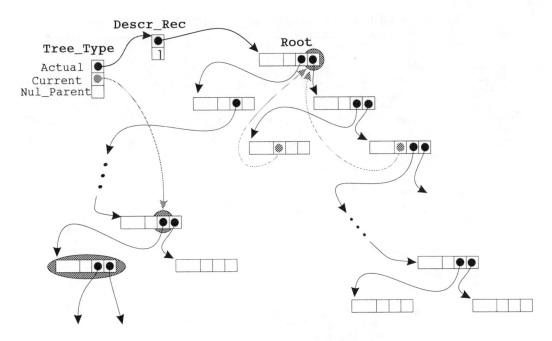

Figure 6.8. Positional paradigm tree representation.

Listing 6.5. `Tree_Binary_Pos_Polymorphic_Cntl Place_Holder` **support.**

```
with Unchecked_Deallocation;
package body Tree_Binary_Pos_Polymorphic_Cntl is
   procedure Free is new
            Unchecked_Deallocation (Place_Holder'Class, Holder_Class_Ptr);
   procedure Free is new Unchecked_Deallocation (Tree_Descriptor, Desc_Ptr);
   procedure Recycle (Point: in out Holder_Class_Ptr) renames Free;

procedure Initialize (Object: in out Place_Holder) is
   begin -- Initialize
      null;
   end Initialize;
   ---------------------------------------------------------
procedure Finalize (Object: in out Place_Holder) is
   begin -- Finalize
      null;
   end Finalize;
   ---------------------------------------------------------
procedure Adjust (Object: in out Place_Holder) is
   begin -- Adjust
      null;
   end Adjust;
```

Listing 6.6. Binary tree, positional paradigm tree navigation.

```
procedure Move_To_Root (Tree: in out Tree_Type) is
   begin -- Move_To
      Tree.Current   := Tree.Actual.Root'Access;
      Tree.Nul_Parent:= null;
   end Move_To_Root;
------------------------------------------------------
procedure Move_To_Parent (Tree: in out Tree_Type) is
   begin -- Move_To
      if Empty (Tree) then -- empty tree
         raise Empty_Tree;
        elsif At_Root(Tree) then -- current undefined
         raise No_Parent_Of_Root;
        elsif Current_Null (Tree) then
         Tree.Current:= Tree.Nul_Parent;
        else
         Tree.Current:= Tree.Current.all.Parent_Node;
      end if;
   end Move_To_Parent;
------------------------------------------------------
procedure Move_To_Left_Child (Tree: in out Tree_Type) is
   begin -- Move_To
      if Empty (Tree) then
         raise Empty_Tree;
        elsif Current_Null (Tree) then
         raise Invalid_Position;
        else
         Tree.Nul_Parent:= Tree.Current;
         Tree.Current   := Tree.Current.all.Left_Node'Access;
      end if;
   end Move_To_Left_Child;
------------------------------------------------------
procedure Move_To_Right_Child (Tree: in out Tree_Type) is
   begin -- Move_To
      if Empty (Tree) then
         raise Empty_Tree;
        elsif Current_Null (Tree) then
         raise Invalid_Position;
        else
         Tree.Nul_Parent:= Tree.Current;
         Tree.Current   := Tree.Current.all.Right_Node'Access;
      end if;
   end Move_To_Right_Child;
```

tree or a null location. If a location in the tree is null, it cannot have child nodes. Before navigating the current position to the appropriate anchor, the `Nul_Parent` component is set to the current anchor,

```
        Tree.Nul_Parent:= Tree.Current;
```

then the current position is set to

```
Tree.Current:= Tree.Current.all.Left_Node'Access;
```

for navigating to the left child node, or to

```
Tree.Current:= Tree.Current.all.Right_Node'Access;
```

for navigating to the right child node.

There are two tree grafting procedures, one to graft a single object to the tree, and a second to graft another tree onto the current position of the tree. They appear in Listing 6.7. Grafting may occur only at a `null` position in a tree. If the current location is not empty, the `Invalid_Graft` exception is raised. The procedure that grafts a single object to the tree at the current location uses the

Listing 6.7. Binary tree positional paradigm grafting procedures.

```
procedure Graft (Object: in out Place_Holder'Class;
                 Tree  : in out Tree_Type) is
   begin -- Graft
      if Current_Null (Tree) then
          Tree.Current.all:= new Place_Holder'Class'(Object);
          Tree.Current.all.Parent_Node:= Tree.Nul_Parent;
        else
          raise Invalid_Graft;
      end if;
   end Graft;
-------------------------------------------------------
procedure Graft (Subtree: in out Tree_Type;
                 Tree   : in out Tree_Type) is
   begin -- Graft
      if Subtree.Actual.Shared > 1 then
          raise Invalid_Graft;
        elsif Empty (Tree) then
          if not Empty (Subtree) then
              Tree:= Subtree;
              Subtree.Actual  := null;
              Subtree.Current:= null;
          end if;
        elsif Current_Null (Tree) then
          if not Empty (Subtree) then
              Tree.Current.all:= Subtree.Actual.Root;
              Tree.Current.all.Parent_Node:= Tree.Nul_Parent;
              Subtree.Actual.Root:= null;
              Subtree.Current:= Subtree.Actual.Root'Access;
          end if;
        else
          raise Invalid_Graft;
      end if;
   end Graft;
```

current anchor to attach a new `Node_Record`, place the object in the record, and place the address of its parent's anchor in the record:

```
Tree.Current.all:= new Node_Record;
Tree.Current.all.The_Node:= Object;
Tree.Current.all.Parent_Node:= Tree.Nul_Parent;
```

The procedure that grafts a subtree to a position in a tree first checks to see if the tree is empty, in which case the subtree becomes the entire tree as long as the subtree itself is not empty. If the tree is not empty, the subtree is attached at the current location's anchor, the `Parent_Node` anchor is set using the `Nul_Parent` component in the tree, and the subtree is detached from the current tree:

```
Tree.Current.all:= Subtree.Actual.Root;
Tree.Current.all.Parent_Node:= Tree.Nul_Parent;
Subtree.Actual.Root:= null;
Subtree.Current.all:= Subtree.Actual.Root'Access;
```

The positional paradigm pruning procedure appears in Listing 6.8. The procedure finalizes and then reinitializes the `Subtree` parameter and then places the subtree whose root is the current node in the `Tree` into `Subtree`. The `Tree.Current` component is reset to `null`, and `Tree.Nul_Parent` is set to the value of `Subtree.Current.all.Parent_Node` before `Subtree.Current.all.Parent_Node` is set to `null`.

Listing 6.8. Binary tree positional paradigm pruning procedure.

```
procedure Prune (Tree    : in out Tree_Type;
                 Subtree: in out Tree_Type) is
   begin -- Prune
      if Tree.Actual.Shared > 1 then
         raise Invalid_Prune;
      else
         Finalize (Subtree);
         Initialize (Subtree);
         if not Empty (Tree) then
            if not Current_Null (Tree) then
               Subtree.Actual        := new Tree_Descriptor;
               Subtree.Current       := Subtree.Actual.Root'Access;
               Subtree.Actual.Root   := Tree.Current.all;
               Tree.Current.all      := null;
               Tree.Nul_Parent       := Subtree.Actual.Root.Parent_Node;
               Subtree.Actual.Root.Parent_Node:= null;
            end if;
         end if;
      end if;
   end Prune;
```

Listing 6.9. `Tree_Type` **positional paradigm controlled support.**

```
procedure Initialize (Tree: in out Tree_Type) is
   begin -- Initialize
   Tree.Actual := new Tree_Descriptor;
   Tree.Current:= Tree.Actual.Root'Access;    Tree.Nul_Parent:= null;
   end Initialize;
   ---------------------------------------------------
procedure Finalize (Tree: in out Tree_Type) is
   procedure Erase_Subtree (Tree_Ptr: in out Holder_Class_Ptr) is
      begin -- ERASE_SUBTREE
         if Tree_Ptr /= null then
            Erase_Subtree (Tree_Ptr.Left_Node);
            Erase_Subtree (Tree_Ptr.Right_Node);
            Finalize (Tree_Ptr.all);   Free (Tree_Ptr);
         end if;
      end Erase_Subtree;
   begin -- Finalize
      if Tree.Actual.Shared > 1  then
         Tree.Actual.Shared:= Tree.Actual.Shared - 1;
         Tree.Actual := null;
         Tree.Current:= null; Tree.Nul_Parent:= null;
        elsif not Empty (Tree) then
         Erase_Subtree (Tree.Actual.Root);
         Tree.Current:= null;   Free (Tree.Actual);
      end if;
   end Finalize;
   ---------------------------------------------------------
procedure Adjust (Tree: in out Tree_Type) is
   Orig: Desc_Ptr:= Tree.Actual;
   procedure Rec_Clone (Srce, Trgt: in      Ptr_Addr) is
      begin -- Rec_Clone
         Trgt.all:= new Place_Holder'Class'(Srce.all.all);
         if Tree.Current = Srce then
            Tree.Current:= Trgt;
         end if;
         if Tree.Nul_Parent = Srce then
            Tree.Nul_Parent:= Srce;
         end if;
         if Srce.all.Left_Node /= null then
            Rec_Clone
               (Srce.all.Left_Node'Access, Trgt.all.Left_Node'Access);
            Trgt.all.Left_Node.Parent_Node:= Trgt;
         end if;
         if Srce.all.Right_Node /= null then
            Rec_Clone
               (Srce.all.Right_Node'Access, Trgt.all.Right_Node'Access);
            Trgt.all.Right_Node.Parent_Node:= Trgt;
         end if;
      end Rec_Clone;
   ---------------------------------------------------------
   begin -- Adjust
      Tree.Actual:= new Tree_Descriptor;
      Rec_Clone (Orig.Root'Access, Tree.Actual.Root'Access);
   end Adjust;
```

The `Initialize`, `Finalize`, and `Adjust` procedures appear in Listing 6.9. The `Initialize` procedure prepares the `Tree` parameter by establishing it as an empty tree. The `Finalize` procedure is more complex because it was written with representation sharing in mind. If a tree representation is shared, `Finalize` simply detaches `Tree` from the representation and decrements the sharing count. Otherwise, `Finalize` must restore the nodes of the tree to the dynamic space allocation manager. This is done recursively by calling the recursive procedure `Erase_Subtree`, which recursively erases the left and right subtrees of non-`null` nodes before returning `Free(Tree_Ptr)`, the node record to the dynamic space manager. `Free` is an instantiation of `unchecked_deallocation`:

```
procedure Free is new
        Unchecked_Deallocation (Node_Record, Node_Ptr).
```

The `Adjust` procedure duplicates the tree by performing a recursive traversal of the tree while creating a duplicate with the second parameter. The tree traversal method is a variation of a depth-first tree search algorithm, which is discussed in Section 6.4.1.

6.3 Binary Trees, Recursive Paradigm

6.3.1 Abstraction

In Section 6.2.1, a binary tree is viewed as an ordered pair (i, S) where i is a natural number and S is an infinite sequence $s_1, s_2, \ldots, s_k, \ldots$ of objects representing the nodes in the tree, where only a finite number of objects in the sequence are not empty. The nonlinear nature of a tree was achieved by the way the objects in the sequence are traversed, $2*i$ and $2*i+1$. The recursive paradigm views a tree as either empty or containing three items - an object called the root, and two subtrees, referred to as the left subtree and the right subtree. This leads quite naturally to viewing a binary tree as a triple, $T = (L, r, R)$, where L and R are possibly empty binary trees, and r, called the root, is the object at the root of the tree. An empty tree is indicated by the triple (β, β, β), with three empty coordinates.

While the positional paradigm navigates from one position in the tree to another, the recursive paradigm navigates from tree to subtree. In navigating from tree to subtree, the paradigm views only the object at the root of a tree. Processing usually involves recursive calls and passing either the left subtree or

Listing 6.10. `Tree_Binary_Polymorphic_Cntl` **specifications.**

```
with Ada.Finalization; use Ada.Finalization;
package Tree_Binary_Polymorphic_Cntl is

type Place_Holder is abstract new controlled with private;
   procedure Initialize (Object: in out Place_Holder);
   procedure Finalize (Object: in out Place_Holder);
   procedure Adjust (Object: in out Place_Holder);

type Holder_Class_Ptr is access Place_Holder'Class;
   procedure Recycle (Point: in out Holder_Class_Ptr);

type Tree_Type is new controlled with private;
   procedure Initialize (Tree: in out Tree_Type);
   procedure Finalize (Tree: in out Tree_Type);
   procedure Adjust (Tree: in out Tree_Type);

   Tree_Underflow, Tree_Overflow, Root_Exists: exception;

function Empty (Tree: Tree_Type) return boolean;
function Empty_Tree return Tree_Type;

generic
   type Extended_Type is new Place_Holder with private;
function Root_Value (Tree: Tree_Type) return Extended_Type;

function Root_Of (Tree: Tree_Type) return Holder_Class_Ptr;

procedure Graft (Object: in      Place_Holder'Class;
                 Tree  : in      Tree_Type );
procedure Graft (Subtree: in      Tree_Type;
                 Tree   : in      Tree_Type);

procedure Prune (Tree   : in      Tree_Type;
                 Subtree: in out Tree_Type);

function Left_Subtree (Tree: Tree_Type) return Tree_Type;
function Right_Subtree (Tree: Tree_Type) return Tree_Type;

procedure Update_Root (Tree  : in      Tree_Type;
                       Object: in      Place_Holder'Class);

procedure Swap (Source: in out Tree_Type;
                Target: in out Tree_Type);
```

right subtree to the recursive process. The specifications of a package that supports the recursive paradigm appear in Listing 6.10.

Given the tree $T = (L, r, R)$, the function `Left_Subtree` returns L, and the function `Right_Subtree` returns R. A precondition to grafting an object or a tree to a given tree, T, is that T is empty, $T = (\{\}, \{\}, \{\})$. If an object, o, is grafted, the result of the graft operation is $T' = (\{\}, o, \{\})$. If the object is a tree,

Listing 6.11. Recursive paradigm binary search tree interface package.

```
with Tree_Binary_Polymorphic_Cntl;
package PTS_Pak is
   package tre renames Tree_Binary_Polymorphic_Cntl;

   type Number_Type is new tre.Place_Holder with
      record
         Value: integer;
      end record;

end PTS_Pak;
```

O, then $T' = O$.

If a tree T is pruned and the result is placed in a tree S, then the post-condition of the pruning operation is that $T' = (\{\}, \{\}, \{\})$ and $S' = T$. For a tree T, $T = (L, r, R)$, the reporter function Root_Of returns a copy of r, the tree's root, and Empty returns the result of the test $T = (\{\}, \{\}, \{\})$.

To illustrate the use of the recursive paradigm for binary trees, consider the binary search tree example in Section 6.2.1. Listing 6.11 illustrates a client interface between a recursive polymorphic tree package and a recursive solution to the binary search tree insert procedure. A procedure that illustrates the positional paradigm implementation of the algorithm appears in Listing 6.2. Compare this to the procedure in Listing 6.12. With the recursive paradigm, the algorithm recursively descends from subtree to subtree. At each tree, the algorithm checks to see if the root is empty. If it is, the object is inserted at the root; otherwise, a comparison is made between the object to be inserted and the object at the root. If the new object is less than the object at the root, the procedure recursively descends to the left subtree; otherwise, the procedure recursively descends to the right subtree.

Listing 6.12. Binary search tree Insert for the recursive paradigm.

```
procedure BS_Insert (No  : in out Number_Type;
                     Tree: in      tre.Tree_Type) is
   begin -- BS_Insert
      if tre.Empty (Tree) then
         tre.Graft (No, Tree);
       elsif No.Value < Root(Tree).Value then
         BS_Insert (No, tre.Left_Subtree(Tree));
       else
         BS_Insert (No, tre.Right_Subtree(Tree));
      end if;
   end BS_Insert;
```

With the positional paradigm, the current position in the tree has to be moved before and after recursive calls. The recursive tree paradigm lends itself to recursive processing in that the recursive paradigm moves from tree to tree, always viewing the root of a tree. Hence, the recursive tree representation directly supports the construction of the algorithm.

6.3.2 Representation

The private declarations that appear in Listing 6.13 support the recursive paradigm. This representation uses the "access all" and "Aliased" features to recursively access the anchor points to subtrees. Recall that the aliased feature allows the access components of the records to be addressed indirectly. Defining Tree_Type with an access all declaration allows the 'Access attribute to create values that are accepted as Tree_Types.

Listing 6.14 contains the controlled representation for recursive Tree_Type. Initializing a tree is simply a matter of creating a space for the address of the root and making the address of the root null. However, finalizing is a more complex task. Before a node in the tree may be finalized, the left and right subtrees of the node must be finalized. This is accomplished with a recursive procedure, Erase_Subtree, which performs a recursive depth-first tree traversal. Tree traversals are discussed in Section 6.4. Before freeing the root record, the finalize procedure calls Erase_Subtree. When Erase_Subtree is not passed a null pointer, it recursively calls Erase_Subtree twice - to erase the left and right subtrees - before freeing the Node_Record.

Listing 6.13. Private declarations for Tree_Binary_Polymorphic_Cntl.

```
private
   type Place_Holder is abstract new controlled with
      record
         Left_Node : aliased Holder_Class_Ptr:= null;
         Right_Node: aliased Holder_Class_Ptr:= null;
      end record;
      -------------------------------------------------
   type Tree_Anchor is access all Holder_Class_Ptr;

   type Tree_Type is new controlled with
      record
         Anchor: Tree_Anchor;
         Base  : boolean:= true;
      end record;

end Tree_Binary_Polymorphic_Cntl;
```

Listing 6.14. `Tree_Binary_Polymorphic_Cntl` **body.**

```
with Unchecked_Deallocation;
package body Tree_Binary_Polymorphic_Cntl is
   procedure Free is new
                     Unchecked_Deallocation     (Place_Holder'Class,
Holder_Class_Ptr);
   procedure Free is new Unchecked_Deallocation (Holder_Class_Ptr,
Tree_Anchor);
   procedure Recycle (Point: in out Holder_Class_Ptr) renames Free;

procedure Initialize (Object: in out Place_Holder) is
   begin -- Initialize
      null;
   end Initialize;
-----------------------------------------------------
procedure Finalize (Object: in out Place_Holder) is
   begin -- Finalize
      null;
   end Finalize;
-----------------------------------------------------
procedure Adjust (Object: in out Place_Holder) is
   begin -- Adjust
      null;
   end Adjust;
-----------------------------------------------------
procedure Initialize (Tree: in out Tree_Type) is
   begin -- Initialize
      Tree.Anchor     := new Holder_Class_Ptr;
      Tree.Anchor.all:= null;
      Tree.Base       := true;
   end Initialize;
-----------------------------------------------------

procedure Erase_Subtree (Tree_Ptr: in out Holder_Class_Ptr) is
   begin -- Erase_Subtree
      if Tree_Ptr /= null then
         Erase_Subtree (Tree_Ptr.Left_Node);
         Erase_Subtree (Tree_Ptr.Right_Node);
         -- Finalize (Tree_Ptr.Node);
         Free (Tree_Ptr);
      end if;
   end Erase_Subtree;
-----------------------------------------------------
procedure Finalize (Tree: in out Tree_Type) is
   begin -- Finalize
      if Tree.Base then
         Erase_Subtree (Tree.Anchor.all);
         Free (Tree.Anchor);
      end if;
   end Finalize;
```

Listing 6.14. (cont.)

```
procedure Adjust (Tree: in out Tree_Type) is
   Original: Holder_Class_Ptr:= Tree.Anchor.all;
   procedure Clone (Srce, Trgt: in out Holder_Class_Ptr) is
      begin -- Clone
         if Srce /= null then
            Trgt:= new Place_Holder'Class'(Srce.all);
            Clone (Srce.Left_Node, Trgt.Left_Node);
            Clone (Srce.Right_Node, Trgt.Right_Node);
         end if;
      end Clone;
      ----------------------------------------------------
   begin -- Adjust
      Tree.Anchor.all:= null;
      Clone (Original, Tree.Anchor.all);
   end Adjust;
   -------------------------------------------------------

function Empty_Tree return Tree_Type is
   Answer: Tree_Type;
   begin -- Empty_Tree
      return Answer;
   end Empty_Tree;
   -------------------------------------------------------

function Empty (Tree: Tree_Type) return boolean is
   begin
      return Tree.Anchor.all = null;
   end Empty;
   -------------------------------------------------------

procedure Graft (Object: in      Place_Holder'Class;
                 Tree   : in      Tree_Type ) is
   begin -- Graft
      if not Empty (Tree) then
         raise Root_Exists;
      else
         declare
            New_Node: Holder_Class_Ptr:= new
                                   Place_Holder'Class'(Object);
         begin
            New_Node.Left_Node := null;
            New_Node.Right_Node:= null;
            Tree.Anchor.all:= New_Node;
         end;
      end if;
   exception
      when storage_error => raise Tree_Overflow;
   end Graft;
```

Listing 6.14. (cont.)

```
function Root_Value (Tree: Tree_Type) return Extended_Type is
   begin -- Root_Value
      if Tree.Anchor.all = null then
         raise Tree_Underflow;
       else
         return Extended_Type(Tree.Anchor.all.all);
      end if;
   end Root_Value;
   --------------------------------------------------------
function Root_Of (Tree: Tree_Type) return Holder_Class_Ptr is
   begin -- Root_Of
      if Tree.Anchor.all = null then
         raise Tree_Underflow;
         else
         return new Place_Holder'Class'(tree.Anchor.all.all);
      end if;
   end Root_Of;
   --------------------------------------------------------

procedure Swap (Source: in out Tree_Type;
                Target: in out Tree_Type) is
   Temp: Holder_Class_Ptr;
   begin
      Temp              := Target.Anchor.all;
      Target.Anchor.all:= Source.Anchor.all;
      Source.Anchor.all:= Temp;
   end Swap;
   --------------------------------------------------------

function Left_Subtree (Tree: Tree_Type) return Tree_Type is
   Answer: Tree_Type;
   begin -- Left_Subtree
      if Tree.Anchor.all = null then
         raise Tree_Underflow;
       else
         Answer.Anchor:= Tree.Anchor.all.Left_Node'Access;
         Answer.Base  := false;
         return Answer;
      end if;
   end Left_Subtree;
   --------------------------------------------------------
function Right_Subtree (Tree: Tree_Type) return Tree_Type is
   Answer: Tree_Type;
   begin -- Right_Subtree
      if Tree.Anchor.all = null then
         raise Tree_Underflow;
        else
         Answer.Anchor:= Tree.Anchor.all.Right_Node'Access;
         Answer.Base  := false;
         return Answer;
      end if;
   end Right_Subtree;
```

Listing 6.14. (cont.)

```
procedure Update_Root (Tree   : in      Tree_Type;
                       Object: in      Place_Holder'Class) is
   begin -- Process_Root
      if Tree.Anchor.all = null then
         raise Tree_Underflow;
       else
         declare
            New_One: Holder_Class_Ptr;
         begin
            New_One:= new Place_Holder'Class'(Object);
            New_One.Left_Node := Tree.Anchor.all.Left_Node;
            New_One.Right_Node:= Tree.Anchor.all.Right_Node;
            Free (Tree.Anchor.all);
            Tree.Anchor.all:= New_One;
         end;
      end if;
   end Update_Root;
   --------------------------------------------------------

end Tree_Binary_Polymorphic_Cntl;
```

The bodies of the grafting procedures appear in Listing 6.14. Recall that a precondition of grafting is that the tree must be empty. The procedure for grafting a single object first checks to make sure the tree is empty. If it is not, an exception is raised; otherwise, the node for holding the root is prepared and attached to the tree.

The procedure that grafts an entire tree to an empty tree first checks to make sure the two tree parameters are not pointing to the same tree. Once it is determined that Tree is empty, the grafting process is accomplished by moving the address of the root from Subtree to Tree and then making Subtree an empty tree.

The pruning process, which appears in Listing 6.14, first finalizes the Subtree where the result is to be placed and then reinitializes. After that, the address of the root of Tree is placed in Subtree and then Tree is made empty.

Fundamental to the recursive processing are the Left_Subtree and Right_Subtree navigation procedures. The algorithms in these procedures first check for an empty tree, raise an exception if the tree is empty and then form Tree_Type, which contains the address to the anchor position for the root of the left or right subtree.

6.4 Tree Traversals

Tree traversal algorithms are concerned with visiting the nodes of a tree in various specified orders. Each traversal algorithm visits each node in the tree a predetermined number of times and in a particular order. The **Depth-first** family of tree traversals describes an important collection of traversal algorithms that occur frequently in the solution of many classic problems. The other major family of tree traversals is the family of **Breadth First** tree traversals. There are 15 traversals in the depth-first family and 2 in the breadth-first family.

This section discusses the construction of iterators for binary trees. Building iterators for n-ary trees is left as exercises. Building a user-controllable iterator for lists was simplified by the linear structure of lists. The linear structure limits the number of alternatives that must be considered while traversing the list. In a binary tree, the iteration process faces two alternatives at each node, proceeding either to the left child or right child. In either case, there must be a back-up mechanism, which allows the iteration process to return to the untried branch and continue in that direction.

There are three categories of binary tree iterators: two categories follow predetermined patterns for visiting the nodes; the third category contains problem-specific iterators, whose tree traversal patterns depend on the contents that have been observed in the nodes. These categories are classified as follows:

1. **Depth-first iterators**: These iterators, also called **natural order iterators**, traverse down the tree to leaf nodes, either down the left side, as indicated in Figure 6.9, or down the right side of the binary tree.
2. **Breadth-first iterators**: These iterators, also called **level-by-level iterators**, visit all nodes at level 0, then all nodes at level 1, and so forth, until all nodes have been visited.
3. **Other schema**: These are other methods of traversing trees.

6.4.1 Depth-first

Observe in Figure 6.9 that as the arrows are followed around the tree, each node is visited three times. The first time the node is entered from its parent. The second time is on the return from its left child. The third time is on the return from its right child. The process performed the first time the node is visited is called a **pre-order** process. A process performed after visiting the left child, but before visiting the right child, is called an **in-order** process. A process performed

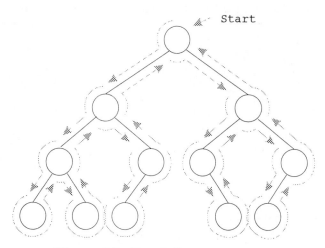

Figure 6.9. Depth-first sequence.

after visiting both children is called a **post-order** process. A depth-first tree search that applies only one of these processes is referred to as a pre-order traversal, an in-order traversal, or a post-order traversal, as appropriate. Figure 6.10 illustrates the relative order of the calls to the three processes.

Depth-first tree iterators may be constructed using either the recursive paradigm or the positional paradigm. Listing 6.15 illustrates the depth-first tree traversal using the positional paradigm; the recursive tree paradigm version appears in Listing 6.16. In both representations, a test is performed to make sure that the current node in the tree is not empty. If it is not, the code to perform the

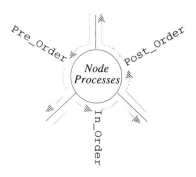

Figure 6.10. Depth-first node processes.

Listing 6.15. Depth-first tree traversal, positional paradigm.

```
procedure Pos_DFTT (Tree: in out Tree_Type) is
   procedure DFTT (Tree: in out Tree_Type) is
      begin -- DFTT
         if not Current_Null (Tree) then
            -------------------------------
            --  pre-order code here
            -------------------------------
            Move_To_Left_Child (Tree);
            Rec_DFTT (Tree);
            Move_To_Parent (Tree);
            -------------------------------
            --  in-order code here
            -------------------------------
            Move_To_Right_Child (Tree);
            Rec_DFTT (Tree);
            Move_To_Parent (Tree);
            -------------------------------
            --  post-order code here
            -------------------------------
         end if;
      end DFTT;
   begin -- Pos_DFTT
      Move_To_Root (Tree);
      Rec_DFTT (Tree);
   end Pos_DFTT;
```

pre-order code is performed. After the code is performed, the traversal precedes
to the left subtree. For the positional paradigm, this requires three lines of code,
to set the current position down to the subchild, make the recursive call, and then
return back to the parent node. The recursive paradigm carries out this process
in one statement, by making the recursive call and passing the appropriate subtree
as a parameter to the recursive call.

One should note the simplicity of the depth-first algorithm in Listing 6.16
compared to the algorithm in Listing 6.15. This is due to the way that the
recursive tree representation lends itself to recursive processing. This natural
relation is worth exploiting and should encourage programmers to consider using
the recursive paradigm instead of the positional paradigm as much as possible.

One should not lose sight of the relationship between recursion and stacks,
which is such that every recursive algorithm may be rewritten as a nonrecursive
algorithm that uses a loop and a stack. A depth-first tree traversal can be
accomplished with a stack as follows: The stack would contain records, and each
record would contain the address of an object in the tree and a number (one
through three). The number is used to indicate the first through third time the

Listing 6.16. Depth-first tree traversal, recursive paradigm.

```
procedure Rec_DFTT (Tree: in out Tree_Type) is
   begin -- Rec_DFTT
      if not Empty (Tree) then
         ---------------------------------
         --  pre-order code here
         ---------------------------------
         Rec_DFTT (Left_Subtree (Tree));
         ---------------------------------
         --  in-order code here
         ---------------------------------
         Rec_DFTT (Right_Subtree (Tree));
         ---------------------------------
         --  post-order code here
         ---------------------------------
      end if;
   end Rec_DFTT;
```

node is visited. Using the notation (Address, No) to indicate the record, the following pseudocode describes a depth-first tree traversal:

```
Push (Root address, 1) into the stack;
while the stack is not empty loop
    Pop (Address, No);
         if Address not null then
         case No of
            when 1 =>
                perform pre-order code;
                Push (Address, 3);
                Push (Right Child Address, 1);
                Push (Address, 2);
                Push (Left Child Address, 1);
            when 2 =>
                perform in-order code;
            when 3 =>
                perform post-order code;
         end case;
         end if;
end loop;
```

6.4.2 Breadth-first

A second type of tree traversal is a breadth-first tree traversal. The nodes in Figure 6.11 are numbered in the order in which they would be visited in a breadth-first tree search if the nodes at each level are traversed in a left-to-right fashion. A breadth-first tree traversal is performed using a queue as an intermediate structure for maintaining information about the nodes that need to

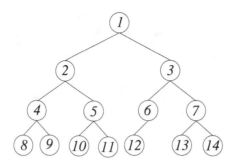

Figure 6.11. Breadth-first tree traversal.

be traversed. The breadth-first algorithm and its use of a queue closely parallel the depth-first algorithm and its use of a stack.

The structure of a level-by-level tree traversal is described in pseudocode as follows:

```
enqueue (pointer to the root);
while (the queue is not empty)
   and (problem dependent condition) do
   dequeue (pointer) -- to access a node
     if the node is not empty then
        [[possible problem specific code]]
        enqueue (left child pointer)
        enqueue (right child pointer)
     end if;
end while;
```

The implementation of a breadth-first iterator is left as an exercise.

6.4.3 Other Schema

Other traversal schema may be developed using various structures to hold intermediate information. One common traversal is based on a **priority queue**. A priority queue is like a queue in that there are a front and a rear and the dequeue procedure for priority queues is like that for queues. However, the enqueue procedure for priority queues uses an additional value, called the object's **priority**, to position the object in the queue so that all objects with lower priority are closer to the rear and all objects with higher priority are positioned closer to the front of the queue. Priority queue-based search algorithms are frequently used to search trees that represent the tree of all possible moves in a game.

6.5 Complete Trees

Frequently, objects are stored in trees that satisfy a problem-specific relationship between each node and its children. Many of these applications locate objects by starting at the root of the tree and traversing down the arcs using the application-specific relationship to locate the desired object. Naturally, the time required to reach the desired object depends on the length of the path from the root to the object. That, in turn, is bound by the length of the longest path from the root to any node. As a result, O (the length of longest path) bounds the timing of many tree processes.

The shortest possible length of the longest path in a binary tree with n nodes is log n. A **full tree** is a tree with n nodes whose longest path from the root is of length log n. A **complete tree** is a tree with n nodes such that if the nodes are numbered in the order in which they would be traversed in a left-to-right breadth-first tree search, then for each node i, $i > 1$, the parent of node i is node $i/2$. Simply stated, a complete tree is a tree that is full on each level, except possibly the lowest level. If the lowest level is not full, all the nodes in that level appear on the left side of the level with no vacant positions to the left of any node on the last level.

Although complete trees appear to be very restrictive, they have many applications. One advantage to them is that if the maximum number of nodes for a complete tree may be predetermined, there is an efficient static implementation for complete trees.

A bound, complete tree package is constructed using an array and based on the breadth-first numbering of the nodes. Specifically, a complete tree of n nodes may be represented in an array of n locations with the following node-to-array index correspondence: The root corresponds to index 1. For a node with index i, if the node has one child, a left child, the index to the child's array location is $2*i$. If the node has a second child, a right child, that child's index is $2*i+1$. Equivalently, for a node with index i, $i > 1$, its parent has index $i/2$. Consequently, in an array representation of a complete tree, simple arithmetic calculations implement the arc traversals.

The relationship between the nodes in a complete tree and the array representation of a complete tree appears in Figure 6.12. Because of the simplicity of this relationship, a package to directly support complete trees is normally not developed. Instead, packages are usually developed to support structures based on complete trees, like heaps, which appear in the next chapter.

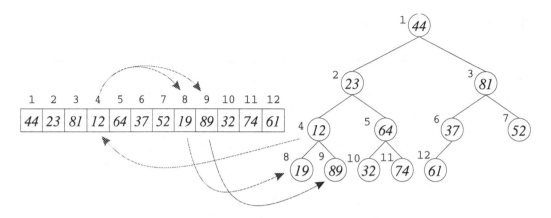

Figure 6.12. Complete tree, array representation.

6.6 *N*-ary Trees

If each node in a tree may have *n* or less children per node, the tree is called an *n*-ary tree. An *n*-ary tree has no limit on the number of children per node. Figure 6.13 illustrates an example of an *n*-ary tree. Only a few subprograms in the specification of the binary tree package in Listing 6.1 depend on the two children-per-node limit. Certainly, the functionality of the constructors and observers is sufficient for *n*-ary trees. However, it should be obvious that the binary tree navigation and constructors must be replaced by navigation and constructors appropriate for *n*-ary trees.

Binary trees are sufficient for all tree applications. Although sufficient, they may not be convenient. However, it is surprisingly convenient to use the relationship when building an *n*-ary tree package. Figure 6.14 illustrates the

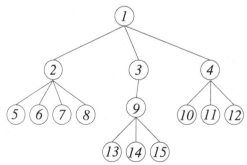

Figure 6.13. Example of an *n*-ary tree.

representation of the unbound tree in Figure 6.13 as a binary tree. The representation associates the left child navigation in a binary tree to navigation to the first child of a node in an *n*-ary tree. The right child navigation in a binary tree corresponds to navigating to a sibling of the current node. For a given *n*-ary tree node, access to the children of an *n*-ary tree's node is down the left child of the binary tree representation of the *n*-ary tree. Access down the right child in the binary tree corresponds to traversing to a sibling of the node. Access to the parent of an *n*-ary tree's node in the binary tree representation might be indirect. In the binary tree representation, a parent of a node is found by traversing up the tree toward the root until a left child arc is traversed. When a left child arc is traversed, the parent of the starting node is found.

In the binary representation, there are no siblings of the root. The first child of a node is accessed by traversing down the left branch. The other children are accessed by traversing the right branch from the first child and subsequent children nodes.   The relationships between *n*-ary tree traversals and their representations in a binary tree appear in Table 6.1.

The relationship between binary trees and unbound trees suggests a method for building the body of an *n*-ary tree package that makes direct use of a binary tree package to represent an *n*-ary tree. In fact, building that package is obvious,

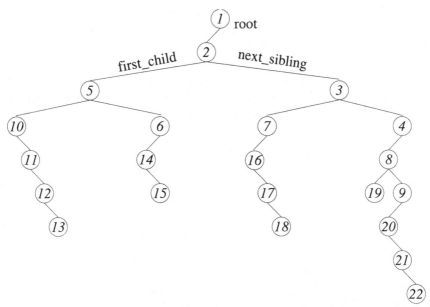

Figure 6.14. The *n*-ary tree in Figure 9-8 as a binary tree.

Table 6.1. Binary Tree and *n*-ary Tree reposition relations.

Tree_Nary	Tree_Binary
Positional	
Move_To_Root	Move_To_Root
Move_First_Child	Move_Left_Child
Move_Next_Sibling	Move_Right_Child
Move_To_Parent	Move_To_Parent
Move_Previous_Sibling	
Recursive	
Child_Subtree	Left_Subtree
Sibling_Subtree	Right_Subtree

once the binary representation of an *n*-ary tree is completely understood. However, building an *n*-ary tree package based on a binary tree package is more an academic exercise than a practical one. For this reason, it is left as an exercise.

Listing 6.17 contains a child unit for a binary tree package that supports *n*-ary trees, `Tree_Binary_Polymorphic_Cntl.Nary`. This child unit provides support that assists clients in viewing a binary tree as an *n*-ary tree. The fundamental differences between an n-ary tree package and a binary tree package are due to the arbitrary number of children per node. The recursive paradigm requires subtle changes in the graft and pruning procedures and a renaming of the navigation functions to reflect the *n*-ary tree view.

The *n*-ary tree recursive paradigm is supported through a pair of functions, `Child_Subtree` and `Siblings_Subtree`. These two functions are sufficient to provide navigation under the recursive paradigm. The characteristics of the root of an *n*-ary tree are identical to those of a binary tree. Specifically, the root in an *n*-ary tree has no parent and no siblings. Hence, attempts to move to a parent or sibling of the root raise an exception. Also, siblings cannot be grafted to the root. However, a subtree may have siblings.

Although the analogy between the two structures is useful, there are several places where the analogy fails. The most obvious places are in the grafting and pruning procedures. Recall that grafting can occur in a binary tree only when the tree is empty. Also, after pruning from a binary tree, the tree is empty. In *n*-ary trees, grafting can occur anywhere in the tree. When a subtree is grafted at a specified location, the object at that location becomes the next sibling of the object being grafted. Correspondingly, when a subtree is pruned, the next sibling of the subtree moves into the place of the subtree being grafted.

The pair of grafting procedures for *n*-ary trees are analogous to the grafting procedures for binary trees. The grafting procedures provide a means for grafting

Listing 6.17. `Tree_Binary_Polymorphic_Cntl.Nary` **specifications.**

```
package Tree_Binary_Polymorphic_Cntl.Nary is

procedure Nary_Graft (Object: in out Place_Holder'Class;
                      Tree   : in      Tree_Type );

procedure Nary_Graft (Subtree: in      Tree_Type;
                      Tree   : in      Tree_Type);

procedure Nary_Prune (Tree   : in      Tree_Type;
                      Subtree: in out Tree_Type);

function Child_Subtree (Tree: Tree_Type) return Tree_Type;

function Sibling_Subtree (Tree: Tree_Type) return Tree_Type;

end Tree_Binary_Polymorphic_Cntl.Nary;
```

a single node or an entire tree. The procedure that grafts a single object attaches any record at the root as a sibling of the record being grafted before being attached to the tree. When a subtree is grafted, the process of attaching the current root correctly as a sibling is more complicated because the item being grafted may already have siblings. As a result, a recursive procedure, `Rec_Attach`, searches through the siblings and attaches the current root at the end of the sibling list of the subtree being attached.

As was the case for the binary procedures for grafting single objects into a tree, the *n*-ary tree procedures build a tree with a single node and pass the tree to the corresponding overloaded grafting procedure for subtrees. This is illustrated for the `Graft_Child` in Listing 6.18. After testing for possible exceptions, it calls a procedure that prepares a tree with the object and calls the `Graft_Child` procedure for subtrees. Note how the procedure captures and reraises exceptions after recycling the newly recreated subtree space.

When a subtree is pruned from an *n*-ary tree, a sibling subtree must be attached at the anchor. If a first child had been pruned, then the next sibling of that child node must be attached at the first child anchor. Recall that in a binary tree, pruning always produces a null anchor point. This is not necessarily the case in an *n*-ary tree.

6.7 Measurement

Trees present an opportunity for good timings for algorithms that must manipulate large amounts of data. From a timing viewpoint the reasons for looking at trees

Listing 6.18. `Tree_Binary_Polymorphic_Cntl.Nary` **body.**

```
package body Tree_Binary_Polymorphic_Cntl.Nary is
procedure Nary_Graft (Object: in out Place_Holder'Class;
                      Tree  : in      Tree_Type ) is
   New_Node: Holder_Class_Ptr:= new Place_Holder'Class'(Object);
   begin -- Nary_Graft
      New_Node.Left_Node:= null;  New_Node.Right_Node:= Tree.Anchor.all;
      Tree.Anchor.all   := New_Node;
   exception
      when storage_error => raise Tree_Overflow;
   end Nary_Graft;
   ----------------------------------------------------------
procedure Nary_Graft (Subtree: in      Tree_Type;
                      Tree   : in      Tree_Type) is
   procedure Rec_Attach (This, That: in out Holder_Class_Ptr) is
      begin -- Rec_Attach
         If That = null then
            That:= This;
          else
            Rec_Attach (This, That.Right_Node);
         end if;
      end Rec_Attach;
      ----------------------------------------------------------
   begin -- Nary_Graft
      if not empty (SubTree) then
         Rec_Attach (Tree.Anchor.all, Subtree.Anchor.all.Right_Node);
         Tree.Anchor.all    := Subtree.Anchor.all;
         Subtree.Anchor.all:= null;
      end if;
   end Nary_Graft;
   ----------------------------------------------------------
procedure Nary_Prune (Tree   : in      Tree_Type;
                      Subtree: in out Tree_Type) is
   begin -- Nary_Prune
      Subtree:= Empty_Tree;
      if not Empty (Tree) then
         SubTree.Anchor.all               := Tree.Anchor.all;
         Tree.Anchor.all                  := Tree.Anchor.all.Right_Node;
         Subtree.Anchor.all.Right_Node:= null;
      end if;
   end Nary_Prune;
   ----------------------------------------------------------
function Child_Subtree (Tree: Tree_Type) return Tree_Type is
   Answer: Tree_Type;
   begin -- Child_Subtree
      return Left_Subtree (Tree);
   end Child_Subtree;
   ----------------------------------------------------------
function Sibling_Subtree (Tree: Tree_Type) return Tree_Type is
   Answer: Tree_Type;
   begin -- Sibling_Subtree
      return Right_Subtree (Tree);
   end Sibling_Subtree;

end Tree_Binary_Polymorphic_Cntl.Nary;
```

may be summarized with the following example: Assume that n data objects have been organized into a tree structure in such a way that all possible node positions are filled starting at the root and proceeding down each level of the tree until all n objects have been placed. Further, objects may be found by starting at the root node and looking at each node as the tree is traversed down to the desired node. In this scenario, the timing for an algorithm is of the same order of magnitude as the length of the path from the root to the desired object. If the n objects are placed in the tree in the fashion described, then the algorithm search time is bound by $O(\log n)$.

This translates into desirable results such as the following: In a well-organized tree with a billion nodes, an object may be found in time $O(1,000,000,000)$, which is about 30. The next chapter investigates the basic method of organizing trees and attempting to maintain $O(\log n)$ timing for trees with n nodes.

6.8 Explorations

1. Some people may be confused about an n-ary tree being made available as a child package of a binary tree package.

   a. Construct the specifications of a `Tree_Nary_Polymorphic_Cntl` package.
   b. Construct the body for `Tree_Nary_Polymorphic_Cntl` by taking full advantage of the `Tree_Binary_Polymorphic_Cntl` and its `.Nary` child unit.

2. Construct the specifications and body for a `Tree_Binary_Pos_Polymorphic_Cntl.Nary`, a positional paradigm n-ary tree support child package based on the positional paradigm binary tree support package.

7

Tree Applications

7.1 Tree Restructuring

7.1.1 Binary Search Trees Revisited

Binary search trees were introduced in Chapter 6. This chapter looks into variations of binary search trees. One possible set of specifications for a binary search tree appears in Listing 7.1. These specifications totally encapsulate the tree; no `Tree_Type` is made available. The package is instantiated with the client's `Object_Type` and a linear ordering function, "<", for `Object_Type`. The package defines two objects A and B to be equivalent when

$$(A < B) = (B < A).$$

Equivalent objects are not allowed in binary search trees. Two exceptions are made visible by the package. `No_Match` is raised when seeking a particular object in the `Delete` procedure, the `Copy_Object` procedure, and the `Exists` functions. The `Equivalent_Exists` exception is raised when there is an attempt to `Insert` an object that is equivalent to an object that already exists in the tree.

The `Exists` function returns `true` if there is an object in the tree that is equivalent to the function's parameter. The `Delete` procedure either deletes an object in the tree that is equivalent to the parameter passed to it or raises the

Listing 7.1. Binary search tree specifications.

```
generic
   type Object_Type is private;
   with function "<" (Left, Right: Object_Type) return boolean;
package Tree_Binary_Search_Pt_En is

   Equivalent_Exists: Exception;
   No_Match          : Exception;

   procedure Insert (Object: in    Object_Type);

   procedure Delete (Object: in    Object_Type);

   function Copy_Object (The_Match: Object_Type ) return Object_Type;

   function Exists (Object: Object_Type) return boolean;

   type Process_Type is access
      procedure (Object  : in     Object_Type;
                 Continue: in out boolean );

   procedure Iterate (Process: Process_Type );

end Tree_Binary_Search_Pt_En;
```

No_Match exception. Copy_Object works in a similar fashion. The iterator passes the objects in the tree one at a time in the order defined by the instantiating "<" function.

The Insert procedure and the beginning of the body for the binary search tree package appear in Listing 7.2. The binary search tree package instantiates a binary tree package, Tree_Binary_Pt_Lpt, with the client's Object_Type. The_Tree is the Tree_Type used to represent the binary search tree. Note the function Equivalent that builds a test for equivalence using the instantiating procedure "<". Equivalence is used throughout the body of the package in several of the procedures and functions.

The Insert procedure appearing in Listing 7.2 is based on the recursive binary search tree procedure, Rec_Attach, from the previous chapter. If the tree is empty, Insert grafts the object to the root.   Otherwise, it calls the Rec_Insert procedure to recursively traverse the tree until an equivalent object is encountered or until the node is placed. If an equivalent object is encountered, an exception is raised.

From the viewpoint of abstraction, there is no real difference between the ordered list package discussed in Chapter 5 and the binary search tree described here. Both abstractions provide the same services. The decision to choose one package over the other should be based on the efficiency of the package.

Listing 7.2. Binary search tree `Insert`.

```
package body Tree_Binary_Search_Pt_En is
   package My_Tree is new Tree_Binary_Pt_Lpt (Object_Type);
   use My_Tree;

   The_Tree: Tree_Type;

function Equivalent (Left, Right: Object_Type) return boolean is
   begin -- Equivalent
   return ((Left < Right) = (Right < Left));
   end Equivalent;

procedure Insert (Tree: in out Tree_Type;
                   Data: in      integer) is
   Continue: boolean:= true;
   Arc: Path_Info_Type:= none;
   procedure Rec_Insert (Tree: in      tree_type;
                         arc: in out Path_Info_Type) is
      begin -- Rec_Insert
      if Empty(Tree) then
            Graft ((Data, Equal_Balance), Tree);
            arc:= none;
         elsif Data < Root_Of(Tree).Object then
            Rec_Insert (Left_Subtree(Tree), arc);
            -- AVL Code
         else
            Rec_Insert (Right_Subtree(Tree), arc);
            -- AVL Code
      end if;
      end Rec_Insert;
      -------------------------------------------------
   begin -- Insert
      Rec_Insert (Tree, Arc);
   end Insert;
```

Obviously, a binary tree package uses more space, because of the additional access type per node. However, the ordered list package has unfavorable timing characteristics when compared to the potential timing characteristics of a binary search tree. Specifically, if an ordered list contains n objects, the time to insert an object is bound by the order of the size of the list, is $O(n)$. However, if the binary search tree is a full tree with n objects, the time required to access any object is bound by $O(\log n)$. Since there are many applications based on maintaining objects in a linear ordering, an efficient implementation is desirable.

Inserting or retrieving an object in a binary search tree in $O(\log n)$ time is based on the assumption that the tree is full. A more honest appraisal would be that the time to insert or seek an object in a binary search tree is bound by

$$O(\text{Length of longest path in the tree}).$$

Unfortunately, the `Insert` procedure does not restructure the tree as new objects are inserted to keep the length of the longest path in the tree in the range of $O(\log n)$. For example, assume the objects stored in a binary search tree are integers and they are passed to the `Insert` procedure in the following order: 45, 57, 53, 70, 94, 87, and 90. The binary search tree that is constructed by the `Insert` procedure appears in Figure 7.1. However, if the same values were entered in a different order, the result might be the tree that appears in Figure 7.2. The tree in Figure 7.2 is much more desirable than the tree in Figure 7.1. In general, it is possible to build a tree with n objects and have the longest path in the tree be $O(\log n)$. The length of the longest path bounds the maximum time required to insert or access an object in the tree.

It is not desirable for the order in which the objects are placed in the structure to have a serious impact on the timing results of the various procedures in the package. It would be desirable if the tree could be restructured as nodes are added so that the timing of all operations would be bound by $O(\log n)$ and that the restructuring procedures themselves do not have serious timing problems. The restructuring itself must be time-efficient. This result is achieved by modifying the `Insert` and `Delete` procedures for a binary search tree so that when necessary, the tree is restructured to maintain the length of the longest path close to $O(\log n)$.

A procedure to `Delete` an object from a binary search tree is left as an exercise. An object is deleted by promoting its left or right child to the parent's position in the tree and recursively continuing this process until a node with no children may be removed from the tree.

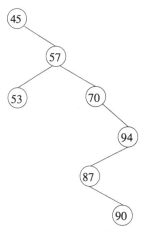

Figure 7.1. Node placement without restructuring.

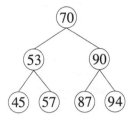

Figure 7.2. Balance tree example.

There are two classical tree restructuring methods, AVL trees and B-trees. AVL tree restructuring is described in Section 7.1.2, and B-trees are discussed in Section 7.1.3.

7.1.2 AVL Trees

As stated earlier, the timing for many tree procedures is bound by the length of the longest path in the tree. Therefore, it is desirable to maintain a tree with n nodes so that the length of the longest path in the tree is bound by log n, $O(\log n)$. Recall that the longest path from the root to a node in a full tree with n nodes is $O(\log n+1)$. If a binary search tree is almost full, then any node in the tree may be accessed within $O(\log n)$ arc traversals. A desirable situation would be an automatic tree restructuring system that bounds the length of the longest path in a tree of n nodes to $O(\log n)$. A tree with this characteristic is called a **height-balanced tree**.

There is an efficient height-balancing algorithm called the **AVL tree rebalancing**. The AVL algorithm is named after two Russian mathematicians who discovered the algorithms, G. M. Adelson-Velskii and E. M. Landis. The AVL algorithm is quite elegant in that it requires the maintenance of a minimum of additional information with each node and performs each tree restructuring in a constant amount of time.

Each node in the tree is assigned a height-balancing value equal to the length of the longest path down its left subtree minus the length of the longest path down its right subtree. The tree is maintained to keep the height-balance value in the range -1 .. +1. Therefore, each node is assigned a height-balance value of +1, 0, or -1, which we indicate with the symbols '+', '=', and '-'. As nodes are placed into the tree, only the nodes in the path from the root to the newly placed node need rebalancing. The rebalancing process starts with the newly placed node being assigned a balance value of ' = '. Other nodes are rebalanced by traversing up the path from the new node to the root as follows:

1. When the rebalancing algorithm traverses back toward the root along the left arc of a node, the rebalancing algorithm performs the following process on the node, depending on its current balance:

   '+':   Restructure the tree as described in the AVL restructuring algorithm (described ahead) and terminate the rebalancing process, since no additional nodes need be rebalanced.

   '=':   Rebalance the node as '+' and traverse to the parent and continue rebalancing.

   '-':   Rebalance the node as '=' and terminate the rebalancing procedure, since no additional nodes need rebalancing.

2. When the rebalancing algorithm traverses back toward the root along the right arc of a node, the rebalancing algorithm performs the following process on the node, depending on its current balance:

   '+':   Rebalance the node as '=' and terminate the rebalancing, since no additional nodes need be rebalanced.

   '=':   Rebalance the node as '-' and continue the algorithm after traversing up to the parent.

   '-':   Restructure the tree as described in the AVL restructuring algorithm and terminate the rebalancing, since no additional nodes need be rebalanced.

There are four AVL restructuring cases, which may be viewed as two pairs of mirror images. They appear in Figure 7.3 and are referred to as the R-R case (back up a right branch to a node, then a right branch again to the node that became unbalanced), the L-L case, the R-L case, and the L-R case. The R-R and L-L cases are mirror images, as are the L-R and R-L cases. This section discusses the L-L and L-R cases in detail. The R-R and R-L cases are left as exercises. Note that the four cases refer to the relative position of the newly attached node with respect to the node that became unbalanced.

There are two advantages to the AVL tree balancing algorithms. First, the algorithms are fast, as they contain no loops. Second, the effects of rebalancing are localized. When restructuring occurs, the effects of rebalancing are within the subtree being rebalanced and no further rebalancing is necessary between the

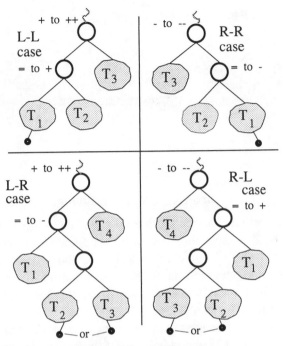

Figure 7.3. AVL cases.

location where the rebalancing occurs and the root of the tree.

The L-L rebalancing case appears in Figure 7.4. For an L-L restructuring to occur, a node is attached to the tree and all the nodes that are in the path back to the root are rebalanced following the rules described above, until a node with a '+' balance is encountered. From the viewpoint of the node that became unbalanced, the newly attached node was down a left subtree, then another left subtree, as indicated in Figure 7.4. If X is the node that went out of balance and Y is the left child of X, the nodes are rotated, as indicated in Figure 7.4. Node Y becomes the new root of the subtree. The repositioning makes X the right child of Y and the right subtree of Y becomes the left subtree of X.

In the L-L case, both the X and Y nodes become balanced. The rebalancing is obtained by observing that before the new node was attached, if n is the length of the longest path in T_1, then the longest path in T_2 and T_3 are also n. Note that the new node might have been attached as the left child of Y, which implies that $n = 0$. The R-R case is a mirror of this case.

The L-R restructuring case appears in Figure 7.5. In this case, a node with a "+" balance is about to become unbalanced because the path from X to the newly attached node traverses down a left branch, then a right branch. This

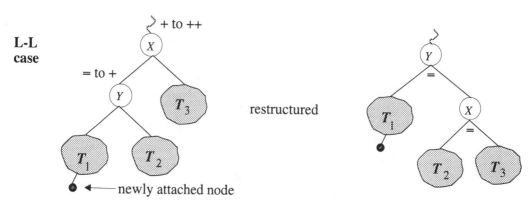

Figure 7.4. L-L rebalancing.

rebalancing algorithm focuses on three nodes, labeled X, Y, and Z. Y is the left child of X, and Z is the right child of Y. The node Z moves up to become the parent of both X and Y, with Y as its left child and X as its right child.

There are three possible final rebalancings that may be assigned to the nodes X, Y, and Z. The three cases depend on where the new node had been attached to the tree, either to T_2, or to T_3, or if Z itself was the newly attached node. If n was the length of the longest path in trees T_2 and T_3, then the lengths of the longest paths in T_1 and T_4 would be $n+1$. If the new node was attached to T_2 then the new balance for Y is "=". The balance for Z is '-', and the balance for X is '='. The case when the new node is attached to T_3 produces balances of '+' for Y, '=' for X, and '=' for Z.

The third rebalancing in the L-R case is when Z is the newly attached node. In this case, trees T_2 and T_3 are empty. As a result of the restructuring, all three nodes, X, Y, and Z, have balance '='.

L-R case

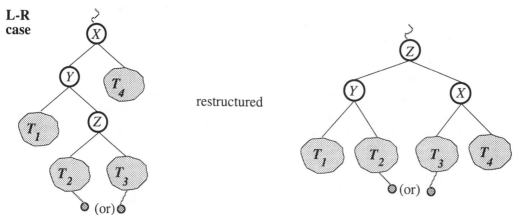

Figure 7.5. L-R case.

Figure 7.6 illustrates the result of AVL tree balancing on the sequence of data leading to the tree in Figure 7.1. Figure 7.6 [i] and [ii] show the balancing after the second and third nodes are attached. In Figure 7.6 [ii], the node whose value is 45 goes out of balance and leads to an R-L rebalancing. Figure 7.6 [ii] illustrates the tree after rebalancing. Next, nodes with values 70 and 94 are attached. As a result, the node with value 57 becomes unbalanced, Figure 7.6 [iv]. This requires an R-R restructuring, which leads to the rebalancing in Figure 7.6 [iv]. When the node with the value 87 is attached, the root, with value 53, becomes unbalanced. An R-R restructuring produces a root with value 70. When 87 is attached, a restructuring occurs at 53, which places 70 at the root. Finally, as the node with value 90 is attached, the node with value 94 becomes unbalanced, leading to an L-R rebalancing. Figure 7.6 [v] illustrates the final structure of the tree after all the nodes have been attached and the tree has been restructured.

The AVL tree Delete procedure must address the issues of node balancing as it removes a node from the tree. If the deleted node was a terminal node, the delete process must work its way back up the path to the root rebalancing nodes in a fashion similar to when nodes are attached.

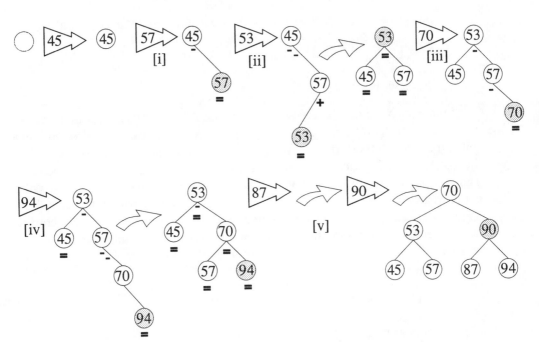

Figure 7.6. AVL examples.

If the node is not a terminal node, then the node is replaced by either its left subtree's rightmost child or its right subtree's leftmost child. The replacement is given the balance of the deleted node. This process continues until a terminal node is removed. After that, a rebalancing, as mentioned in the previous paragraph, is applied starting with the parent of the terminal node. Details of the design of the algorithm are left as an exercise.

Height-balanced restructuring is a feature that should be included in a binary search tree package. Using height-balanced restructuring, like AVL tree balancing, is an implementational detail, hidden from users. This may be accomplished by storing with each node the necessary balance information. For example, if the ordered tree package employs the `Tree_Search_Pt_En` package, the body of the package would include the following declarations to support a height-balanced tree:

```
private
   type Balance_Type is ('+', '=', '-');
   type Tree_Node is
      record
        Object : Object_Type;
        Balance: Balance_Type:= Balanced;
      end record;

   package B_T is new Tree_Binary_Pt_Lpt (Tree_Node);

   type Tree_Type is
      record
        Tree: B_T.Tree_Type;
      end record;
```

The implementation of a binary search tree with AVL tree restructuring is left as an exercise for the reader. Fundamentally, this is accomplished by first building four procedures to perform the four restructurings. The next step is modifying the binary search `Insert` procedure to perform height-balancing. When the `Insert` procedure observes that a node is becoming unbalanced, it calls the appropriate AVL restructuring algorithm. An additional parameter should be added to the `Rec_Insert` procedure to advise the algorithm which restructuring should occur. This information determines the restructuring algorithm that is to be used.

7.1.3 B-trees

The time required to seek an object in a tree depends on the length of the path from the root to the object being sought. The AVL tree restructuring guarantees that the longest path from the node to any leaf is of order $O(\log n)$, where n is the number of nodes in the tree. This directly affects the maximum time required to access a node. The length of the longest path from the root to all terminal nodes may be reduced by placing more than one object at each node and allowing more than two children per node. In particular, if a node contains k objects, the k objects may be use to distinguish between $k+1$ children, as indicated in Figure 7.7.

A tree structure that places more than one object in each node and with desirable timing characteristics for its algorithms is a **B-tree**. For each B-tree, there is a number b that has the following properties:

1. The root contains between 1 and $2b$ objects.
2. Every other node contains between b and $2b$ objects.
3. The number of children of a node is 0 or $k+1$ where k is the number of objects in the node.

It should be noted that there are many variations of B-trees, called B^* and B^+ trees. The description here contains elements of some of these variations.

The restructuring algorithms for B-trees are substantially different than the AVL restructuring algorithms. As new objects are placed in the tree, the algorithm shuffles objects between nodes in order to fill a node and its siblings before attempting to create new nodes. The process of creating new nodes is called **node splitting**. When a object cannot be placed in a node because the node and its siblings are filled, the $2b$ objects in the node and the new object are placed in order. The node is split and replaced by two nodes containing b objects each, with the median object of the $2b+1$ objects acting as the parent of the two

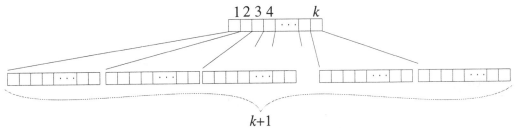

Figure 7.7. K objects per node with k+1 children.

new nodes. An attempt is then made to place the median object and its two children into the tree.

There are three basic node insertions cases:

I₁. If there is room in the node or in one of its siblings, the object is inserted without any node splitting. If the available space is not in the node, but in one of its siblings, objects are shuffled, as indicated in Figure 7.8, to make room for the insertion.

I₂. If an object is to be inserted in a node **other than the root** and the node is full, the node is split, as illustrated in Figure 7.9. This may cause additional node splitting further up the tree.

I₃. If a object is to be inserted in the **root** node and the node is full, the node is split, as illustrated in Figure 7.9, and the median object becomes the only value in the new root of the tree.

Before a node is split, all of its siblings must be filled. This increases the utilization of space. Consider the scenario illustrated in Figure 7.8. The number 77 should be placed in the third child node, but no space is available in that node. The only space is in the third node. As a result, values are shuffled across the children and to and from the parent node to maintain the tree's order and to provide space for placing the new value, 77, which is then inserted.

Consider a B-tree with $b = 2$. Figure 7.9 illustrates a node split that occurs in the root of the B-tree. Since the object with value 18 cannot fit into the node, that object, along with the four other objects, are ordered according to their values. When the five objects are placed in order, the object with value 26 is the

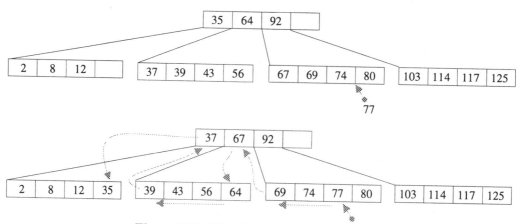

Figure 7.8. Shuffling nodes in a B-tree.

Figure 7.9. Simple node splitting example.

middle object. It becomes the lone object in the node, and the node is given two child nodes. The left node contains the two objects with values smaller than 26 and the right child node contains the two objects with values greater than 26.

Figure 7.10 illustrates node splitting when it does not occur at the root. In this case, the object with value 60 must be inserted in the second child of the root. That node is full; therefore, it is split. When the split occurs, the object with value 53 is promoted to the root.

Sometimes, when an object is promoted to its parent node, that node may become full. In this case, the process of node splitting is repeated, and the repetition continues up the tree as necessary to maintain the tree as a B-tree.

Figure 7.11 illustrates a ripple effect of node splitting. When an object with value 37 is added to the node, the node is split. 37 is the value of the median object that is promoted to its parent. But the parent node must be split, and the object with value 53 is the median value, which is promoted. However, there is no parent; hence 53 become the lone value in the new root of the B-tree.

Just as there are three possible cases for inserting values into a B-tree, there are three cases that must be considered for deleting nodes from a B-tree. These three cases mirror the three insertion cases. Elaborating these cases is left as an exercise for the reader.

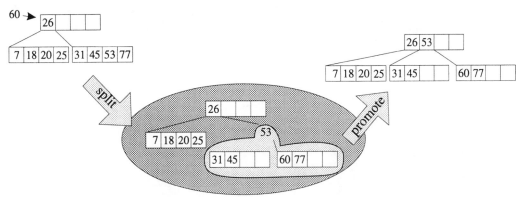

Figure 7.10. Node split with promotion example.

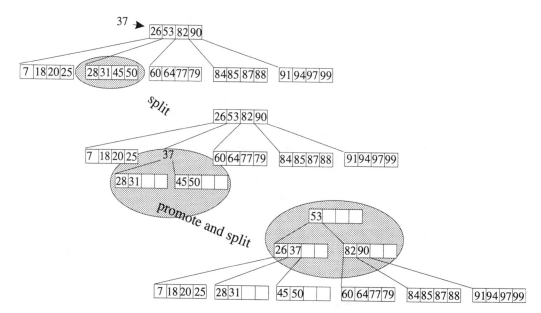

Figure 7.11. Value promotion ripple effect.

Figure 7.12 illustrates a deletion case. The node with value 45 is to be
removed. The node containing this value has a sibling with more than $b = 2$

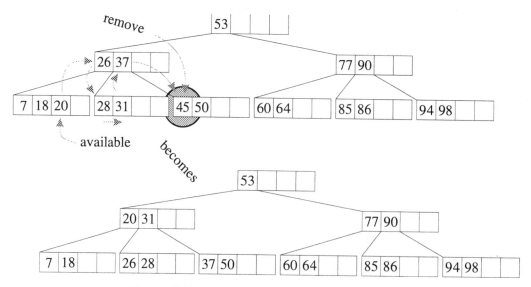

Figure 7.12. B-tree node deletion, case D2.i.

values. The node whose value is 20 is promoted to replace the node with value 26 in its parent node. The node with value 26 is demoted so that the node with value 31 may be promoted. Finally, the node with value 37 is demoted to satisfy the requirement that the node contain *b* objects.

Figure 7.13 illustrates another B-tree deletion that requires several actions in order to maintain the B-tree. If the object with value 86 is to be deleted, since its node and all of its siblings have exactly *b* values, the node is combined with one of its siblings and the corresponding intermediate value from the parent node. As a result, the parent node must now be processed to maintain the B-tree node requirements. Since the lone sibling of this node has *b* values, a further reduction of the tree occurs. As a result, three nodes are combined into one, forming a new root.

Developing a B-tree package is left as an exercise for the reader. The specifications for a B-tree package are basically the same as those for a binary

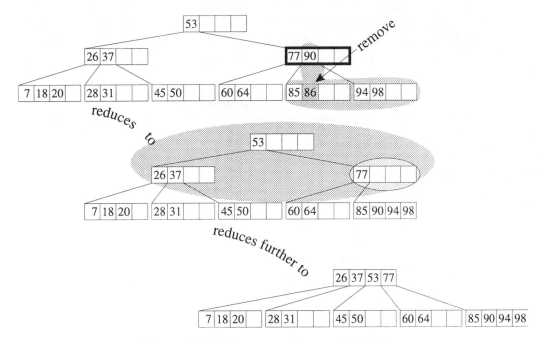

Figure 7.13. B-tree complex node deletion.

search tree but with the additional parameter, B, that controls the number of objects per node:

```
generic
   type Object_Type is private;
   with function "<" (Left, Right: Object_Type)
                                        return boolean;
   B: integer:= 4;
package B_Tree_Pt_En is
       . . .
```

Listing 7.3 illustrates part of the body of the B-tree based on using the Tree_Nary_Pt_Lpt package. The package defines a B_Node as a record with two components, the count of the number of objects actually in the node and an array that may contain up to 2*B objects.

If a node contains *k* objects, the package must maintain the tree in a way that the node must have *k*+1 child nodes. The objects in the node appear in the order defined by the instantiating ordering function. The objects in the *i*th child of a node are all less than the *i*th object in a node, which, in turn, is less than all the objects in the *i*+1st child node. A B-tree package includes an iterator that traverses the values in a B-tree in order according to the linear ordering of the objects in the nodes. The heart of this algorithm is a depth-first tree search that passes the objects in each node to the client's process. There should also be a second iterator that traverses down the tree to a specified object until either it reaches the left or right end of the tree or the instantiating process tells it to stop.

Listing 7.3. B-tree package specifications.

```
with Tree_Nary_Pt_Lpt;

package body B_Tree_Pt_En is

   subtype B_Array_Range is positive range 1 .. 2*B;
   type    B_Array_Type  is array (B_Array_Range) of Object_Type;
   type    B_Node        is
      record
         Actual_Number: natural:= 0;
         Object        : B_Array_Type;
      end record;

   package My_Tree is new Tree_Nary_Pt_Lpt (B_Node);
   use My_Tree;

   The_Tree: Tree_Type;

      . . .
```

Listing 7.4. B-Tree declarations based on access types.

```
package body B_Tree_Pt_En is

   type B_Node;
   type B_Node_Ptr is access B_Node;

   subtype B_Array_Range    is positive range 1 .. 2*B;
   subtype X_B_Array_Range  is positive range 0 .. 2*B;
   type    B_Array_Type     is array (B_Array_Range)   of Object_Type;
   type    B_Ptr_Array_Type is array (X_B_Array_Range) of B_Node_Ptr;
   type    B_Node           is
      record
         Actual_Number: natural          := 0;
         Object       : B_Array_Type;
         Child        : B_Ptr_Array_Type:= (others => null);
      end record;


   The_Tree: B_Node_Ptr:= null;

   . . .
```

Listing 7.4 contains a second set of declarations for building a B-tree package. This set is based on the direct use of access types. In this specification, each node contains three components, the actual count of the number of objects, an array of objects, and an array of access types to the children of the node. Basing the body on the declarations in Listing 7.3 or 7.4 is more a matter of preference. However, there are some efficiencies to be achieved by directly using access types, as described in Listing 7.4. Building packages, based on each set of declarations, and a comparative analysis of these packages is left as an exercise for the reader.

7.2 Heaps

Binary search trees, AVL trees, and B-trees are all based on an ordering relationship, "<", between nodes such that, given a node, its left child, and its right child,

```
Left_Child < Parent
```

and

```
Parent < Right_Child
```

Another important ordering relationship between a node and its children is the linear ordering relationship

        Parent >= *all children*

This parent–child relationship helps maintain a structure called a **heap**. A heap is a complete tree satisfying the parent–child order relationship, ">=",

        Parent >= Child

for all children.

   Figure 7.14 illustrates a heap of integers with the parent–child relationship, ">=". The subscript on each node indicates the position of the nodes in the array that would contain the heap.

   There are two fundamental operations on a heap, removing the root and inserting a new node. When a new node is inserted, it must be placed in such a way as to maintain the parent–child order relationship. When the root is removed, the other nodes must be reset in the tree to maintain the parent/child order relationship. If a heap contains n objects, each operation may be performed in time $O(\log n)$.

   The algorithm for inserting a new node into a heap is called the **sift-up** algorithm. The algorithm for removing the root of a heap and reorganizing the remaining nodes is called the **sift-down** algorithm. To illustrate the sift-up process, consider the heap in Figure 7.15. The heap is based on the parent–child relationship, ">=". A new node, 87, is attached to the heap at the first available location. The newly attached node does not satisfy the heap ordering relationship. This node is **sifted up** the tree until the parent–child relationship is satisfied. When a new node does not satisfy the parent–child relationship, it is swapped

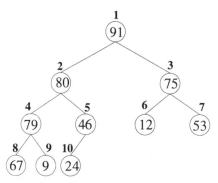

Figure 7.14. A sample heap.

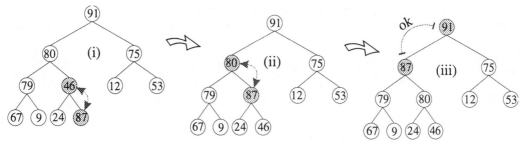

Figure 7.15. Heap sift-up process.

with its parent, sifting up the node in question. This process continues until the parent–child relationship is satisfied.

The sift-down process is illustrated in Figure 7.16. The root has been removed from the heap. To replace the root, the last node is removed from its location and viewed as a potential candidate for the root. However, if the root is attached, the heap relationship is not satisfied. The sift-down process determines whether the candidate, 24 in this example, or one of the children of the root should be promoted. If a child is promoted, the promotion opens up a vacant location and an attempt is made to place the candidate in the vacated position, This comparison and promotion of the "larger" child continues until the candidate is positioned in the tree at a location where the heap condition is satisfied.

The specifications for a package that supports heaps appear in Listing 7.5. The heap is instantiated with the `Object_Type` and the `">="` relationship. Note that heaps are made visible as a **private** type with a discriminant. A user determines the maximum size of a heap with the discriminant when a heap is declared:

```
My_Heap: Heap_Type (25);
```

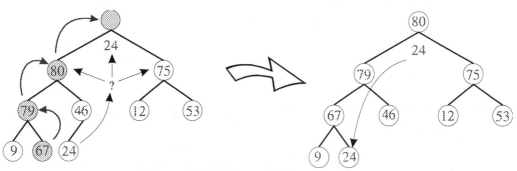

Figure 7.16. Heap sift-down example.

Listing 7.5. `Heap_Pt_Pt` specifications.

```
generic
   type Object_Type is private;
   with function ">=" ( Parent, Child: Object_Type) return boolean;
package Heap_Pt_Pt is

   type Heap_Type (Max_Size: positive) is private;

   Empty_Heap, Heap_Overflow: exception;

procedure Insert ( The_Heap  : in out Heap_Type;
                   The_Object: in     Object_Type);
   -------------------------------------------------------
   -- Pre Cond : Size_Of (The_Heap) < The_Heap.Max_Heap_Size
   -- Post Cond: The_Object is sifted into The_Heap
   -- Exception: Heap_Overflow
   -------------------------------------------------------

procedure Remove_Root ( The_Heap  : in out Heap_Type;
                        The_Object:    out Object_Type );
   -------------------------------------------------------
   -- Pre Cond : The_Heap is not empty
   -- Exception:  Empty_Heap.
   -------------------------------------------------------

function Is_Empty ( The_Heap: Heap_Type ) return boolean;

function No_Of_Objects ( The_Heap: Heap_Type) return natural;

function Are_Equal (Heap_1, Heap_2: Heap_Type) return boolean;

private
   type Heap_array is array (positive range <>) of Object_Type;
   type Heap_Type (Max_Size: positive:= 50) is
      record
         Size: natural:= 0;
         Data: Heap_Array (1 .. Max_Size);
      end record;

end Heap_Pt_Pt;
```

The fundamental procedures in the package are the `Insert` procedure, which places a new node in the heap, and the `Remove_Root` procedure, which removes the root of the heap and reorganizes the heap using the sift-down process. The `Insert` procedure uses the sift-up process to insert a new value in the heap.

Since a static data structure represents a heap, the heap is represented as a record containing two components. The first component maintains the count of the actual number of objects in the heap. The second component is an array that contains the objects in the heap. The heap could be made visible as a `private`, `limited private`, or `controlled` type, depending on the client's needs.

Listing 7.6. Heap `Insert` procedure.

```
procedure Insert (Heap   : in out Heap_Type;
                  Object: in out Object_Type) is
   Parent: natural:= (Heap.Size + 1) / 2;
   Child : natural:= Heap.Size + 1;
   begin
      if Heap.Size = Heap.Max_Size then
         raise Heap_Overflow;
      else
         Heap.Size:= Heap.Size + 1;
         while (Parent > 0) and then
               not ((Heap.Data(Parent) >= Object)) loop
            Swap (Heap.Data(Parent), Heap.Data (Child));
            Child := Parent;
            Parent:= Parent / 2;
         end loop;
         Swap (Object, Heap.Data(Child) );
      end if;
   end Insert;
```

The `Insert` procedure for heaps appears in Listing 7.6. The procedure begins by testing for possible overflow and then proceeds with the sift-up process. The index `Child` is set to where the new node has been placed. `Parent` indicates the location of the parent node of that position. The loop compares the object at the `Parent` location against the new object. If the parent–child relationship is not satisfied, the object at the `Parent` location is swapped with the object being sifted up from the `Child` location and the looping process continues until a location is found where the new object satisfies the parent–child relationship. Once a location is found, the loop terminates.

The time required to perform the `Insert` procedure is bound by the length of the longest path from the root to any node. In a complete tree that is bound by $O(\log n)$, hence the worst-case time for the `Insert` procedure, and the sift-up algorithm contained within, is $O(\log n)$.

The `Remove_Root` procedure is more complex. It contains the sift-down process. The algorithm, which appears in Listing 7.7, performs as follows. First, the procedure tests for a potential exception, an `Empty_Heap`. The object at the root, `The_Heap.Data(1)`, is placed in the procedure's **out** parameter. The size of the heap is reduced. If the heap has become empty, the sift-down process is not performed.

In preparation for the sift-down process, the last node is pruned from the heap and placed in `Candidate`. With the root empty and `Candidate` playing the role of the object that is to be sifted down the heap, the procedure calls the `Sift_Down` process.

Listing 7.7. Heap `Remove_Node` **procedure.**

```
procedure Remove_Root ( The_Heap  : in out Heap_Type;
                        The_Object:    out Object_Type ) is
   Candidate: Object_Type;
   procedure Sift_Down ( The_Heap  : in out Heap_Type;
                         The_Object: in     Object_Type ) is
      Parent  : positive:= 1;
      Child   : positive;
      Continue: boolean := true;
      begin -- Sift_Down
         while Continue loop
            Child:= 2*Parent;
            if Child > The_Heap.Size then
               Continue:= false;
             else
               if ((Child+1) <= The_Heap.Size) and then
                   The_Heap.Data(Child+1) >= The_Heap.Data(Child) then
                   Child:= Child+1;
               end if;
               if The_Object >= The_Heap.Data(Child) then
                  Continue:= false;
                else
                  The_Heap.Data(Parent):= The_Heap.Data(Child);
                  Parent:= Child;
               end if;
            end if;
         end loop;
         The_Heap.Data (Parent):= The_Object;
      end Sift_Down;
      -------------------------------------------------
   begin -- Remove_Root
      if The_Heap.Size = 0 then
         raise Empty_Heap;
        else
         The_Object   := The_Heap.Data (1);
         Candidate    := The_Heap.Data (The_Heap.Size);
         The_Heap.Size:= The_Heap.Size - 1;
         if The_Heap.Size /= 0  then
            Sift_Down (The_Heap, Candidate);
         end if;
      end if;
end Remove_Root;
```

The difficulty in the `Sift_Down` procedure is that the algorithm must compare the new object with the larger of the two children of the vacant node in the heap. Also, each time through the algorithm's loop, the algorithm must determine if the vacant node has two, one, or no children. The combination of the number of child nodes of the vacant node and the relative values of the child nodes leads to the collection of if-else structures. Let's work our way through the maze of conditions that are tested in the loop. First,

```
if Child > The_Heap.Size then
    Continue:= false;
```

determines if the vacant node has any children. If not, the loop is terminated. Next, the procedure tests a pair of conditions. The first condition determines if there are two children. If there are two children, a second test must be made to determine if the second child is larger. As a result,

```
if ((Child+1) <= The_Heap.Size) and then
    The_Heap.Data(Child+1) >= The_Heap.Data(Child) then
    Child:= Child+1;
end if;
```

the parameter Child points to the larger of the two children of the vacant node At this point, The_Object is compared to the larger child,

```
if The_Object >= The_Heap.Data(Child) then
    Continue:= false;
else
    The_Heap.Data(Parent):= The_Heap.Data(Child);
    Parent:= Child;
end if;
```

which terminates the loop, if The_Object is ">=", or else the larger child is promoted to the parent position and the algorithm resets Parent to prepare for the next loop iteration.

When the loop terminates, the algorithm places The_Object, guaranteeing that the heap condition is satisfied. In the worst-case timing scenario for the Sift_Down procedure, the number of loop iterations is bound by the length of the longest path from the root to any node. The longest path in a complete tree with n nodes is $O(\log n)$; hence, the time to perform the sift-down procedure is bound by $O(\log n)$.

7.2.1 Heapsort

The best possible sort time for an arbitrary array of n objects in time $O(n \log n)$. One sort that satisfies this timing is the **heapsort**. The heapsort uses the ordered heap's sift-up and sift-down algorithms to obtain $O(n \log n)$ timing.

The sort has two distinct phases that correspond to multiple applications of the sift-up and sift-down algorithms. An array of numbers may be viewed as a complete tree. The complete tree must be reorganized to form a heap. The reorganization of the complete tree into a heap is accomplished with $n-1$ applications of the sift-up process. Figure 7.17 illustrates an array, its corresponding view as a tree and the tree after the sifting process.

The sift-up algorithm is composed of a pair of nested loops. If the array contained n objects, since the sift algorithm processes all nodes in the tree except the root node, the outer loop iterates $n-1$ times. The inner loop performs the sift-up process on the ith node, for i in $2..n$. The number of iterations of the sift-up algorithm is bound by the size of the path from the node to the root, which is bound by $\log(n)$. Hence the entire sift-up algorithm is bound by $O(n \log(n))$. Since the heap uses the complement of the desired sort ordering, the root of the heap is the number that belongs in the nth array location. When the root is removed, a sift-down process is applied and the item removed from the root may now be placed in the nth location of the array, which became vacant.

Once the heap has been ordered, the second phase does the following, as illustrated in Figure 7.18. The last node in the heap is removed. In the array, this equates to vacating the position in the array where the root should eventually be placed when the objects in the array are ordered. Next, the object in the root is placed in that position. The object that was removed from the array is now used in the sift-down process. This process repeats until the entire tree is processed. As a result, the array is ordered.

The sift-down phase of the heapsort contains a nested pair of loops. The outer loop iterates $n-1$ times, and the inner loop iteration is bound by the length

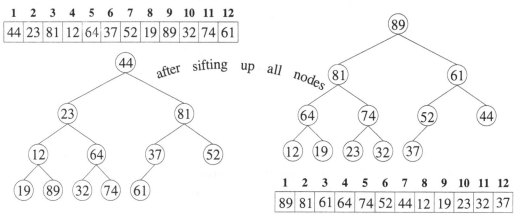

Figure 7.17. Heapsort phase one example.

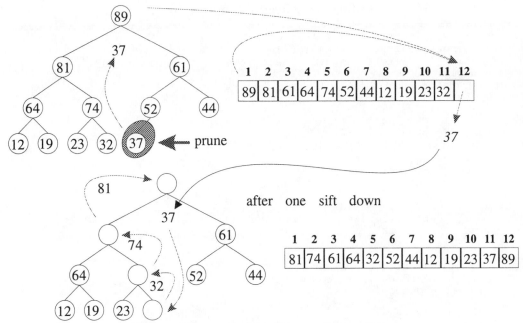

Figure 7.18. Heapsort phase two example.

of the longest path in the tree, log(n). Therefore, the timing of the second phase is also bound by $O(n \log(n))$.

Specifications for a generic heapsort procedure appear in Listing 7.8. The procedure is instantiated with an `Object_Type` and an unconstrained array type containing the `Object_Type`. It is also instantiated with a linear ordering function for the objects in the array. Note that since the heapsort uses the array

Listing 7.8. Generic heapsort specifications.

```
generic
   type Object_Type is private;
   type Object_Array is array (natural range <>) of Object_Type;
   with function "<" (Left, Right: Object_Type) return boolean;
procedure Heap_Sort (Item: in out Object_Array );
   -----------------------------------------------------------------
   -- Precondition : Objects are placed in array positions indexed by
   --                Item (first .. Last_Index)
   --                Item'first = 1
   -- Postcondition: Objects are ordered according to the order
   --                indicated by the collating function "<"
   -- Side Effects : (None)
   -- Exceptions   : constraint error if Item'first /= 1
   -----------------------------------------------------------------
```

Listing 7.9. Generic heapsort body.

```
procedure Heap_Sort (Item: in out Object_Array) is
   Last_Index: natural:= Item'last;
   function ">=" (Left, Right: Object_Type) return boolean is
      begin
         return not (Left < Right);
      end ">=";
   ----------------------------------------------------------

   procedure Order_Heap is
      Outer, Child, Parent: natural;
      Extra: Object_Type;
      begin -- Order_Heap
         for Outer in 2 .. Last_Index loop
            Child:= Outer;
            Parent:= Child / 2;
            while (Parent /= 0) and then (Item(Parent) < Item(Child)) loop
               Extra         := Item (Child);
               Item (Child) := Item (Parent);
               Item (Parent):= Extra;
               Child := Parent;
               Parent:= Child / 2;
            end loop;
         end loop;
      end Order_Heap;
   ----------------------------------------------------------
   procedure Sort_The_Array is
      Fill_Position: natural;       The_Key: Object_Type;
      procedure Sift_Down (The_Heap  : in out Object_Array;
                           The_Object: in      Object_Type ) is
         Parent: positive:= 1;         Child: positive;
         Continue: boolean := true;
         begin -- Sift_Down
            while Continue loop
               Child:= 2*Parent;
               if Child > The_Heap'range'last then
                  Continue:= false;
                else
                  if ((Child+1) <= The_Heap'range'last)
                     and then The_Heap(Child+1) >= The_Heap(Child) then
                     Child:= Child+1;
                  end if;
                  if The_Object >= The_Heap(Child) then
                     Continue:= false;
                   else
                     The_Heap(Parent):= The_Heap(Child);
                     Parent:= Child;
                  end if;
               end if;
            end loop;
            The_Heap (Parent):= The_Object;
         end Sift_Down;
   ----------------------------------------------------------
```

Listing 7.9. Generic heapsort body (cont.)

```
   begin -- Sort_The_Array
      for Fill_Position in reverse 2 .. Last_Index loop
         The_Key:= Item (Fill_Position);
         Item (Fill_Position):= Item (1);
         Sift_Down (Item (1 .. Fill_Position-1), The_Key);
      end loop;
   end Sort_The_Array;
   ----------------------------------------------------
begin -- Heap_Sort;
   if Item'first /= 1 then
      raise constraint_error;
   end if;
   Order_Heap;
   Sort_The_Array;
end Heap_Sort;
```

indices to form the array representation of a complete tree, the constrained array must be over a range starting with index 1.

The heapsort body appears in Listing 7.9. The procedure is composed of two algorithms. The first procedure, `Order_Heap`, views the array as a complete tree and uses the complement of the linear ordering to convert the complete tree into a heap. This is accomplished through application of the sift-up procedure at each node.

The second procedure, `Sort_The_Array`, appears in Listing 7.9. Each time through the outer loop in this procedure, the size of the heap is reduced by removing the last object in the heap and placing it in `The_Key`. The object at the root of the heap is placed into the vacated position. The remainder of the array and `The_Key` are processed with the `Sift_Down` procedure.

The `Sift_Down` procedure in `Sort_The_Array` is fundamentally the same as the `Sift_Down` procedure that appears in Listing 7.7. Since both the sift-up and sift-down procedures perform in time $O(\log n)$ and each is called $n-1$ times, the total time for the heapsort algorithm is $O(n \log n)$.

7.2.2 Priority Queues

A **priority queue** is a structure for storing and retrieving information. The structure is queuelike in that objects are retrieved from the structure by a dequeue operation, which removes objects from the front of the priority queue. However, each object is placed in a priority queue according to a user-assigned priority value. If "<" is the linear ordering for a priority queue $(O_1, O_2, \ldots, O_n)$, then for any two objects O_j and O_k, if $i < k$, then $O_i \leq O_k$.

At first glance, a list seems to be an appropriate structure for representing a priority queue. In fact, the ordered list package could be used with the queue's priority forming the list's order. One potential problem with using a list to represent a priority queue is that the enqueuing procedure contains a loop and the timing of that loop is bound by the size of the list, $O(n)$, where n is the number of objects in the priority queue. An alternative would be to store the objects in a binary tree. If the nodes in the binary tree are height-balanced, the time required to place an object in a priority queue would be bound by $O(\log n)$, where n is the number of objects in the priority queue. This is a much more desirable result.

Heaps are an ideal structure for representing priority queues. In fact, very little must be done to a heap's package to represent a priority queue. The procedures made visible in the heap specification are ideal for building a priority queue package.

Listing 7.10 contains the specifications for a priority queue. The package has three instantiation parameters. The instantiation parameters are the client's `Object_Type` and an ordering function, "<". The package uses the linear ordering to order the objects in the priority queue. The priority of the objects at the front of the queue are "<" the priority of the objects at the rear of the queue.

7.2.3 Huffman Coding

In some applications a variable-length coding for characters reduces storage requirements. One method of reducing the size of text uses the relative frequencies of characters. Variable-length codes assign small code sequences to letters that occur more frequently and longer codes to letters that occur less frequently.

If a variable-length coding scheme is to have good timing characteristics, O(length of the string), one obvious requirement is that the code for any character may not be a prefix of the code for any other character. If one code was a prefix to another, it would be difficult to determine which symbol is being represented.

Huffman coding is a method of developing, encoding, and decoding variable-length codes that are encoded and decoded in linear time. It should be noted that many data compression techniques are based on Huffman coding methods. Huffman coding assumes the existence of information about the relative frequency of characters. A Huffman code is created from a binary tree that is constructed

Listing 7.10. Priority queue specifications.

```
with Heap_Pt_Pt;
generic
    type Object_Type is private;
    type Priority_Type is (<>);
    with function "<" (Left, Right: Priority_Type) return boolean;
package Priority_Queue_Pt_Pt is

    type PQ_Type (Max_Size: positive:= 50) is private;

    Empty_PQ, PQ_Overflow: exception;

    procedure Enq ( Object  : in     Object_Type;
                    Priority: in     Priority_Type;
                    Queue   : in out PQ_Type );
    Procedure Deq ( Queue : in out PQ_Type;
                    Object:      out Object_Type );
    function Is_Empty (Queue: PQ_Type) return boolean;

    function Q_Size (Queue: PQ_Type) return positive;

private
    type Heap_Node is
       record
          Object  : Object_Type;
          Priority: Priority_Type;
       end record;
    function "<" (Left, Right: Heap_Node) return boolean;

    package My_PQ is new Heap_Pt_Pt (Heap_Node, "<");

    type PQ_Type (Max_Size: positive:= 50) is
       record
          Actual: My_PQ.Heap_Type (Max_Size);
       end record;

end Priority_Queue_Pt_Pt;
```

from the frequency information. The binary tree is constructed with the help of a priority queue. It should be noted that Huffman codes are not unique, in that through slight variations of the construction method, several different binary trees could be constructed. Also, given the final binary tree, several codes could be generated from the tree.

Figure 7.19 contains a frequency listing for seven characters. A priority queue of binary trees is constructed from the data, as illustrated in Figure 7.19 a. The frequencies of the characters are used as the priority, but with a "<" ordering. That is, lower frequency is placed at the front of the queue, with higher frequencies to the rear. The trees at the front of the queue are dequeued, and a new binary tree is constructed. The new binary tree is constructed by grafting the

Characters	e	t	a	n	s	o	l
Frequency	65	53	45	45	22	18	13

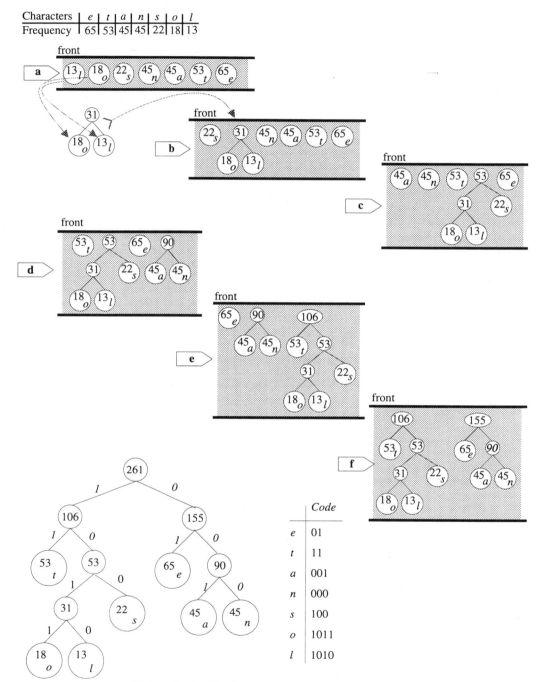

Figure 7.19. Huffman code tree construction.

two dequeued trees as the left and right subtrees of its root. The priority for the newly constructed tree is the sum of the priorities of the two subtrees. The dequeuing, combining, and requeuing results appear in Figure 7.19 b–f.

This process produces a single binary tree, which appears in Figure 7.19. It should be noted, as stated previously, that the tree produced by this process is not unique. Specifically, at any point in the process, interchanging the order of two trees of equal priority in the priority queue results in a different tree.

Once the tree is formed, zeros and ones are assigned to the branches in the tree. The zeros and ones may be assigned in any order, just as long as each arc in a pair of child arcs is assigned two different values, one with a zero, the other with a one. Since there are many possible assignments of zeros and ones to arcs, the resulting Huffman code is not unique.

Given the binary tree with the zero-one assignments, the Huffman code corresponding to the tree is obtained by transcribing the sequence of zeros and ones on the path to each terminal node. Figure 7.19 lists the Huffman code generated by the binary tree. The Huffman code has the distinct advantage that the code for any symbol is never the prefix of the code for another symbol. This means that the time to decode a symbol is O(length of symbol's encoding).

Huffman coding requires three components, one to create a Huffman code, one to encode a string to a Huffman coding, and one to decode the Huffman coding. The processes involved in building a system to generate Huffman codes is described above. Building the coding and decoding components are left as an exercise.

The message encoder simply replaces each letter by its Huffman coding. The decode component is handled most efficiently in a binary tree, a reconstruction of the tree used to create the coding. Two exercise problems suggest methods of building Huffman decoders.

7.3 Dictionary Trees

When processing strings of characters it is desirable to have a method of quickly comparing two strings to see if they match. A tree structure may store strings in a fashion that makes it easy to perform string matching in time O(string length). This type of tree is referred to as a **dictionary tree**.

Figure 7.20 illustrates a dictionary tree containing the words ABLE, BAKER, CHARLIE, BAKE, BAT, QUICK, and QUIZ. The words are stored in an n-ary tree with the first letter of each word appearing in a child node of the root. The nodes at the ends of words are marked with an '*'. To determine if a word is in the

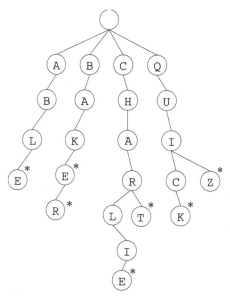

Figure 7.20. Example of a dictionary tree.

tree, a letter-by-letter match is performed as the word is processed against the words in the tree. Words are added to the tree by correctly linking additional nodes to the tree. Sometimes, all the letters in the word must be added, while other times only a few letters need to be added. For example, to add QUIT to the tree in Figure 7.20, only a node containing a 'T' need be added as a child node of the node containing the 'I' in the path 'Q', 'U', and 'I'.

A procedure that creates and prints a dictionary tree appears in Listing 7.11. The package instantiates the *n*-ary tree package with a record that contains a character and an end-of-word mark, EoW. The mark is set to true when the corresponding character is the last character in a word.

7.4 Explorations

1. Complete and test a binary search tree package.
2. Rewrite the body of the binary search tree package to include AVL tree restructuring algorithms using the positional paradigm. This may be accomplished in the following manner:

    a. Build and test a procedure AVL_L_L that performs restructuring for the AVL L-L rebalancing case.

Listing 7.11. Dictionary tree example.

```
with tree_nary_pt_lpt, text_io;
procedure Dictionary is
   package tio renames text_io;
type Node is
   record
      Symbol: character:= ' ';
      EoW   : boolean  := false;
   end record;
      package tre is new tree_nary_pt_lpt (Node);
      use tre;
   Tree: Tree_Type;
   Word_File: tio.File_Type;
   Word: string (1..80);
   W_Size: natural;
procedure Place (Str : in    string;
                 Tree: in    Tree_Type) is
   begin -- Place
      if Empty (Tree) or else Str(Str'First) <= Root_Of(Tree).Symbol then
         if Empty (Tree) or else Str(Str'First) < Root_Of(Tree).Symbol then
            Graft ((Str(Str'First), false), Tree);
         end if;
         if Str'First = Str'Last then
            Update_Root (Tree, (Str(Str'First),true));
           else
            Place (Str(str'First+1..Str'Last), Child_Subtree(Tree));
         end if;
        else
         Place (Str, Sibling_Subtree(Tree));
      end if;
   end Place;
   -------------------------------------------------------
procedure List_Words (Tree: in Tree_Type; Str: in string) is
   begin -- List_Words
      if not Empty (Tree) then
         if Root_Of(Tree).EoW then
            tio.Put (Str & Root_Of(Tree).Symbol); tio.New_Line;
         end if;
         List_Words (Child_Subtree(Tree), Str & Root_Of(Tree).Symbol);
         List_Words (Sibling_Subtree(Tree), Str);
      end if;
   end List_Words;
   -------------------------------------------------------
begin -- Dictionary
   Initialize (Tree);
   tio.Open (Word_File, tio.in_file, "words.dat");
   while not tio.End_Of_File (Word_File) loop
      tio.Get_Line (Word_File, Word, W_Size);
      Place (Word(1..W_Size), Tree);
   end loop;
   tio.Close (Word_File);
   List_Words (Tree, "");
   Finalize (Tree);
end Dictionary;
```

b. Build and test a procedure `AVL_L_R` that performs restructuring for the AVL L-R rebalancing case.

c. Build and test a procedure `AVL_R_R` that performs restructuring for the AVL R-R rebalancing case.

d. Build and test a procedure `AVL_R_L` that performs restructuring for the AVL R-L rebalancing case.

e. Modify the binary tree `Insert` procedure to include AVL balancing and have this procedure call the appropriate restructuring procedure as needed.

3. Rewrite the body of the binary search tree package to include AVL tree restructuring algorithms using the recursive paradigm. Follow the steps in Exercise 2.

4. Build and test a B-tree package based on the use of the `Tree_Nary_Pt_Lpt` package illustrated in Listing 7.3.

5. Build and test a B-tree package based on the use of the `Tree_Nary_Pt_Lpt` package illustrated in Listing 7.4.

6. Complete and test a priority queue package based on heaps.

7. Build and test a procedure that accepts a series of symbols and their relative weights and builds a Huffman coding for those symbols.

8. Build and test a system that accepts a Huffman coding for a set of symbols, accepts strings composed of those symbols, and generates the encodings of the strings.

9. Build and test a system that accepts the Huffman coding of a set of symbols and accepts strings of zeros and ones and decodes them using a binary tree representation of the Huffman codes.

10. Complete and test a dictionary tree package.

11. Given a set of delimiters, a **concordance listing** of a text file is a list of all strings separated by delimiters in the text file. The listing indicates the string and the sequence number of all the records that contain that string. Build and test a concordance listing system based on the dictionary tree package.

12. Develop the preconditions, postconditions, and invariants for the heap `Sift_Down` and `Sift_Up` procedures.

13. Perform a comparative analysis of a B-tree package based on the specifications in Listings 7.3 and 7.4, paying particular attention to space requirements and algorithm timings.

14. A **trie** is an alternative to an *n*-ary tree when there is a predetermined number of child nodes. Research a trie, create specifications, and determine if a trie construction may be efficiently based on an existing binary tree package.

8

Graphs

8.1 Graphs and Digraphs

A **graph**, G, is an ordered pair of sets, $G = (N, A)$. The set N is a finite set, called the **set of nodes**,

$$N = \{n_1, n_2, n_3, \ldots, n_k\}.$$

The finite set A, called the **set of arcs**, is a set of pairs of objects from N,

$$A = \{a_1, a_2, a_3, \ldots, a_m\},$$

where for each i, $a_i = \{n_p, n_q\}$. Figure 8.1 illustrates a simple graph with 6 nodes and 12 arcs. Observe from the figure that two arcs may contain the same pair of nodes. Also, note that an arc may contain the same node twice. The **multiplicity of a node** in a graph is the count of the number of times the node appears in the definitions of arcs. In Figure 8.1, the multiplicity of node 2 is four, not three. The multiplicity of node 6 is five.

A **path** in a graph between two nodes, u and v, is a sequence of arcs

$$p_1, p_2, \ldots, p_d$$

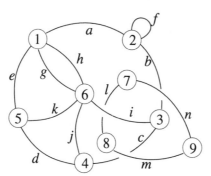

Figure 8.1. A sample graph.

if and only if $u \in p_1$, $v \in p_d$, $p_{i-1} \cap p_i \neq \emptyset$ for all i in $1 \leq i < d$, and for the sequence
of sets $Q_0, Q_1, \ldots, Q_d$ defined by

$$Q_0 = \{u\},$$
$$Q_i = p_i \sim Q_{i-1} \text{ for } i, \; 1 \leq i < d,$$

$Q_d = \{v\}$ and each Q_i contains exactly one element. Simply stated, a path is a
sequence of arcs that links two nodes by starting at one of the nodes and
traversing from node to node by following arcs until the second node is reached.
For example, the sequence of arcs

$$\{a, b, c, j\}$$

is a path between node 1 and node 6. However, the sequence of arcs,

$$\{a, b, j\}$$

is not a path between node 1 and node 6. A path may traverse one or more arcs
several times. A path may also pass through a node several times. For example,
the sequence of arcs

$$\{a, e, f, f, f, b, i, j, c\}$$

is a path between node 5 and node 3.

The **length** of a path is the number of arcs in the sequence. In determining the length of a path, each arc is counted each time it appears in the path. A **cycle** is a path from a node to itself. For example, the arc sequence

$\{a, b, c, d, e\}$

is a cycle from node 1 to itself. $\{f\}$ is also a cycle.

Paths play a fundamental role in the manipulation and use of graphs. A **simple path** is a path that does not properly contain any cycles. Frequently, the **distance between two nodes** is defined as the minimum length of all paths between the nodes, where **length** is an application-dependent value that may be assigned to each arc. Two nodes in a graph are said to be **connected** if a path exists between them.

A graph $G_s = (N_s, A_s)$ is a **subgraph** of a graph $G = (N, A)$ if $N_s \subseteq N$ and $A_s \subseteq A$. A **Euler path** is a path in a graph, if such a path exists, that traverses each arc once. A **Hamiltonian path** is a path in a graph that traverses each node once. Similarly, Euler cycles and Hamiltonian cycles may be defined. There is a simple method of determining if a graph has a Eulerian path. No such simple method exists for determining the existence of Hamiltonian paths. There are several exercise problems elaborating on classical graph problems.

Figure 8.2 illustrates a **directed graph**, also called a **digraph**. A digraph is similar to a graph except that the arcs are defined as ordered pairs, hence giving each arc direction. Formally, a digraph, D, is an ordered pair of sets (N, A). The set N, as with a graph, is a finite set called the set of nodes. The finite set A, called the set of arcs, is a set of **ordered pairs** of objects from N,

$A = \{a_1, a_2, a_3, \ldots, a_m\},$

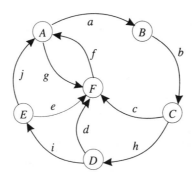

Figure 8.2. A sample digraph.

where for each i, $a_i = (n_p, n_q)$. All graph concepts, like path and cycle, may be extended from graphs to digraphs. The extension of these terms must take into account the direction of arcs. For example, in Figure 8.2, arc a is a path of length one from node A to node B, but not a path from node B to node A. All paths in a digraph must follow the arc directions from one node to the next.

Each graph may be represented by a digraph simply by representing each arc in the graph with a pair of arcs in the digraph. Therefore, digraphs may represent graphs. For this reason, this chapter discusses the representation of digraphs. It is desirable to have a package to represent digraphs that has sufficient features to apply to a large variety of graph and digraph applications. However, the great range of potential graph applications leads to a variety of representation methods depending on whether an application deals simply with connectivity concerns or with more complex relationships between arcs and nodes.

Many graph applications involve not just representing graphs, but using other data objects in the analysis of the graph. Some graph problems involve constructing a tree as part of the analysis of the graph application and, often, using a third structure to assist in developing the tree. Often, the tree that is built is a subgraph of the digraph, called a **spanning tree**. A spanning tree T of a digraph G, $G = (N, A)$, if T is a subgraph G_s, $G_s = (N_s, A_s)$, $N = N_s$ and G_s is a tree.

8.2 Digraph Specifications

Since a digraph is a fairly complex structure, a number of issues arise regarding the structure of a digraph support packages. Three object types come together to define a digraph, a node type, an arc type, and a digraph type. For example, sometimes the node type may be represented as the subrange of some discrete type. For example, the nodes might simply be referred to as nodes numbered 1 through n, where n is the number of nodes in the digraph. Other times nodes may be identified with a label, or name. Typically, the name might be a string of characters. Because of the large variety of applications for digraphs, it is common to have several digraph packages, each supporting the fundamental digraph operations, but allowing a variety of instantiations.

A digraph package must make object types available, like `Digraph_Type`, `Node_Type`, and `Arc_Type`, as well as the constructors, observers, and iterators that assist users in building, maintaining, and gaining information about the graph, its contents, and structure. All digraph packages must include two fundamental operations, a constructor, `Add_Arc`, to attach an arc from one node to another, and an observer, `Arc_Exists`, to determine if an arc exists from one node to

Listing 8.1. Digraph specifications.

```
generic
   type Node_Label_Type is private;
   type Node_Data_Type is private;
   type Arc_Data_Type is private;
   -- Max_No_Nodes is natural; -- FOR STATIC REPRESENTATION
   -- Max_No_Arcs is natural; -- FOR STATIC REPRESENTATION
package Digraph_??_En is

   type Node_Type is private;
   type Arc_Type is private;

   Label_Error, Node_Error, Arc_Error,
   Node_Overflow, Arc_Overflow : exception;

procedure Add_Arc ( From_Node,
                    To_Node  : in       Node_Type;
                    Data     : in       Arc_Data_Type );
procedure Add_Arc ( From_Label,
                    To_Label : in       Node_Label_Type;
                    Data     : in       Arc_Data_Type );
procedure Bind ( Label: in       Node_Label_Type;
                 Data : in       Node_Data_Type;
                 Node :    out Node_Type );
procedure Update_Node ( Node: in       Node_Type;
                        Data: in       Node_Data_Type );
procedure Update_Node ( Label: in       Node_Label_Type;
                        Data : in       Node_Data_Type );
procedure Update_Arc ( From_Node,
                       To_Node  : in       Node_Type;
                       Data     : in       Arc_Data_Type );
procedure Update_Arc ( From_Label,
                       To_Label : in       Node_Label_Type;
                       Data     : in       Arc_Data_Type );

function Arc_Exists ( From_Node, To_Node  : Node_Type ) return boolean;
function Arc_Exists ( From_Label, To_Label: Node_Label_Type )
                                                    return boolean;

function Node (Label: Node_Label_Type ) return Node_Type;
function Label (Node: Node_Type ) return Node_Label_Type;

function Data ( From_Node, To_Node: Node_Type ) return Arc_Data_Type;
function Data ( From_Label, To_Label: Node_Label_Type )
                                               return Arc_Data_Type;
generic
   Type Pass_Type is limited private;
   with procedure Process ( Node      : in       Node_Type;
                            Label     : in       Node_Label_Type;
                            Data      : in       Node_Data_Type;
                            Pass_Thru: in out Pass_Type;
                            Continue :    out boolean );
   procedure Sel_Node_Iterator (Pass_Thru: in out Pass_Type);
```

Listing 8.1. (cont.)

```
generic
   Type Pass_Type is limited private;
   with procedure Process ( Node     : in      Node_Type;
                            Label    : in      Node_Label_Type;
                            Data     : in out Node_Data_Type;
                            Pass_Thru: in out Pass_Type;
                            Continue :     out boolean );
      procedure Con_Node_Iterator (Pass_Thru: in out Pass_Type);

generic
   type Pass_Type is limited private;
   with procedure Process ( To_Node  : in      Node_Type;
                            From_Node: in      Node_Type;
                            Data     : in      Arc_Data_Type;
                            Pass_Thru: in out Pass_Type;
                            Continue :     out boolean );
   procedure Sel_Out_Arc_Iterator ( Node    : in      Node_Type;
                                    Pass_Thru: in out Pass_Type);
generic
   type Pass_Type is limited private;
   with procedure Process ( To_Node  : in      Node_Type;
                            From_Node: in      Node_Type;
                            Data     : in out Arc_Data_Type;
                            Pass_Thru: in out Pass_Type;
                            Continue :     out boolean );
   procedure Con_In_Arc_Iterator ( Node    : in      Node_Type;
                                   Pass_Thru: in out Pass_Type);
generic
   type Pass_Type is limited private;
   with procedure Process ( To_Node  : in      Node_Type;
                            From_Node: in      Node_Type;
                            Data     : in      Arc_Data_Type;
                            Pass_Thru: in out Pass_Type;
                            Continue :     out boolean );
   procedure Sel_In_Arc_Iterator ( Node    : in      Node_Type;
                                   Pass_Thru: in out Pass_Type);
generic
   type Pass_Type is limited private;
   with procedure Process ( To_Node  : in      Node_Type;
                            From_Node: in      Node_Type;
                            Data     : in out Arc_Data_Type;
                            Pass_Thru: in out Pass_Type;
                            Continue :     out boolean );
   procedure Con_Out_Arc_Iterator ( Node    : in      Node_Type;
                                    Pass_Thru: in out Pass_Type);
private
   type Arc_Type is
      . . .

   type Node_Type is
      . . .
end Digraph_??_En;
```

another. Other constructors and observers may be included to provide additional versatility.

One possible specification for a digraph package appears in Listing 8.1. In this illustration, a user instantiates the package with the data types that are associated to each node, `Node_Data_Type`, and arc, `Arc_Data_Type`, as well as a `Node_Label_Type` that the client may associate to a node. `Node_Label_Type` represents the data type that the client plans to use to reference nodes in the digraph. For example, in a large graph, like a map of the United States, the user may wish to use application-specific labels to manipulate the node, like abbreviations for the names of states (MA, PA, NY, . . .). The package provides access to nodes and arcs through references to both `Node_Types` and `Node_Label_Types`.

A careful review of the package raises one question: Where is the `Digraph_Type` defined? Instead of defining a `Digraph_Type`, the package itself encapsulates the digraph. That is, one instantiation of the package supports one digraph. Since many digraph applications normally work with a single digraph, this is a reasonable approach for encapsulating and hiding implementational details. In fact, since there is no `Digraph_Type`, there is no need to reveal the details of the graph representation in the `private` part of the specification. This means the details of the representation may be placed in the body of the package, further hiding them from the client.

Note the collection of iterators provided through the package, iterators to traverse the nodes, in arcs, and out arcs. Given a `Node`, one pair of iterators processes through all the arcs coming into a `Node`, and another pair to process the arcs leaving a `Node`. With this collection of iterators, users may build a large number of digraph algorithms.

8.3 Matrix Representation

The simplest method of representing a digraph is with an *n-by-n* boolean matrix where n is the number of nodes in the digraph (see Figure 8.3). A digraph G is represented with a boolean matrix M with the criteria

$M(i, j)$ is true if and only if there is an arc from node i to node j.

This representation contains only connection information. The user must maintain information about the nodes and arcs elsewhere. However, many digraph problems only need access to connection information to solve certain problems.

	A	B	C	D	E	F
A	F	T	F	F	F	T
B	F	F	T	F	F	F
C	F	F	F	T	F	T
D	F	F	F	F	T	T
E	T	F	F	F	F	T
F	T	F	F	F	F	F

Figure 8.3. Boolean matrix representation of the digraph in Figure 8.2.

The major advantage of this approach is the simplicity and speed of the algorithms for a package's support subprograms. Adding an arc between two nodes is accomplished by setting the appropriate location in the matrix to `true`. Testing for the existence of an arc between two nodes is accomplished by testing to see if the corresponding position in the matrix is `true`.

One advantage frequently mentioned about this approach is the correspondence between connectivity information and matrix operations. If M is the matrix representation of the digraph, the matrix describes all nodes connected with paths of length one. An identity matrix, I, may be thought of as representing all connectivity with paths of length zero. Therefore, the matrix, $M' = I + M$ indicates all node connectivity of paths of length zero or one. That is, $M(i, j)$ is true if and only if there is a path of length zero or one from node i to node j. Applying matrix multiplication to M' provides further connectivity information. Position (i, j) in M'^2 is true if and only if there is a path of length two or less between node i and node j.

With subsequent matrix multiplications the sequence of matrices, $(M'^2)^2$, $((M'^2)^2)^2, \ldots$, is formed. After $\log_2 n + 1$ multiplications, subsequent multiplications produce no changes in the resulting matrix, and the positions in the resulting matrix indicate all node connectivity. That is, a position (i, j) is true if and only if there is a path from node i to node j.

The traversal from node to node through the out arcs of nodes may be realized in terms of matrix manipulations. For example, to traverses the **out arcs** of node i, the algorithm simply processes the ith row of the matrix representation. To view the traversals of the **in arcs** of node i, the algorithm processes the ith column of the matrix.

There are several limitations to this approach. One, mentioned above, is that the matrix representation does not maintain node and arc information; it provides information only about the connections between arcs. The second limitation is that the boolean matrix records only the existence of an arc between two nodes, not the number of arcs between two nodes.

A third possible limitation of the matrix representation is the potential size of the matrix. With n nodes, the matrix is of size n^2. Therefore, for large values of n, the storage requirements for the matrix could be prohibitive. This potentially large storage requirement leads to alternate methods, described in Section 8.4.

For example, if the rows of the matrix could be formed one at a time, the matrix could be represented by **comb vectors**. For sparse matrices, comb vectors have a very favorable time-space tradeoff with substantially reduced storage requirements with only a constant factor increase in the timing of the comb vector algorithms when compared to a boolean matrix representation.

Figure 8.4 illustrates a comb vector representation for the digraph in Figure 8.2. Two arrays are used for the comb vector representation of a boolean matrix. The first array, `Index`, indicates the location in the second array of the first element in the row of the corresponding boolean matrix. The value in position `(i,j)` in the matrix is determined by the computation

```
Comb (Index(i) + j - 1).
```

Under certain circumstances, sparse matrix techniques may be applied to represent the connection matrix.

If the index into the `Comb` array, `Index(i) + j - 1`, is outside the range of the `Comb`, then there is no arc from node i to node j. Otherwise, the existence of an arc from node i to node j is determined by the boolean expression

```
Comb (Index(i) + j - 1) = i
```

For example, in Figure 8.4, node 4 has only one out arc, to node 5. Row 4 of the boolean matrix is represented as follows: The `Index` array in Figure 8.4 indicates that row 4 begins at location 0. Therefore, there is no arc from node 4 to node 1. Since the only arc exiting node 4 goes to node 5, observe that for all

```
Index
  A   B   C   D   E   F
+---+---+---+---+---+---+
| -1| -1| 1 | 2 | 9 | 3 |
+---+---+---+---+---+---+

Comb
  1   2   3   4   5   6   7   8   9  10  11  12  13  14
+---+---+---+---+---+---+---+---+---+---+---+---+---+---+
| A | B | F | C | A | C | D | D | E |   |   |   |   | E |
+---+---+---+---+---+---+---+---+---+---+---+---+---+---+
```

Figure 8.4. Comb vector representation of the digraph in Figure 8.2.

k in the range $1..6$, only when $k = 5$ does

$$\text{Comb (Index(4)} + k - 1) = 4.$$

8.4 Table Representation

A more straightforward alternative to a boolean matrix is a connection table. In many digraph applications there may be a predetermined bound, k, on the maximum number of out arcs for each node. If n is the number of nodes in the digraph, the digraph may be maintained in a table with n rows and k columns. Figure 8.5 illustrates a table representation for the digraph in Figure 8.2.

	1	2	3
A	B	F	
B	C		
C	D	F	
D	E	F	
E	F	A	
F	A		

Figure 8.5. Table representation of the digraph in Figure 8.2.

Suppose a digraph application constructs paths in reverse order. That is, given a particular node, it maintains information on the arc that come into the node. The table in Figure 8.5 illustrates a table of all arcs coming out of a node. This table lends itself to processing arcs in one direction but not in the other. Fortunately, with the approach in Figure 8.5, another table of information for the arcs coming into each node could be constructed.

A set of declarations that describe the table representation for digraphs appears in Listing 8.2. These declarations lead to a static table representation for digraphs. The representation includes three array declarations: an array to hold information on all arcs leaving a node, an array to hold information about arcs entering a node, and an array of node information. The declarations for Graph_Type is a record containing two components, a count of the actual number of nodes in the graph and an array of information on the nodes. The Node_Array is an array of node information. Each node record has six components. The Name component in the Node_Record contains the node's label defined by the client, and the Data component contains the data associated with the node. The remaining four components maintain the in arc and out arc

Listing 8.2. Digraph declarations for a table representation.

```
subtype Arc_Range is positive Range 1 .. Max_No_Arcs;
type Out_Arc_Record is
   record
      In_Node : natural:= 0;
      Out_Node: natural:= 0;
      Data    : Arc_Data_Type;
   end record;
type Out_Arc_Array is array (Arc_Range) of Out_Arc_Record;
type In_Arc_Record is
   record
      Out_Node : natural:= 0;
      Arc_Index: natural:= 0;
   end record;
type In_Arc_Array is array (Arc_Range) of In_Arc_Record;
subtype Node_Range is positive Range 1 .. Max_No_Nodes;
type Node_Record is
   record
      Name         : Node_Label_Type;
      Data         : Node_Data_Type;
      No_In_Arcs   : positive:= 0;
      In_Arc       : In_Arc_Array;
      No_Out_Arcs: positive:= 0;
      Out_Arc      : Out_Arc_Array;
   end record;
type Node_Array is array (Node_Range) of Node_Record;
type Graph_Type is
   record
      No_Of_Nodes: positive:= 0;
      Node       : Node_Array;
   end record;
type Arc_Type is
   record
      Out_Node: natural:= 0;
      Index   : natural:= 0;
   end record;
type Node_Type is
   record
      Index: positive:= 0;
   end record;
```

information. Note that the data associated with each arc are stored once, in an Out_Arc_Record in the Out_Arc component of the Node_Record.

The information in each In_Arc_Record is sufficient for rapid access to arc data. Each In_Arc_Record contains two components, Out_Node and Arc_Index. Together they provide rapid access to the arc's data, which is stored in an Out_Arc_Array. If G is a Graph_Type, and n and k are the contents of the `Out_Node` and `Arc_Index` components, respectively, of a given `In_Arc_Record`, then the data that corresponds to the arc are

```
G.Node(i).Out_Arc(k).Data
```

Both `Node_Type` and `Arc_Type` are defined to provide quick access to the information about a node and an arc, respectively. Each `Node_Type` record contains the index into the graph's `Node` array component. `Arc_Type` contains two pieces of information, the `In_Arc_Records` to access the node and the `Out_Arc` component that contains the arc's information.

There is a classical tradeoff between the matrix representation described in Section 8.3 and the table representation in this section. The matrix method may take more space, but the table method requires more time. For example, to determine if there is an arc from node i to node j requires a constant amount of time to access the matrix representation. However, with the table representation, a sequential search through the ith row of the table for an occurrence of an arc to node j requires $O(k)$ time. However, if k is substantially smaller than n, the time-for-space tradeoff between the boolean matrix and table representation may be worthwhile.

But even the space requirement of the table representation may be improved upon. For example, suppose most nodes have substantially fewer than k arcs. Then much of the space in the table is actually wasted. Another static representation, based on the table approach, is to form a single vector combining all arc information.

A **combined arc vector** is to the table representation what the comb vector is to the boolean matrix. As the list of all out arcs is formed for each node, the list of terminal nodes for the arcs is placed in a vector and the first and last locations where the information was placed are recorded. Figure 8.6 illustrates this for the digraph in Figure 8.2. This approach uses two arrays. One array, `Nhbr`, contains the list of the terminal nodes for all arcs. The other n-by-2 array

	1	2	3	4	5	6
First	1	3	5	7	8	10
Last	2	4	6	7	9	12

	1	2	3	4	5	6	7	8	9	10	11	12
Nhbr	1	2	3	6	4	6	5	1	6	1	2	4

Figure 8.6. Alternate array representation of the digraph in Figure 8.2.

contains indices that indicate the piece in the neighbor array where the terminal nodes appear. For example, in column 1, the `First` and `Last` components locate the beginning and the end of the piece of the `Nhbr` array that corresponds to terminating nodes of the arcs leaving node 1.

The space requirements for this approach are of order $O(n) + O(k)$, the sum of the lengths of the two arrays. That is less than the space required for the table method, $O(nk)$, and the matrix method, $O(n^2)$. The time requirements for the various algorithms that manipulate the representation are of the same order of magnitude as the algorithms that manipulate the table representation. The tradeoff among the alternate approaches and the table method is that the alternate approaches require all out arc information for a specific node to be processed together. However, that is not a serious restriction for many digraph applications.

8.5 Dynamic Representation

A table representation of a digraph uses three arrays. By trading off the size limits of arrays for sequential access, we arrive at a dynamic representation of a digraph. Figure 8.7 illustrates the parallel. The `Graph_Type` points to a list of records containing node information. Each `Node_Record` contains a pointer to the next node record, which has components to maintain the node's `Label` and `Node_Data`. The `Node_Records` in the table representation contained two arrays. Those arrays are replaced by pointers to two lists, an `Out_Arc` list and an `In_Arc` list. The records in the `Out_Arc` list contain four components: a

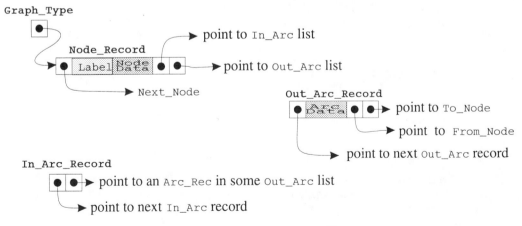

Figure 8.7. A Digraph as lists.

pointer to the next record in the list, the `Arc_Data`, and pointers to the records of the `From_Node` and `To_Node` of the arc.

Declarations to form the dynamic representation for digraphs suggested by Figure 8.7 appear in Listing 8.3. The **private** type, `Node_Type`, is defined as a pointer to a `Node_Record`. Each `Node_Record` contains a pointer to the next node record, the label, the node data, and pointers to the `In_Arc` and `Out_Arc` lists. `Arc_Type` is defined as a pointer to `Out_Arc_Records`, which contain all the information related to an arc, the arc's data, and pointer to the `From_Node` and `To_Node` of the arc, as well as a pointer to the `Next_Out_Arc` in the same `Out_Arc` list. Each `In_Arc_Record` contains two components, the pointer to the next record in the `In_Arc` list, and an `Arc_Type` pointer that points to the `Out_Arc_Record` that contains the arc's information.

Listing 8.3. Dynamic digraph declarations.

```
type Node_Record;
type Node_Type is access Node_Record;


type In_Arc_Record;
type In_Arc_Ptr is access In_Arc_Record;

type Out_Arc_Record;
type Arc_Type is access Out_Arc_Record;

type In_Arc_Record is
   record
      Next_In_Arc: In_Arc_Ptr;
      Arc_Ptr    : Arc_Type;
   end record;

type Out_Arc_Record is
   record
      Next_Out_Arc: Arc_Type;
      Label       : Label_Type;
      Data        : Arc_Data_Type;
      From_Node   : Node_Type;
      To_Node     : Node_Type;
   end record;

type Node_Record is
   record
      Next_Node: Node_Type;
      Data     : Node_Data_Type;
      Out_List : Arc_Type;
      In_List  : In_Arc_Ptr;
   end record;
```

8.6 Applications

Digraphs and graphs have many important applications. Typical of digraph applications is the use of other structures for assistance. For example, to solve some digraph problems, it is necessary to build a spanning tree for the digraph. Sometimes a third structure - a queue, stack, priority queue, or some other linear structure - may be required to maintain certain information while the spanning tree is constructed.

To illustrate a simple digraph application, consider the problem of determining the minimum number of borders that must be crossed to traverse from one state to another in the 48 contiguous United States. Figure 8.8 illustrates a part of the U.S. map as a graph. Each arc in the graph is represented by a pair of arcs in a digraph to represent the connection between adjoining states.

Suppose the border-crossing problem must find a path with the fewest number of border crossings from Washington (WA) to Florida (FL). One method of solving this problem is to build a spanning tree, starting at one of the two states in question and building a spanning tree as follows:

> Place one of the two states in question at the root of the tree. Place the neighbors of the root at the first level of the tree. Now, go across the tree, one level at a time, and for each node, place as child nodes all neighbors of that node that are not already in the tree. Continue this process until the node being sought is placed into the tree. When the node being sought is placed into the tree, the path from that node back to the root is a solution to the border-crossing problem.

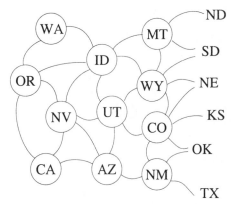

Figure 8.8. United States map as a digraph.

The construction of the tree one level at a time is analogous to a level-by-level tree traversal, hence a queue could be used to assist in constructing the tree. Figure 8.9 illustrates part of a spanning tree that might be constructed in finding a shortest path from Washington to Florida. It should be noted that there may be more than one spanning tree, hence more than one solution to the border-crossing problem. If the nodes were added to the spanning tree in a different order, a different tree would be created. For example, if Idaho was placed in the second level of the tree before Oregon, Nevada would appear as a child node of Idaho instead of Oregon.

Figure 8.10 illustrates a static method of representing both the tree and the queue in one structure. The structure is an array of records with two components, one for storing access to the node and an index indicating the location of the node's parent. The first location in the array contains the root of the tree, Washington. Since Washington is the root of the tree, the index zero is placed with it to indicate that it has no parent. As each node is placed, the location of its parent is placed with it. Hence Oregon and Idaho appear in the tree with the index **1**, indicating the location of their parent.

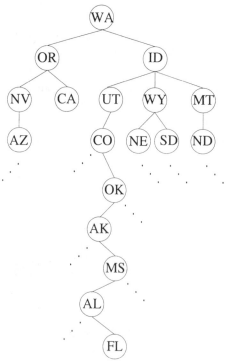

Figure 8.9. Border-crossing spanning tree of Figure 8.8.

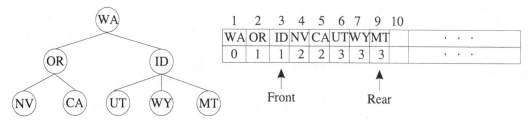

Figure 8.10. Combined tree/queue for the border-crossing problem.

The array also contains the queue, as indicated by the indices `Front` and `Rear`. The queue in Figure 8.10 illustrates the queue after Idaho is processed but before the `Front` pointer is changed to begin processing the next node. The result of processing Idaho was the placement of three nodes in the array that represents both the tree and the queue: Utah, Wyoming, and Montana. Next, the `Front` pointer would be incremented and Nevada would be processed. Completing this application is left as an exercise.

8.7 Explorations

1. Build and verify a `Digraph_Range_En` package based on the boolean matrix representation.
2. Build and verify a `Digraph_Range_En` package based on the comb vector representation of a boolean matrix.
3. Build and verify a `Digraph_Pt_En` package based on the table representation.
4. Build and verify a `Digraph_Pt_En` package based on the combined arc vector representation.
5. Build and verify a `Digraph_Pt_Lpt` package based on a linked list representation using a linked list of arcs with linked lists of nodes.
6. Build, test, and validate a system to solve border-crossing problems.
7. Read about CPM, the critical path method. Build a package to find critical paths through a digraph.
8. Build, test, and validate a system to find Euler paths and cycles.
9. Build, test, and validate a system to find Hamiltonian paths and cycles.
10. Build, test, and validate a system to test four-color planar maps.
11. None of the packages described in this chapter maintains multiple arcs between two nodes. Evaluate the possible ramifications of incorporating the possibilities of multiple arcs between any two nodes.

12. Several of the packages in this chapter contain examples of iterators that are encapsulated as generic procedures. Reconstruct these iterators as nongeneric procedures, with the user procedure that completes the algorithm passed as a procedure access parameter.

9

Sets

9.1 Specifications

Sets are a fundamental building block for mathematical systems. Sometimes, when building the representation of an object type a software developer must apply set fundamentals to model the problem and its solution.

Sets are collections of elements. A **universal set**, **U**, is the collection of all elements from which sets may be derived. Sets are formed by collecting elements from a universal set. Like every other object type, sets have certain fundamental attributes and operations. Let x be an element in the universal set, and let A be a set. The notation $x \in A$ indicates x is a **member of** the set A. Correspondingly, $x \notin A$ indicates that x is not a member of A. A set is normally indicated using the notation, $\{ \ldots \}$, to indicate the elements in the sets. Within the braces, two types of notation are used to indicates the elements. If a set is finite, the elements in the set may be listed. For example,

$$\{1, 2, 3, 4, 5\}$$

indicates a set composed of the integers between and including 1 and 5. Set membership may also be indicated with the notation

$$\{x \mid P(x) \},$$

where x is a free variable and P a boolean expression. The set consists of all elements x for which $P(x)$ is true. The set of integers between and including 1 and 5 may be indicated as

$$\{x \mid (x \in I^+) \wedge (1 \le x) \wedge (x \le 5)\},$$

where I^+ indicates the universal set of positive integers.

Set A is **a subset of** set B, $A \subseteq B$, if and only if, for all $x \in A$, $x \in B$. A is a **proper subset of** B, $A \subset B$ or $A \subsetneq B$, if and only if $A \subseteq B$ and there is an $x \in B$ such that $x \notin A$. Set A is a **superset of** set B if and only if $B \subseteq A$. A is a **proper superset** of B if and only if B is a proper subset of A. Set A **equals** set B if and only if $A \subseteq B$ and $B \subseteq A$.

Four fundamental binary and one fundamental unary operation are defined for sets. They are the following:

1. The **union** of two sets is the collection of all objects in either set, $A \cup B = \{x \mid x \in A \vee x \in B\}$.

2. The **intersection** of two sets is the collection of all objects that are in both sets, $A \cap B = \{x \mid x \in A \wedge x \in B\}$.

3. The **difference** of two sets, $A - B$, is the collection of all objects in A that are not in B, $A - B = \{x \mid x \in A \wedge x \notin B\}$.

4. The **symmetric difference** of two sets, $A \oplus B$, is the union of the two set differences, $A \oplus B = (A - B) \cup (B - A)$.

5. The **complement** of a set A, $\overline{A}$, is the collection of all objects not in A, $\overline{A} = \{x \mid x \notin A\}$.

These operations do not form a minimal collection of set operations. For example, from deMorgan's laws,

$$A \cup B = \overline{A} \cap \overline{B}.$$

Hence, union may be described in terms of complement and intersection. Similarly, difference and symmetric difference may be reduced to descriptions in terms of complement and intersection.

The symbols for union and intersection are not in the standard ASCII characters sets. Typically, the arithmetic symbols "+" and "*" are used to

Listing 9.1. Set specifications.

```
generic
   . . .
package Set_??_?? is
   subtype Set_Type is ... ;

   Set_Overflow, Element_Already_In_Set, Element_Not_In_Set: exception;

   procedure Include ( Element: in    Element_Type;
                       To_Set : in out Set_Type);
   function Cardinality (The_Set: in Set_Type) return natural;
   procedure Clear (The_Set: in out Set_Type);
   procedure Copy ( from_The_Set: in    Set_Type;
                    to_The_Set  :    out Set_Type );
   procedure Swap ( Left_Set, Right_Set: in out Set_Type );

   function Difference ( Left_Set, Right_Set: in Set_Type) return Set_Type;
   function "-" ( Left_Set, Right_Set: in Set_Type) return Set_Type
      renames Difference;

   function Intersection (Left_Set,
                             Right_Set: in Set_Type) return Set_Type;
   function "*" (Left_Set, Right_Set: in Set_Type) return Set_Type
      renames Intersection;
   function "&" (Left_Set, Right_Set: in Set_Type) return Set_Type
      renames Intersection;
   function "and" (Left_Set,
                     Right_Set: in Set_Type) return Set_Type
      renames Intersection;

   function Is_Empty (The_Set: in Set_Type) return boolean;
   function Are_Equal (Left_Set,
                         Right_Set: in Set_Type) return boolean;
   function Is_Element ( Element: Element_Type;
                         The_Set: Set_Type) return boolean;

   function Is_Proper_Subset (Left_Set,
                                Right_Set: in Set_Type) return boolean;
   function "<" (Left_Set, Right_Set: in Set_Type) return boolean
      renames Is_Proper_Subset;
   function Is_Proper_Superset (Left_Set,
                                  Right_Set: in Set_Type) return boolean;
   function ">" (Left_Set, Right_Set: in Set_Type) return boolean
      renames Is_Proper_Superset;

   function Is_Subset (Left_Set, Right_Set: in Set_Type) return boolean;
   function "<=" (Left_Set, Right_Set: in Set_Type) return boolean
      renames Is_Subset;
   function Is_Superset (Left_Set, Right_Set: in Set_Type) return boolean;
   function ">=" (Left_Set, Right_Set: in Set_Type) return boolean
      renames Is_Superset;
```

Listing 9.1. (cont.)

```
generic
   with procedure Process ( Element : in out Element_Type;
                            Continue:    out boolean);
   procedure Iterate (The_Set: in out Set_Type);

   procedure Remove ( Element : in     Element_Type;
                      From_Set: in out Set_Type);

   function Union (Left_Set, Right_Set: in Set_Type) return Set_Type;
   function "+" (Left_Set, Right_Set: in Set_Type) return Set_Type
      renames Union;
   function "or" (Left_Set, Right_Set: in Set_Type) return Set_Type
      renames Union;

   function Sym_Diff (Left_Set, Right_Set: in Set_Type) return Set_Type;
   function "xor" (Left_Set, Right_Set: in Set_Type) return Set_Type
      renames Sym_Diff;

private
   .  .  .

end Set_??_??;
```

represent union and intersection, respectively. An advantage of using "+" and "*"
is that these symbols may be overloaded in Ada. A set package specification
appears in Listing 9.1. Fundamentally, the package supplies subprograms that
include the fundamental operations users apply to sets and their elements.

Note that the generic instantiation parameters and the **private** declarations
have not been included with the specifications. They are missing because they
depend on the method of representation employed. The choice between different
representations depends on the structure of the universal set and the set
application under consideration.

9.2 Static Representation

Perhaps the simplest sets to represent are those whose universal set may be
represented by a contiguous range of an ordinal type. Such a universal set may
be encapsulated as

```
subtype Universal_Range is ordinal_type range low .. high;
```

Each set composed from this universal set may be represented as an array,

```
type Set_Type is array (Universal_Range) of boolean;
```

where a value of **true** indicates the element that corresponds to that index is in the set and **false** indicates the element corresponding to the index is not in the set. Sets may be declared and initialized as empty with a declaration like

```
P: Set_Type:= (others => false);
```

An element E in the Universal_Range is in a set P if and only if

```
P(E) = true;
```

The set operations of union, intersection, and complement are directly implemented through the boolean operations of **or**, **and**, and **not**, respectively.

Listing 9.2 illustrates the generic instantiation parameters, declarations, and types associated with a static representation of sets over an ordinal range. The instantiation parameters for the static set package whose elements are over a range of an ordinal type must include replacements for *ordinal_type*, *low*, and *high*. The package defines Element_Type and Set_Type. The **private** declarations include

```
type Set_Type is array (Element_Type) of boolean;
```

Listing 9.2. Ordinal range of set declarations.

```
generic

   type Universal_Range is (<>);
   Low : Universal_Range:= Universal_Range'first;
   High: Universal_Range:= Universal_Range'last;

package Set_??_?? is

   subtype Element_Type is Universal_Range range Low .. High;

   type Set_Type is private;
      .
      .
      .

private

   type Set_Type is array (Element_Type) of boolean;
```

The representation of sets as boolean arrays lends itself to simplify algorithms for the set operations. For example, determining if an element E is a member of a set S is accomplished through the boolean expression

```
if S (E) then
    return true;
  else
    return false;
end if;
```

If P and Q are two sets, then forming the intersection set, I, of two sets is accomplished with the **for** loop

```
for Index in Element_Type loop
   I (Index):= P(Index) and Q(Index);
end loop;
```

Completing the bodies of the various algorithms is left as an exercise for the reader.

One potential problem with representing sets with **boolean** arrays is the size of the arrays. The array may be packed, using each bit in a byte to represent a position in the array. Even with packing, each set requires

```
Set_Type'storage_size = (High - Low + 7)/8,
```

where High and Low are two of the Set_Pt_Lpt package's generic instantiation parameters.

If (High - Low) is very large, but the actual maximum sizes of sets is known, there is another alternative for static representations of sets. The generic instantiation parameters and declarations for an alternate static representation appear in Listing 9.3. The alternate representation requires an additional instantiation parameter, Max_Size, that establishes the maximum size of sets. The type declarations made visible are the same as before, but the private declaration for Set_Type is substantially different. In the alternate static representation, sets are represented with a record that contains two components, the count of the number of objects in the set and an array to contain the objects. Since Element_Type is an ordinal type, the elements in each set may be placed in the Element_Array, ordered according to their ordinal values.

A comparison of this approach to the boolean array static representation illustrates some of the classical tradeoffs between algorithm execution time and space requirements. For example, when a set is represented with a boolean

Listing 9.3. An alternate static representation of sets.

```
generic

   type Universal_Range is (<>);
   Low        : Universal_Range:= Universal_Range'first;
   High       : Universal_Range:= Universal_Range'last;
   Max_Set_Size: positive       := 16;

package Set_??_?? is

   subtype Element_Type is Universal_Range range Low .. High;

   type Set_Type is private;

      .
      .
      .

private

   type Element_Array is
      array (1 .. Max_Set_Size) of Element_Type;

   type Set_Type is
      record
         No_Of_Elements: natural:= 0;
         Elements      : Element_Array;
      end record;
```

array, testing an element for set membership is performed in a constant amount
of time. When the set is represented with a record and the array in the record
contains an ordered list of the element in the array, the time required to test for
set membership is

$$O(\log \; (set\_size)).$$

On the other hand, all basic set operations have algorithms that perform in
time

$$O(size \; (Universal\_Set))$$

for the `boolean` array representation, but the record containing an ordered array
approach may use mergesortlike algorithms and perform in time

$$O(sum \; of \; set \; sizes).$$

This is illustrated by the algorithm in Listing 9.4. Completing the body of a sets package using the record containing an ordered array of elements is left as an exercise.

Finally, part of the tradeoff between the two methods is the potential constraint_error that may be raised if Max_Set_Size is not chosen to be sufficiently large. Removing this potential error leads naturally to a dynamic representation with the array replaced by a list of elements, which is discussed in Section 9.3.

Listing 9.4. Union algorithm for static representation.

```
function Union (Set_1, Set_2: Set_Type) return Set_Type;

   Answer: Set_Type;
   Index_1, Index_2: natural:= 1;

   procedure Move_Rest (  Index: in out natural;
                          The_Set: in Set_Type );

      begin
      while Index <= The_Set.No_Of_Elements loop
         Answer.No_Of_Elements:= Answer.No_Of_Elements + 1;
         Answer.Elements (Answer.No_Of_Elements):= The_Set.Elements (Index);
         Index:= Index + 1;
      end loop;
      end Move_Rest;

   begin
   while (Index_1 <= Set_1.No_Of_Elements)
         and (Index_2 <= Set_2.No_Of_Elements) loop
      Answer.No_Of_Elements:= Answer.No_Of_Elements + 1;
      if Set_1.Elements (Index_1)<Set_2.Elements (Index_2) then
         Answer.Elements    (Answer.No_Of_Elements):=   Set_1.Elements
(Index_1);
         Index_1:= Index_1 + 1;
       elsif Set_1.Elements (Index_1) > Set_2.Elements then
         Answer.Elements    (Answer.No_Of_Elements):=   Set_2.Elements
(Index_2);
         Index_2:= Index_2 + 1;
       else
         Answer.Elements    (Answer.No_Of_Elements):=   Set_1.Elements
(Index_1);
         Index_1:= Index_1 + 1;
         Index_2:= Index_2 + 1;
       end if;
   end loop;
   if Index_1 <= Set_1.No_Of_Elements then
      Move_Rest (Index_1, Set_1);
    else
      Move_Rest (Index_2, Set_2);
   end if;
   end Union;
```

9.3 Dynamic Representation

When the elements that form the universal set cannot be simply described as a
subrange of an ordinal type, a dynamic representation is appropriate.   The
package must be instantiated with the type representing the universal type used
to represent the set elements:

```
generic
   type Element_Type is limited private;

   with function "="
      ( Left, Right: Element_Type) return boolean;
   with procedure Copy
      ( Source: in      Element_Type;
        Target:     out Element_Type );
   with procedure Swap
      ( Source: in out Element_Type;
        Target:     out Element_Type );
package Sets_Lpt_Lpt is
         .  .  .
```

As a limited private type, the representation of the values of an element may
be structured or involve indirection. Since the elements are limited private,
the package requires an "=" function in its instantiation, as well as the typical
Copy and Swap subprograms to manipulate objects. The dynamic sets package
instantiates the List_Lpt_Lpt package:

```
package Set_List is new List_Lpt_Lpt (Element_Type);
```

The Set_Type

```
type Set_Type is limited private;
```

is represented as

```
private
   type Set_Type is
      record
         ElementS: Set_List.List_Type;
      end record;
```

This package is influenced by the Sets package described in Booch's *Software
Components in Ada*.

Building a reliable sets package requires some care to guarantee that one and only one copy of each member in a set appears in the list. To illustrate, consider the `Union` function appearing in Listing 9.5. The `Union` algorithm first copies one of the two sets into the `New_Set`. `Union` contains a subprogram `Check_And_Add`, which checks one element. If it is not in the set being formed, it is added to the set. A new set iterator, `Process_Right_Set`, is created by instantiating the set package iterator with `Check_And_Add`. The `Union` algorithm simply copies the first set and then checks to see if the second set is not empty. If it is not empty, `Process_Right_Set` is called to traverse the elements and pass them to `Check_And_Add` for possible inclusion in the union of the two sets.

`Unchecked_Add` is a support procedure used by the package. This procedure simply appends the element to the set without checking, because the checks are performed before the procedure is called. Practically all of the basic set operations may be built by using the sets package iterator to create algorithms for the various set processes. Completing the body of the dynamic sets package is left as an exercise for the reader.

Listing 9.5. `Union` algorithm for dynamic representation.

```
function Union ( Left_Set, Right_Set: in Set_Type) return Set_Type is

    New_Set: Set_Type;
    Working: Set_Type;

    procedure Check_And_Add ( Element : in out Element_Type;
                              Continue:     out boolean) is

        begin
        Continue:= true;
        if not Is_In (Element, New_Set) then
            Sets.Unchecked_Add (Element, New_Set);
        end if;
        end Check_And_Add;

    procedure Process_Right_Set is
        New Set_List.Iterate (Check_And_Add);

begin
Sets.Copy (Right_Set, Working);
Sets.Copy (Left_Set, New_Set);
if not Set_List.At_Front (Working.Element_List) then
    Set_List.Move_To_Front (Working.Element_List);
    Process_Right_Set (Working.Element_List);
end if;
return New_Set;
end Union;
```

9.4 Hashing Representation

For many set applications, the number of objects in the universal set is extremely large. This may preclude the use of either of the two static representations described earlier. If the dynamic representation is used and the sets formed from the universal set are large, the time required to determine the existence of an element in a set is bound by the size of the set. It is desirable to reduce this search time. This may be accomplished by representing sets by combining the flexibility of the dynamic representation with the potential speed improvement of hashing, which is described in Chapter 12. Hashing may be applied to any object type, not just strings. One method of applying hashing to the representation of sets, as illustrated in Figure 9.1, is to represent each set with a hash table of lists. Given an element, the hash function selects a list from the hash table. If the hash table contains k locations, the time to search that list for an occurrence of the element is reduced by a factor of k.

Listing 9.6 illustrates the instantiation parameters for the specifications of a generic Hashed_Sets package. If the Object_Type is limited private, then the package must also be instantiated with an "=" function for the Object_Type. Naturally, the user of the package must also supply a Hash function for the Object_Type.

Since the user supplies the hash function and may be aware of other factors relative to the application, the user may override the default Table_Size. A relationship may exist between the hashing function and the choice of the table size that produces better performance than other choices. Hashing is discussed in detail in Chapter 12. The Hashed_Sets package may be derived from a list-based set package. The derivation is left as an exercise for the reader.

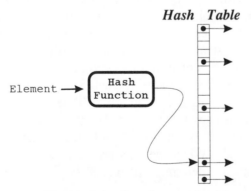

Figure 9.1. Set element hashing.

Listing 9.6. Formal parameters for hash set.

```
with List_Pt_Lpt;

generic
   type Object_Type is private;
   with function Hash (Object: Object_Type) return natural;
   Table_Size: positive;
   with function "=" (Left, Right: Object_Type) return boolean;
package Set_Pt_Lpt
   type Set_Type is limited private;
   ...
```

9.5 Hamming Codes

Sets form a powerful mathematical system with numerous applications. An important application is the use of sets to create error-correcting codes. **Error-detecting codes** are coding systems that add additional information to the data so that upon reception of the data the receiver may determine if the transmission media introduced an error into the data. An **error-correcting code** is a coding system that includes additional information with the data so that upon reception it may be determined if an error was introduced during transmission and if there is sufficient information to correct the error.

Error-detecting and error-correcting codes operate under certain limits to their performance capabilities. The limit is usually defined in terms of the probabilities of certain types of errors. The discussion in this section is limited to error situations where there is a very high degree of probability that there will be at most one bit in n that is in error for some predefined n. The simplest example of error-detecting code systems is **parity checks**. A parity check adds an additional bit to the data bits. A zero or one is included so that the count of the number of one bits is either even or odd. If the count is made odd by the parity bit, the parity check system is said to produce **odd parity**.

For example, eight bits of data are stored in parallel on a typical nine-track tape. Nine-track tapes are extremely reliable, hence there is extremely high probability that no more that one bit in nine will be stored and retrieved with an error. Figure 9.2 illustrates three parity checks. If the eight data bits in each column are as indicated, the parity bits are selected so that the number of one bits in each column is odd. When the data are read, a test, usually performed in hardware, may quickly determine if the data were received correctly by

bit 0	1	0	1
bit 1	1	0	0
bit 2	0	0	1
bit 3	1	1	0
bit 4	0	1	1
bit 5	0	1	1
bit 6	0	1	0
bit 7	1	1	1
parity	1	0	0

Figure 9.2. Parity checking example.

performing a parity check. This parity check is frequently referred to as a **latitudinal**, across the tape, parity check.

Using magnetic tapes as an illustration, parity may be used to perform error correcting. Frequently when data are stored on a magnetic tape, they are stored one block at a time on the tape. That is, there is a block of data followed by an unused piece of tape. Besides performing the latitudinal parity checks described above, at the end of each block a longitudinal check may be performed on each row. That is, as the data are placed on the tape, the system may maintain a count of the number of 1's stored in each track of the tape and place one additional column of data so that the number of 1's in each track is odd. When a block of data is read, the system may use the latitudinal parity check in each column to determine if a column is in error. If only one column contains an error, when the entire block is read, the longitudinal parity check may be used to determine which track contains the error. If there is only one latitudinal and one longitudinal parity error, that pair of checks may be used to locate the bit that is in error.

Usually, the blocks of data on a magnetic tape are extremely large. Fortunately, tapes and their hardware are extremely reliable, and these pairs of parity checks are useful in correcting the occasional errors that occur. However, with most data communications over the airwaves and on various networks, there is more electronic noise and hence a higher probability that errors will appear in the data received over various communications media. Further, as the distance over which data are communicated becomes larger, the need for error correction becomes very important because it may be difficult or impossible to retransmit the data.

A family of important error-correcting codes, discovered by Richard Hamming, is based on the use of set concepts. Assume that a data transmission facility has a very high probability of producing zero or one bits in error for each eight bits transmitted. The simplest Hamming code is constructed that transmits four bits of data along with four error-correcting bits. Given four data bits, the four error-correcting bits are selected as follows using the Venn diagram in Figure 9.3: Associate each of the four data bits to one of the four areas formed by the intersection of two or more sets, areas labeled [3], [5], [6], and [7]. There is an area in each circle that does not contain a data bit. Place a 0 or 1 in each of these areas so that the parity on each set is odd. Finally, place a 0 or 1 in the remaining area so that the entire Venn diagram has odd parity.

Assume four data bits have been associated to the four areas of the Venn diagram:

```
[0] [1] [2] [3] [4] [5] [6] [7]
             1       0   1   0
```

Since set *A* consists of areas [1], [3], [5], and [7] and contains only one 1, a 0 is placed in area [1] to produce odd parity in set *A*. Set *B* consists of the areas [2], [3], [6], and [7]. It contains two 1s, and so a 1 is placed into area [2] to give set *B* add parity. Set *C* is like set *A*; hence area [4] has a 0 placed in it. This produces the result

```
[0] [1] [2] [3] [4] [5] [6] [7]
     0   1   1   0   0   1   0
```

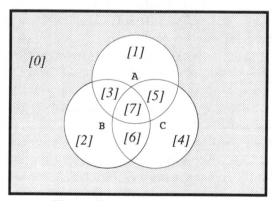

Figure 9.3. Venn diagram.

Finally, the universal set, consisting of all areas, currently has odd parity. Thus, a 0 is placed in area [0], yielding

```
[0]  [1]  [2]  [3]  [4]  [5]  [6]  [7]
 0    0    1    1    0    0    1    0
```

With this coding scheme, if any one bit is changed, it may be corrected by associating the eight bits to the eight areas in a Venn diagram. To illustrate, assume the pattern

```
[0]  [1]  [2]  [3]  [4]  [5]  [6]  [7]
 0    0    1    1    0    1    1    0
```

is received. The parity for the three sets is checked. Set A contains the areas in positions [1], [3], [5], and [7]. This set no longer has even parity, so the error is in set A. Set B contains areas [2], [3], [6], and [7]. This has odd parity. Therefore, if an error exists, it is in $\bar{B}$. Finally, set C contains areas [4], [5], [6], and [7]. This area has even parity; hence there is an error in set C. An odd parity test on the universal set, U, indicates that an error exists in the universal set. It should be noted at this time that if there is a positive indication of a parity error, as we have for sets A and C, and there is no indication of an odd parity error in U, that is an indication of the rare event that two bits were modified and no error correction may occur. Given the results of the parity tests, the error is in $A \cap \bar{B} \cap C \cap U = (A \cap C) - B$, which is area [5]. Once the bit in [5] is changed, the parity test for all three sets is satisfied. After bit [5] is changed, we have

```
[0]  [1]  [2]  [3]  [4]  [5]  [6]  [7]
 0    0    1    1    0    0    1    0
```

This error-correcting code is based on using three sets. It involves $2^3 = 8$ bits and 4 (3+1) error-correcting bits. This approach may be applied using a larger number of sets if the system has a lower error transmission probability. In general, a Hamming code based on n sets corresponds to 2^n bits, of which $n+1$ bits are used for error correction. Naturally, a larger value of n presumes a lower probability of error.

9.6 Bags

Bags are a setlike structure. The fundamental difference between a set and a bag is that elements may appear in a bag more than once. That is, it is necessary to keep track of the multiplicity of each object in the bag. It is natural to draw analogies between sets and bags and have some consistency between the operations on bags and the operations on sets. With sets the basic relationship between sets and elements, set membership, is performed with a boolean function. For bags, the basic relationship between bags and elements is carried out with an ordinal function:

```
function Multiplicity (Element: Element_Type;
                       Bag     : Bag_Type ) return natural;
```

The bag operations are analogous to the set operations, but the definitions must be modified to address the issues raised by counting the number of occurrences of objects rather than just observing their presence or absence.

Let U be a universal set and A a bag. For $x \in U$, if x is in bag A, $x \in_B A$, the multiplicity of x in A, $|x|_A$, is the number of occurrences of x in A. Consider the bag equivalents of set union and intersection. **Bag union**, $\cup_B$, is defined as

$$|x|_{E \cup_B F} = |x|_E + |x|_F.$$

Bag intersection, $\cap_B$, is defined so that

$$|x|_{E \cap_B F} = \min(|x|_E, |x|_F).$$

The other bag operations may be derived from these by analogy to the corresponding set operations.

The representation of bags is analogous to the various representation of sets. If a bag is defined over a range of an ordinal type, where the set representation was defined with the declarations

```
subtype Universal_Range is ordinal_type range Low .. High;
type Set_Type is array (Universal_Range) of boolean;
```

the equivalent declarations for bags are

```
subtype Universal_Range is ordinal_type range Low .. High;
type Bag_Type is array (Universal_Range) of natural;
```

With these declarations, the algorithms to carry out the various set operations are analogous to the set algorithms. For example, the union of two bags, $U = P \cup_B Q$, is accomplished with the statement sequence

```
for Index in Element_Type loop
   U (Index):= P(Index) + Q(Index);
end loop;
```

The dynamic representation of bags requires a modification of the dynamic representation of sets. Specifically, before instantiating the list to represent bags, a Bag_Record must be declared to hold each object along with its multiplicity,

```
type Bag_Record is
   record
      Count : natural:= 0;
      Object: Object_Type;
   end record;
```

then use this record to instantiate Bag_List,

```
package Bag_List is new List_Pt_Lpt (Bag_Record);
```

and define Bag_Type as

```
subtype Bag_Type is Bag_List.List_Type;
```

Completing the static and dynamic bag packages is left as a exercise.

9.7 Explorations

1. Complete and test a set package based on the use of boolean arrays.
2. Complete and test a set package based on the representation of sets with a record containing two components, one component to represent the count of the number of objects in the set and an array to hold the objects.
3. Complete and test a set package based on the representation of sets by lists.

4. Complete and test a bag package based on the use of integer arrays storing the count of the number of occurrences of each object in the bag.
5. Complete and test a bag package based on the representation analogous to the static set representation based on the use of records.
6. Complete and test a bag package based on the representation of sets by lists.
7. Build a generalized Hamming error-correcting code package that includes an instantiation parameter that allows a user to select the number of sets to be used to perform encoding and decoding.
8. Experiment with a set package based on the use of hashing.
9. Perform an analysis of the time and space tradeoffs between set representations that use hashing and those that do not.

10

Strings

10.1 Specifications

Practically every software system must manipulate sequences of characters or bytes. **Bytes** are addressable eight-bit memory locations. In Ada 83, characters are represented with seven-bits. In Ada 95, characters are ISO standard eight-bit character representations, including eight-bit extended ASCII. The material in this chapter makes a distinction between bytes and characters only when necessary.

Many peripheral devices are controlled by command sequences embedded in a sequence of bytes. The sequences of bytes may contain the coding for both control information and printable characters. For example, to display information on a printer, a sequential collection of bytes, containing both the printer's control information and the text to be displayed, is assembled and transmitted to the device. Also, information entered from a keyboard forms a sequence of both control codes and display characters. When control keys, like the "ENTER" and "ESC" keys, are pressed, a code is transmitted just like the codes for printable characters. It is up to the hardware and software interfaces as to how these codes are interpreted.

A **string** is an array of characters, or bytes, regardless of whether the contents are control information or printable characters. For the purposes of this discussion, the ASCII, or an extended ASCII, code scheme is assumed for characters. The **length** of a string is the count of the number of characters, or bytes, in the string. The length of a string should not be confused with the size of the array that holds a string. For example, a particular string might contain 10 characters, but it might be contained in an array of 25 bytes.

Unfortunately, in Ada 83 characters are defined in seven bits, not eight. Therefore, one must distinguish between strings of characters and string of bytes. Fortunately, this problem disappears in Ada 95.

The ordinal value of a character, `character'pos`, is the `natural` number derived by interpreting its bit pattern as a binary number. This also corresponds to the character's position in the ASCII, or extended ASCII, code scheme. A string whose length is zero is referred to as a **null** string. If *Str* is a nonnull string, and

$$1 \leq i \leq length(Str),$$

then *Str (i)* is the *i*th character in the string. Two strings, *Str1* and *Str2*, are **equivalent** if

$$length\ (Str1) = length\ (Str2).$$

If the strings are not null,

$$Str1\,(i) = Str2\,(i)\ \forall\ i \in [\,1, length(Str1)\,].$$

Given two strings, *Str1* and *Str2*, the string *Str1* is said to **precede** the string *Str2*, if there is a *j*,

$$1 \leq j \leq Min\,(length(str1),\ length(str2)),$$

and either

    a. *j = 1* and *Str1(1) < Str2(1)*, or
    b. *j > 1*, *Str1(1) < Str2(1)* and *Str1(i) < Str2(i)* $\forall\ i \in [1,\ j)$.

For certain types of string applications, other definitions for string equivalence and precedence might be more appropriate. Several of these are described in the Explorations section.

10.1.1 String Constructors

The selection of a particular collections of string constructors might depend on the particular string application. The set of constructors described here is not minimal, but it is sufficient for a large number of string applications. Seven constructors are listed in Table 10.1.

Append, also called **concatenation**, attaches one string to the end of another string. In Ada the & symbol is used as a binary string append operator. If

```
Str1 = "this, that, "
```

Table 10.1. String constructors.

Constructor	Description
Append	Attach one string to the end of another string.
Clear	Remove all characters from a string and make the string a null string.
Copy	Copy the contents of one string into another. The result is that the two strings are equivalent.
Delete	For i and j, remove the substring $Str(i..j)$ from the string Str. The new value formed is the concatenation, $\&$, of the two pieces of Str that precede and follow the piece removed: $Str\ (1..i\text{-}1)\ \&\ Str\ (j\text{+}1..length\ (Str))$
Insert	Given two strings, $Str1$ and $Str2$, and an index i, insert the string $Str2$ into the string $Str1$ at location i. The new string value formed is $Str1\ (1..i\text{-}1)\ \&\ Str2\ \&\ Str1\ (1..length\ (Str1))$
Prepend	Place one string at the beginning of another. Prepend is equivalent to $Insert\ (Str1,\ Str2,\ 1)$.
Overlay	Replace the characters in the string $Str1$ starting at position i with the contents of string $Str2$.

and

      `Str2 = "these and those."`

then `Append`ing `Str2` to `Str1`, `Str1:= Str1 & Str2`, produces

      `Str1 = "this, that, these and those."`

    `Clear` changes the value of a string variable to a null string, a string of length zero. Depending on the type of representation, the implementational details of `Clear` may vary from placing a predefined **null** value in array locations to simply **nulling** an access pointer.

    `Copy` duplicates the contents of one string to another string. `Delete` removes a portion of a string. For example, if

      `Str = "Now is a good time to do it"`

the procedure `Delete (Str, 10, 14)` removes the 10th through 14th characters, inclusive, producing the result

      `Str` `= "Now is a time to do it".`

    `Insert` places a second string into the initial string starting at an indicated position. If

      `Str1 = "This is a very good time to do it".`

and

      `Str2 = "not "`

the procedure call `Insert (Str1, Str2, 9)` produces

      `Str1 = "This is not a very good time to do it".`

Note that `Append` is equivalent to `Insert`ing at the end of `Str1`. `Prepend` is equivalent to `Insert`ing at position 1.

The string constructor `Overlay` changes the value of a string object by changing the characters in a substring of the string. For example, if the value of a string is

```
"The quick brown fox jumped over the lazy dog."
```

and if the string value `"green"` is `Overlayed` at position `11`, then the new value of the string object is

```
"The quick green fox jumped over the lazy dog."
```

10.1.2 String Observers

Table 10.2 summarizes eight string observers. Four of them are sufficient: `Precede`, `Is_Null`, `Length_Of`, and `Position_Of`. The remaining four may be derived from `Precede`. They are included for the sake of clarity. The ordering observers use a combination of the relative orderings of the characters along with the lengths of the strings. For example, the string `"bat"` precedes the string `"bats"`. Two strings, `Str1` and `Str2`, are **equivalent** if and only if

```
NOT(Str1 < Str2) AND NOT(Str2 < Str1)
```

which, by DeMorgan's laws is equivalent to

```
NOT ((Str1 < Str2) OR (Str2 < Str1))
```

The observer `Length_Of` reports on the number of characters in the string. `Position_Of (Str1, Str2)` determines if `Str2` is a substring of `Str1` and reports on the position of the first occurrence of `Str2` in `Str1`. If `Str2` is not in `Str1`, the function may report this result in one of two ways: either by returning an illegal string position, like `0`, or by raising an exception. Although some might consider this an exception, many string applications search for substrings expecting that the substring may not be in the string. Hence, raising exceptions would not be a suitable method of reporting the search's failure.

`Is_Null`, or `Is_Empty`, is a observer that reports on the string being `null`, or empty.

Table 10.2. String selectors.

Selectors	Description
Equivalent	A boolean function that is true if the values of two strings are the same.
Precede	A boolean function that returns true if the first string precedes the second string.
<=	A boolean function that returns true if the first string either precedes or is equivalent to the second string.
Follows	Identical to NOT Precede_Or_Equivalent.
>=	Identical to NOT Precede.
Length_Of	An natural-valued function that returns the length of the value of a string object.
Position_Of	Given two strings *Str1* and *Str2*, this function helps determine if the value of *Str1* appears in *Str2*. It is an natural-valued function that returns the location in *Str2* of the first character of *Str1*'s value if it appears in *Str2*. Otherwise, it returns the value of *0* if the value of *Str1* does not appear in *Str2*.
Is_Null	Returns true if the string is null.

10.1.3 String Exceptions

A string package implies two exceptions, not including additional exceptions that may be implementation-dependent. The `Insert` and `Overlay` constructors may raise a `string_position_error` if the position for the insert or overlay operation is not a valid position in the string under construction. Another exception is `not_a_substring`, if the implementor of the package decides to raise exceptions when the `Substring_Of` observer does not find the substring being sought.

A third exception, `string_overflow`, may be raised when the implementation of the package employs a static representation for strings. This exception may be raised by several constructors when they produce results that are too large for the static representation where the result is placed.

The implementor of a string package faces several issues, the most important one being the choice of representation. There is a large number of choices, such as

1. Should Ada's predefined `strings` be employed directly?
2. Should another static representation be employed?
3. Should a dynamic representation be employed?

Each choice has its own collection of tradeoffs. For example, some packages require their own housekeeping support, some of which might have to be visible to package users.

10.2 Static Representations

It is only natural to immediately consider ways of representing strings as arrays of characters directly applying Ada's `string` type. By definition, arrays are of fixed size. Variables defined using an unconstrained array type must be bound when the variable is defined. Strings may vary greatly in size however. For many string applications, an upper bound on the size of strings may frequently be predetermined. When an upper bound on the size of strings is predetermined, arrays, or a fixed-size structure containing arrays, are an appropriate means of representing strings.

When arrays represent strings, there should be a method of distinguishing between the length of the string and the size of the array containing the string. There are three basic methods of representing strings within static structures:

1. Direct use of Ada's `string` type. The predefined unconstrained array type, `string`, does not include a method of distinguishing between the length of a string and the size of the array containing the string.
2. Terminating strings with sentinels.
3. Maintaining a count of the number of characters in the string.

The following subsections explore these methods.

10.2.1 Ada Strings

Ada's support for strings is very elementary. The type `string` is predefined as
an unconstrained array:

```
string is array (positive range <>) of character;
```

Hence, when one declares a `string` variable,

```
My_String: string (1..80);
```

only the holder for the string is declared. An aggregate may be used to initialize
the space, but it is up to the user to devise a method, if necessary, to distinguish
between the size of the array and the length of the string contained in the array.
Although Ada's support for strings is limited, it is worth considering as the basis
upon which other static methods may be built.

The fundamental complaint about Ada's `string` type centers on the effects
of strong type checking. Specifically, as strings and pieces of strings are being
manipulated and combined to create new strings, users must be cautious when the
results of string operations are placed into an array. If the size of the new string
does not exactly match the size of the array where the result is to be placed, an
exception, `constraint_error`, is raised. For example, if a concatenation of
several pieces of strings are joined together to form a new string and place it in
a variable,

```
My_String (1..xx):= Able & " a piece " & Sam (5..35);
```

a `constraint_error` is raised if xx is not equal to the size of the string
expression. The problem of matching the size of the result string to the size of
the location when the string is assigned to a variable may be handled in one of
two ways, as illustrated with the function and procedure depicted in Listing 10.1.
The `Assign` function accepts the length of the variable where the string is placed
and produces the result in a string of the same size:

```
My_String:= Assign ( Able & " a piece " & Sam (5..35),
                     My_String'length);
```

The `Assign` procedure

```
Assign (To_Str    => My_String ,
        Str_value => Able & " a piece " & Sam (5..35) );
```

Listing 10.1. String assignment algorithms.

```
function Assign ( Str_Value  : in    string;
                  Result_Size: in    natural) return string is

   Result: string (1..Result_Size);

  begin
   Result (1..Str_Value'length):= Str_Value;
   return Result;
  end Assign;

procedure Assign (   To_Str:    out string;
                  Str_Value: in     string) is

  begin
   To_Str (1..Str_Value'length):= Str_Value;
  end Assign;
```

determines the size of the string value being assigned and uses its size to properly range the piece of the array where the value is placed.

Although these subprograms place string values correctly, they do not address the problem of distinguishing between the values in locations in the **string** variable that contain the string's value and the remaining positions in the array. The next two sections illustrate two traditional methods of clarifying the location of the string's value within an array. A third alternative would be to **erase** the contents of the other array locations, where **erase** means that a specific character value, which has been predetermined for this purpose, is placed in the remaining locations. A value typically employed for this purpose is character'first, also referred to as ASCII.nul. This is accomplished in the Assign function with the statement sequence

```
    if str_value'length < result_size then
       result (str_value'length+1 .. result_size):=
                        (others => character'first);
    end if;
```

before the return statement. A similar change could be made in the Assign procedure.

Let's take a look at the tradeoffs associated with filling a string with some fill character. Naturally, this removes the fill character from the set of characters that may appear in the string. The character does not have to be character'first; any character could be used. By placing the fill character in the rest of the string, the length of strings may be determined in time $O(\log$ array length$)$. The algorithm in Listing 10.2 finds the length of the string value contained in the

Listing 10.2. A string `Length` function.

```
function Length ( Str: string) return natural is

   Low    : natural:= 0;
   High   : natural:= Str'Length+1;
   Middle: natural;

   begin
   while (Low + 1) < High loop
      Middle:= (Low + High) / 2;
      if Str (Middle) /= character'first then
         Low:= Middle;
       else
          High:= Middle;
      end if;
   end loop;
   return High-1;
   end Length;
```

string variable. The algorithm is basically a bisection method search that looks for the location of the first position in the array that contains `character'first`. The length of the string is one less than the index of the first occurrence of `character'first` in the array.

To achieve the log timing for this algorithm requires that a fill character be placed in all array locations that do not contain the string's value. This requires time, including the time to initialize each empty string with the fill character.

10.2.2 TurboPascal-like Strings

One popular method of maintaining strings in arrays stores the string's value in consecutive array locations and uses an extra location to store the actual size of the string. This is the method employed in Borland's TurboPascal, an excellent Pascal system. In TurboPascal, string variables are defined in a manner similar to Ada's unconstrained arrays. A string type defined as

```
type Message_Type = string [25];
```

in TurboPascal is actually represented as an array of 26 `char` variables:

```
string [n] = array [0 .. n] of char;
```

The first location in the array is used to maintain a count of the number of locations actually used to contain a string value. For example, the string, "The quick brown fox" would be stored as

```
   0   1    2    3    4    5    6    7              17   18   19
 ┌────┬───┬────┬───┬────┬────┬────┬───────        ┬────┬────┬────┬────┐
 │ 19 │'T'│'h' │'e'│' ' │'q' │'u' │'i'    .  .  . │'f' │'o' │'x' │    │
 └────┴───┴────┴───┴────┴────┴────┴───────        ┴────┴────┴────┴────┘
```

String variables of different lengths may be defined:

```
VAR Small: str [3];
    Large: str [200];
```

The value of the string is stored in locations 1 .. k, where k is the length of the string. The length k is encoded in location zero:

```
integer (Small [0]) = length of string in Small.
```

An advantage of this representation is immediate access to the length of the string value in each object. A disadvantage of the approach used in TurboPascal is the size of the location where the string length is kept, which is an eight-bit character location. Hence, only a value in the range 0 .. 255 can be stored. Therefore, the maximum size of strings is 255 characters. It should be said that this is only a minor disadvantage. Many string applications either fit within this bound or can be made to do so.

This upper bound on the size of TurboPascal strings may easily be overcome in Ada by representing strings in a record with a discriminant, as

```
type TP_String (Max_Size: natural) is
   record
      Size  : natural range 0 .. Max_Size:= 0;
      Symbol: string (1..Max_Size);
   end record;
```

When variables of this type are declared, they are initialized as null strings, with the automatic initialization, which places a zero in the record's Size component.

This string representation has the typical problem of static representations, namely, the predetermined limit on the size of the array in each TP_String record. On balance, the implementation of the algorithms for the various constructors and observers is straightforward. Even additional support, like string

Listing 10.3. TP_strings package specifications.

```
package Turbo_Strings is
   type TP_String (Max_Size: positive:= 40) is private;

   function "<" ( Left : in     TP_String;
                  Right: in     TP_String ) return boolean;
   function "<" ( Left : in     TP_String;
                  Right: in     string ) return boolean;
   function "<" ( Left : in     string;
                  Right: in     TP_String ) return boolean;

   procedure Append ( IN_STRING    : in     TP_String;
                      TO_THE_STRING: in out TP_String );
   procedure Append ( In_String    : in     string;
                      To_The_String: in out TP_String );
   procedure Clear ( The_String: in out  TP_String );
   procedure Copy ( From_The_String: in     TP_String;
                    To_The_String  :    out TP_String );
   procedure Copy ( From_The_String: in     string;
                    To_The_String  :    out TP_String );
   procedure Copy ( From_The_String: in     TP_String;
                    To_The_String  :    out string );
   procedure Delete ( In_The_String     : in  out TP_String;
                      From_The_Position: in     positive;
                      To_The_Position  : in     positive );
   procedure Delete ( In_The_String     : in  out TP_String;
                      From_The_Position: in     positive;
                      To_The_Position  : in     positive );
   procedure Insert ( The_String     : in     string;
                      To_The_String  : in out TP_String;
                      At_The_Position: in     positive );
   procedure Insert ( The_String     : in     TP_String;
                      To_The_String  : in out TP_String;
                      At_The_Position: in     positive );

   function  Is_Null ( The_String: TP_String ) return boolean;
   function  Length_Of ( The_String: TP_String ) return natural;
   function Position_Of ( Substring : TP_String;
                          The_String: TP_String;
                          Start_At  : positive:= 1) return natural;
   function Position_Of ( Substring : string;
                          The_String: TP_String;
                          Start_At  : positive:= 1) return natural;
   procedure Prepend ( The_String   : in     string;
                       To_The_String: in out TP_String );
   procedure Prepend ( The_String   : in     TP_String;
                       To_The_String: in out TP_String );
   procedure Replace_Substring ( In_The_String   : in out TP_String;
                                 At_The_Position: in     positive;
                                 With_The_String: in     STRING );
   procedure Replace_Substring ( In_The_String   : in out TP_String;
                                 At_The_Position: in     positive;
                                 With_The_String: in     TP_String );
```

Listing 10.3. TP_strings specifications (cont.)

```
function  Get_Substring (The_String        : TP_String;
                         From_The_Position : positive;
                         To_The_Position   : positive;
                         Return_Size       : positive) return TP_String;
function  Get_Substring (The_String        : TP_String;
                         From_The_Position : positive;
                         To_The_Position   : positive;
                         Return_Size       : positive) return STRING ;

String_Overflow, String_Position_Error : exception;

private
   type Char is array (positive range <>) OF character ;
   type TP_String (Max_Size : positive := 40) is
      record
         Size : natural := 0;
         Strng: Char (1..Max_Size);
      end record ;

end Turbo_Strings ;
```

I/O, is easy to build. For example, a get_line procedure for TP_Strings may directly use text_io.get_line:

```
procedure Get_Line (Str:     out TP_String) is
   begin
      Text_IO.Get_Line (Str.Symbol, Str.Size);
   exception
      when constraint_error => raise String_Overflow;
   end Get_Line;
```

If, through the analysis of the system being designed and needing string support, a software developer can determine the maximum size of strings, the TP_Strings representation is an excellent, and efficient, method for representing strings. The only potential efficiency problem with this approach relates to the efficient use of memory. Specifically, if the maximum size of strings is substantially larger than the actual size manipulated by the system, the amount of storage reserved for strings could affect system performance.

Once a package developer makes a decision to have a package export its own string type, the number of constructors and observers must be increased, or the existing ones must be overloaded, to assist package users through a collection of subprograms for the conversion and interaction between TP_Strings and Ada's strings. This is illustrated with the package specifications for TurboPascal-like strings appearing in Listing 10.3.

Note that it is unnecessary to provide I/O support for TurboPascal-like strings because the package provides subprograms for passing string values between Ada's `strings` and `TP_Strings`, allowing users to perform their own string I/O with the existing Ada `string` I/O support.

Building the body of a strings package based on `TP_Strings` is not a difficult matter and is left as an exercise for the reader.

10.2.3 The Sentinel Method

When a specific character does not appear in string values, the sentinel method could be an appropriate means of representing strings. This is the method employed in C and Modula-2. In Modula-2, strings are maintained in any `array of char`. However, Modula-2's standard `ReadString` procedure in the module `InOut` places strings in arrays of characters in such a way that if the string does not fill the array, the string is terminated with an `ASCII.nul` character. Also, Modula-2's `InOut`'s `WriteString` is consistent with `ReadString` in that when a string is processed by `WriteString`, all characters are printed until either an `ASCII.nul` is encountered or all characters in the array are printed. For example, the string `"Small one"` would appear as

1	2	3	4	5	6	7	8	9	10	
'S'	'm'	'a'	'l'	'l'	' '	'o'	'n'	'e'	chr(0)	. . .

One disadvantage to this approach is the time required, *O(string length)*, to determine the length of a string. This also affects several string constructors, which need to know the position of the end of a string. However, the bodies of string constructors and observers are easy to build. This approach may directly use Ada strings. A package to support this approach should be built as a generic package, whose instantiation parameter is the sentinel value

```
generic
   sentinel: character := character'first;

package Modula-2-like_Strings is
   . . .
```

Another decision that must be addressed when building this package is whether to use Ada's `string` type, either directly or indirectly; that is, whether to use

Ada `strings` or export a `private` type. An advantage of having the package declare a `private` type is that the initialization of that type, with the sentinel value in the first array location, may be guaranteed. If string initialization is provided, a package specification similar to the one in Listing 10.3 is necessary.

Construction of the specifications and body for a Modula-2-like strings package is left as an exercise for the reader.

10.3 Dynamic Representations

10.3.1 Strings as Lists

The complete opposite to the static methods for representing strings is the direct representation of a string as a list of characters, one character per list record. This is illustrated in Figure 10.1.

Despite the simplicity of this approach, there is one very obvious disadvantage: the overhead for each record in the string representation. Allocating an access component with each character's record requires the memory overhead for access types. This overhead may range from two to eight bytes per record, depending on the method for representing access types on a particular system. If we assume four bytes are required for the access component in each record, then 20 percent of each record is allocated to each character and 80 percent is allocated for the access component. That is, the space cost is five bytes per character for each character in the string.

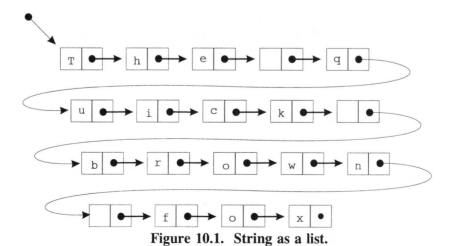

Figure 10.1. String as a list.

The effects on constructing and timing the various constructor and observer algorithms are as one would expect when comparing list-based structures to array-based structures. The use of array indexes and ranges and random access to array locations are replaced by pointers and the strict sequential access of lists. Other than that, there is a great deal of similarity between array-based and list-based string processing algorithms.

Building a simple list-based string package is a nice academic exercise, but the memory overhead precludes the use of this package for serious string applications.

10.3.2 Strings as Piecewise Lists

Figure 10.2 illustrates an alternative to the straight list approach described in Section 10.3.1. This approach breaks the string into pieces, stores the pieces of the string in records, and forms the records into a list. The piecewise list illustrated in Figure 10.2 stores up to six characters per record. If the access component used to link strings requires four bytes, then the space utilization approaches 60 percent efficiency, six bytes for the characters and four bytes for the access component.

Figure 10.2 also illustrates a potential space utilization problem for dynamically allocated piecewise strings, namely, a last piece that is not fully utilized. The example illustrated in Figure 10.2 shows a last piece containing only one character. Hence, this piece has a space cost of 10 bytes for that one character.

The specifications for a piecewise string package are essentially the same as the specifications for the TurboPascal-like string package appearing in Listing 10.3. The description of the private type, PW_Strings, appears in

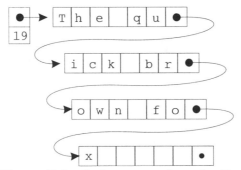

Figure 10.2. Strings as a piecewise list.

Listing 10.4.   The List_Pt_Lpt module may be used to assist in the representation of PW_Strings. The private declarations indicate the structure of PW_Strings, which includes a component that provides access to the piecewise list, the length of the string, and other components that assist in navigating the string. Included in each PW_String record is an array, where a copy of the current piece is kept. This array component is used by several string manipulating subprograms as a buffer to improve the speed of access to characters in the string. Selection of an appropriate piece size is application-dependent. Therefore, it is appropriate for a piecewise representation to include a generic instantiation parameter like

```
        Piece_Size: positive:= 8;
```

with a reasonable default value. If the software developer can predetermine the expected size of strings, piece size may be optimized. For example, if most strings are expected to be 15 or more characters long, a piece size of 15 may be appropriate. However, users should avoid very large piece sizes, because of the potential memory requirements that may be associated with this approach.

Listing 10.4. Piecewise string representation.

```
with List_Pt_Lpt;
generic

  Piece_Size: in positive:= 10;

package Piecewise_Strings is

  type PW_String is limited private;

               ...  -- SPECIFICATIONS OF SUBPROGRAMS

private

  type Char is array (0 .. Piece_Size-1) of character;

  package Str_Lst is new List_Pt_Lpt (Char);
  use Str_Lst;

  type PW_String is
     record
        List          : Str_Lst.List_Type;
        Length        : natural:= 0;
        Logical_Index : natural:= 0;
        Piece_Index   : natural RANGE 0 .. Piece_Size:= 0;
        Current_Piece : Char;
     end record;

end Piecewise_Strings;
```

To illustrate the potential memory utilization problems, consider a case where a piecewise representation is instantiated with a piece size of 50. Further assume that 50 is the average size of strings, but with a very small standard deviation in string size. For each string whose length is in the range 45 to 49, there may be a similar number of strings with lengths in the range 51 to 55. Although each string in the first group has good space utilization, every string in the second group requires two pieces. resulting in poor space utilization for these strings, in the range of about 50 percent.

The piecewise representation of strings does represent some challenges to the implementor when building the bodies of the string constructors and observers. However, most of the processing of the string constructors and observers is sequential. The only nonsequential operation entails the initial position of some operations. Listing 10.5 illustrates several navigation procedures for strings. These procedures provide navigation and access support for the package's constructors and observers. The procedure `Set_Position` accepts a string and a position and initializes the various components in the string in preparation for access to the string. The function `Current_Char` returns the character indicated by the current index into the string. `Set_Position` attempts to reduce the amount of list access by comparing the new index to the old. If they are the same, no change occurs. If they access the same piece, only the `Piece_Index` component is modified; otherwise, the algorithm sequentially processes the list and places a copy of the appropriate piece in `Current_Piece`. The procedures `Increment_Index` and `Decrement_Index` provide relative processing access by associating the repositioning request in the string to an appropriate call to `Set_Position`.

10.3.3 Tradeoffs

The tradeoffs between the various list representations are the typical ones that occur between static and dynamic representations, namely, the speed of static representations versus the unboundedness of dynamic representations. A comparison between the two dynamic approaches leaves no questions about the large overhead of the straight list method. The only remaining question is: What is an appropriate choice for the `Piece_Size` in the piecewise list representation? Under certain circumstances it has been shown that if L is the average length of strings and a is the overhead per record for access pointers, then the piece size that minimizes wasted memory is $\sqrt{2aL}$.

Listing 10.5. Navigation processes for piecewise strings.

```
procedure Set_Position ( Str   : in out PW_String;
                         Index: in      natural ) is

   begin
   if Index = 0 then
      Str.Logical_Index:= 0;
    elsif ((Index-1) mod Piece_Size)
          = ((Str.Logical_Index-1) mod Piece_Size) then
      Str.Logical_Index:= Index;
      Str.Piece_Index  := (Index-1) mod Piece_Size;
    else
      Str:= (Str.List, Str.Length, Index, (Index-1)
             mod Piece_Size, Str.Current_Piece );
      Move_To_Front (Str.List);
      if (Index-1)/Piece_Size > 0 then
         for IX in 1 .. (Index-1)/Piece_Size loop
            Move_Towards_Rear (Str.List);
         end loop;
      end if;
    Str.Current_Piece:= Current_Object (Str.List);
    end if;
   end Set_Position;

procedure Increment_Index ( Str       : in out PW_String;
                            Increment: in     positive ) is

   begin
   Set_Position (Str, Str.Logical_Index + Increment);
   end Increment_Index;

procedure Decrement_Index ( Str       : in out PW_String;
                            Increment: in     positive ) is

   begin
   Set_Position (Str, Str.Logical_Index - Increment);
   end Decrement_Index;

function Current_Char (Str: PW_String) return character is

   begin
   return Str.Current_Piece(Str.Piece_Index);
   end Current_Char;
```

The piecewise method does present some challenges when coding the bodies of the constructors and observers. For example, inserting one string in another may require the manipulation of characters between pieces and adjusting each piece from the position where the insertion was made to the end of the string. However, there is no reason why this algorithm should not function in the same order of magnitude of time as the array-based algorithm, $O(n)$.

10.4 String Search Algorithms

Fundamental to practically every string processing application is the searching within one string for the occurrences of a second string,

```
... := Position_Of (Sub_String, The_String);
```

The simplest algorithm, sometimes called **the obvious algorithm**, searches The_String for occurrences of the first character in the Sub_String. At each such occurrence it performs pairwise matches between corresponding characters in the two strings until a pairwise match fails, or until the substring is located. The algorithm is discussed in Section 10.4.1. This approach makes no use of any information about the structure of the substring.

Alternate algorithms, which appear in Sections 10.4.2 through 10.4.4, make use of the structure of the substring. Section 10.4.2 describes the simplest of these, a variation of **the obvious algorithm**, selects a unique character in the substring, a character whose occurrences in the The_String are expected to be rare, and centers the initial search process for this character; and then checks the characters that surround it for the desired substring. The next two sections describe two important string search algorithms.

10.4.1 The Obvious Algorithm

Listing 10.6 contains an example of the obvious algorithm. This example searches through a string contained in a PW_String for an occurrence of a substring contained in an Ada string. This algorithm makes use of the string navigation subprograms described in Listing 10.5. To illustrate the potential time for the algorithm, assume the substring being sought is

```
DABADABADO
```

and the search is through a large string like

```
DABADABADABADABADABA ... DABADABADABADABADABADABADABADO
```

Listing 10.6. The obvious algorithm.

```
function Position_Of ( Substring : string;
                       The_String: PW_String;
                       Start_At  : positive:= 1) return natural is

   Answer  : natural   := 0;
   Str_Copy: PW_String:= The_String;
   Found_It: boolean   := false;

begin
for Index in 1..(The_String.Length-Substring'length+1) loop
   Set_Position (Str_Copy, Index);
   if Current_Char (Str_Copy) = Substring (1) then
      Found_It:= true;
      for Index in 2 .. Substring'length loop
         Increment_Index (Str_Copy,1);
         if Current_Char(Str_Copy) /= Substring(Index) then
            Found_It:= false;
            exit;
         end if;
      end loop;
      if Found_It then
         Answer:= Index;
         exit;
      end if;
   end if;
end loop;
return Answer;
end Position_Of;
```

As the search progresses, the substring is compared a character at a time to the string

```
DABADABADABADABADABA ... DABADABADABADABADABADABADABADO
||||||||||x
DABADABADO
```

In this example, the search fails with the last character. Note that this search time is the length of the substring. Because the search fails, the substring is moved up one character and compared with the larger string

```
DABADABADABADABADABA ... DABADABADABADABADABADABADABADO
 x
 DABADABADO
```

This time the search fails at the first character. Unfortunately, every fourth substring search takes time in the order of the length of the substring. Since the substring being sought is found at the end of the large substring, the entire search time is of order

$$O(\text{length of string 1 * length of small string 2}).$$

Despite the potential time problem for this search technique, the maximum time is reached only when there are unusual relationships between the two strings, as illustrated with the previous example. The next three sections describe three search techniques that improve upon the potential upper bound described here.

10.4.2 A Human Variation

When humans search for a substring in a string, they frequently use a simple variation of the search described above. The human variation of substring searching usually begins with an analysis of the substring. The analysis usually involves finding something unique in the substring, like a symbol, or small sequence of symbols, that does not occur frequently. This special symbol is then used in the sequential search of the other string and comparisons are made surrounding this special letter.

An illustration of this search method is typical of the method employed when solving word matrix puzzles. A **word matrix puzzle** is a rectangular arrangement of letters and the puzzle solver is given a list of words that appear in the matrix. The words may appear in any row, column, or diagonal of the matrix and be spelled left to right or right to left. A method frequently employed in solving these puzzles is to search for a word by first looking for a special letter in the word and seeing if the rest of the word might surround the letter. For example, if the word `"dazzle"` is sought in a word matrix, the searcher would probably look for the letter `"z"` - actually look for a pair of `"z"`s - and see if the word surrounds the letters.

The rationale behind this approach is that fewer `"z"`s than `"d"`s will appear in the word matrix, and hence less time will be spent making comparisons with other letters in the string being sought.

Consider the example from Section 10.4.1. In the substring

        DABADABADO

the letter o occurs only once. Now the other string is searched to look for occurrences of this letter. Fortunately, in this case only one o occurs in the other string, and hence no time is wasted comparing the other letters in the string being sought, except for the one occurrence of an O.

The two algorithms described in the next two sections perform their searches by making use of information available in the string being sought. In the example discussed in Section 10.4.1, when the comparison

```
DABADABADABADABADABA . . . DABADABADABADABADABADABADABADO
|||||||||x
DABADABADO
```

was made, there is enough information in the comparisons to indicate that the next test should be made **not** by moving the string one character, but by moving it four characters

```
DABADABADABADABADABA . . . DABADABADABADABADABADABADABADO
      ||||||
      DABADABADO
```

and continuing the comparison with the seventh character, the B and not repeat a comparison of the beginning characters, DABADA. Algorithms for these improved search strategies are described next.

10.4.3 Knuth-Morris-Pratt Algorithm

Let S_1 and S_2 be two strings. The Knuth-Morris-Pratt (KMP) algorithm searches S_1 for occurrences of S_2 in time,

$$T = O(\text{length}(S_1) + \text{length}(S_2)).$$

Assume S_1 is being searched for an occurrence of S_2. Simply stated, the goal of the KMP algorithm is not to back up. That is, once the jth symbol in S_1, $S_1(j)$, is found the algorithm does not look back at any $S_1(i)$, for $i < j$. For example, consider the strings used as an example in Section 10.4.1. After the first comparison of the characters in S_1 to those in S_2,

```
DABADABADABADABADABA . . . DABADABADABADABADABADABADABADO
|||||||||x
DABADABADO
```

there is enough information from the successful character-by-character comparisons so that the comparisons continue the search

```
DABADABADABADABADABABA ... DABADABADABADABADABADABADABADO
| | | | |?
DABADABADO
```

as indicated with the "?". That is, there is enough information in the successful character-by-character comparisons so that the second string may be positioned appropriately so that the comparisons may continue where the last failure occurred. It should be noted that when a comparison succeeds, the character in S_1 at that position is known, but when a comparison fails, all that is known is that the character **is not** the same in this case, it was not an O. It was not know that the character was an A.

The key to the KMP algorithm is the formation of a table associated to the positions in S_2 that indicate how to slide the string S_2 when the character-by-character match fails at that position. Table 10.3 illustrates three strings and their corresponding slide tables. String (a) in Table 10.3 is the string appearing in several examples above, "DABADABADO". A quick look at the rationale for each slide value could be instructive. The reasons for the slide values for the nine symbols are as follows:

1. The first D does not have a match so, obviously, move the string over one position and try again.
2. The symbol does not match the A, therefore, it might be a D, so the string must be slid over one so the symbol may be compared to the starting symbol, D.
3. The symbol does not match the B, therefore, the string must be slid over to check against the leading D.
4. Same reason as (2) and (3).

Table 10.3. KMP table examples.

```
        D A B A D A B A D O
        1 1 2 3 5 5 6 7 9 4
                (a)

          S I M P L E
          1 1 2 3 4 5
              (b)

          X Y Z X Y Z
          1 1 2 4 4 5
              (c)
```

5. This symbol does not match the D, therefore, it will not match the leading D, so slide the string over and continue the comparisons with the next character.
6. Same reasons as (2), (3), and (4).
7. Same as (6).
8. Same reason as (5).
9. The lack of a match to the O must be adjusted with the matches to the previous five symbols. Therefore the string is slid only four places, and the symbol compared to the O will be compared to the A in position 6.

Listing 10.7 describes a type declaration for the offset table used by the KMP algorithms and the specification for the procedure that builds the table. The algorithm for building the slide table appears in Listing 10.8 without explanation. Developing a detailed rationale for the algorithm is left as an exercise for the reader.

The preprocessing algorithm that produces the table that supports the KMP algorithm is performed in time of the order of the length of the string being sought. The KMP algorithm does not backtrack. Therefore, the search algorithm performs in time of the order of the length of the string being searched. As a result, the entire search is performed in time of the order of the sum of the lengths of the two strings.

Listing 10.7. KMP support specifications.

```
package KMP_Support is

type Slide_Array is array (positive range <>) of natural;

procedure KMP_Scan ( The_String : in      string;
                     String_Size: in      positive;
                     Table      : in out slide_array );

end KMP_Support;
```

10.4.4 Boyer-Moore Algorithm

The Boyer-Moore algorithm was published in the same year as the KMP algorithm. The Boyer-Moore algorithm uses the KMP algorithm but builds upon it with a second approach. Fundamentally, the Boyer-Moore algorithm uses two slide tables, a KMP-like slide table and a second table. Also, the Boyer-Moore

Listing 10.8. KMP table construction algorithm.

```
procedure KMP_Scan ( The_String : in        string;
                     String_Size: in        positive;
                     Table       : in out slide_array ) is

   Index_1: natural:= 1;
   Index_2: natural:= 0;

begin
Table (1):= 0;
while Index_1 < String_Size loop
   while (Index_2 > 0) and
         then The_String (Index_1) /= The_String (Index_2) loop
      Index_2:= Table (Index_2);
   end loop;
   Index_1:= Index_1 + 1;
   Index_2:= Index_2 + 1;
   if The_String (Index_1) = The_String (Index_2) then
       Table (Index_1):= Table (Index_2);
     else
       Table (Index_1):= Index_2;
   end if;
end loop;
end KMP_Scan;
```

algorithm performs its matching comparisons working from right to left instead of from left to right.

The KMP-like table is prepared making use of the results of the right-to-left comparisons. Table 10.4 illustrates the slide table for several strings. A comparison of strings (a) and (d) in Table 10.4 helps gain an understanding of the interaction between the various matches and the right-to-left comparisons. In string (a), if a match occurs with the rightmost symbol, an O, and since there is no other O in the string, the entire string must be moved past the O when a match fails on other symbols in the string. In string (d), note that if the match fails on the second character from the right, the A, the string is moved only eight positions, because the failure to match against the A might be because the symbol at that location is an O.

The second table makes use of the character in the larger string that did not match the corresponding character. This character may or may not be in the string being sought. It describes how far the string should slide knowing where the rightmost occurrences of this character appears in the string being sought. For example, if the word "APPEAR" is sought, the table entries for the characters in this string would be

```
  - A P E R
  6 1 3 2 0
```

Table 10.4. Boyer-Moore KMP-like tables.

```
        D    A    B    A    D    A    B    A    D  O
        10   10   10   10   10   10   10   10   10 1
                           (a)


                  S   I   M   P   L  E
                  1   1   2   3   4  5
                           (b)


                  X   Y   Z   X   Y  Z
                  1   1   2   4   4  5
                           (c)


        O    D    A    B    A    D    A    B  A  D
        10   10   10   10   10   10   10   10 8  1
                           (d)
```

where " - " indicates all the characters not appearing in the string being sought. Each value indicates the distance of the first occurrence of that character from the right-hand end of the pattern.

Let S be the string being searched and P the pattern being sought. The Boyer-Moore algorithm performs the search as follows: Let i_S be the index used in scanning the string S and i_P be the index used in scanning the pattern P. Initially,

$$i_S = i_P = length\ of\ P.$$

When the characters at the indices match, both indices are decremented. When there is no match, i_P is reset to the *length of P*. i_S is reset to the larger of the two values obtained in the KMP-like table at position i_S and in the second table at i_P, before i_P is reset. Building the Boyer-Moore algorithm and its support is left as an exercise.

10.4.5 Comparisons

A comparison of the three search algorithms - the obvious algorithm, the KMP algorithm, and the Boyer-Moore algorithm - indicates that for small patterns, the obvious algorithm is as good as any. In practice, most matches fail with the first or second character. Hence, there is not much gained with the overhead of the KMP algorithm versus the obvious algorithm. However, a glance at the slide table for the Boyer-Moore algorithm indicates that for many patterns, the Boyer-

Moore algorithm makes large jumps while scanning the string. Experiments show that as patterns get larger, the Boyer-Moore algorithm is substantially faster, in the order of two or three to one, than either the obvious algorithm or the KMP algorithm.

10.5 Tradeoffs

The choices between the various static and dynamic representations of strings depends on the application. From a user's point of view, it is desirable to select the least complex representation of strings. From our experience, and no scientific survey, we believe that most software developers make their choice of string representation based not on what might be an appropriate representation for the application, but on the string representation with which they are most experienced. In many cases, this is not necessarily bad.

We find that two packages seem to cover all possible situations with good reliability and efficiency, the TP_Strings package and the piecewise dynamic representation. As long as a reasonable upper bound on the size of strings being manipulated may be predetermined, TP_Strings is a practical first choice. When in doubt, the piecewise strings package is a good compromise that performs with reasonable efficiency over a wide range of applications.

10.6 Explorations

1. For string applications involving text processing, the normal ASCII collating order might not be appropriate. In particular, for some applications, the ASCII collating order of characters,

```
A..Z, a..z
```

might not be suitable for certain text-processing applications. In some cases, it might be desirable to maintain the ASCII collating order but ignore the case of alphabet characters. That is, consider A equivalent to a, B equivalent to b, and so forth.

Another alternative might be to maintain the ASCII collating order for all nonalphabetic characters and the ASCII collating order between any alphabetic character and any nonalphabetic character, but use the collating order

$$AaBbCcDd \ldots YyZz.$$

Build observers, `No_Case_Equivalent` and `No_Case_Precede`, that perform the normal equivalent and precede selections except that the upper and lower cases of each alphabet character are considered equivalent. Also build `Alpha_Precede` that uses the `AaBbCc` ... collating order for alphabet characters.

2. Evaluate the time-space requirements for your solution of Exercise 1.
3. Is an `Alpha_Equivalent` observer necessary? Explain.
4. In the ASCII scheme, the numerals come before the alphabetic characters and the control and special characters are dispersed around the numeric and alphabetic characters. Build a package that includes all of the string processing features but allows a user to specify a unique collating order.
5. Evaluate the various factors that must be considered when building a string package for an EBCDIC or other encoding scheme.
6. Build a package that uses a translation table that allows a user to modify all or part of the ASCII collating order of characters. This package should include procedures to modify all or part of the table as well as display the new table both in its collating order as well as in ASCII order with each character's new collating value. Also include procedures that allow a user to determine if several characters might have the same collating value, which may or may not be desirable, depending on the application.
7. How many of the exercises in this section could be handled with a translation table? Explain. Evaluate the use of a translation table versus other approaches to implementing alternative collating orders.
8. Modify the string package with an instantiation option that allows a user to decide whether the function `Position_Of` returns an exception, `Not_A_Substring`, or a value of zero when the search does not find the substring.
9. Develop a written description, and appropriate assertions, for the KMP algorithm for creating the support table.
10. Build the Boyer-Moore modification of the KMP table builder.
11. Build a Boyer-Moore support package including the Boyer-Moore pattern-searching algorithm.
12. Create the specification and body for a complete `TP_Strings` package.

13. Create the specification and body for a complete dynamic piecewise string package.
14. Analyze the problems surrounding the use of the Boyer-Moore algorithm for pattern searching within the dynamic piecewise string package.
15. Build a Boyer-Moore pattern-search subprogram within the piecewise strings package.
16. Investigate the various Ada string packages, like `Ada.Strings.Bound` and `Ada.Strings.Unbound`, with respect to their limitations and the timing characteristics of their subprograms.
17. Construct the KMP tables for the following strings:

```
abcdefghij          abcaefgaij          abcdabghab
abcdabchabc         abcdabcdab          abcdabcdabcde
```

18. Construct the Boyer-Moore tables for the strings in Exercise 17.

11

Sorting

Organizing information, seeking information, and updating collections of information stored in various structures consume both a large portion of software development efforts and enormous amounts of program execution time. This chapter addresses the fundamentals that surround the organization of arrays of data. The searching and updating of collections of information stored in arrays appears in Chapter 12.

The term **sorting**, the topic discussed in this chapter, refers to the process of organizing collections of objects into sequential structures according to a linear ordering relationship that defines an ordering of the objects. The ordering relation is also referred to as a **collating** relationship. In the simplest cases, the objects to be collated are represented by an ordinal data type and the objects are placed into an array, with a linear order relation between the objects.

This chapter begins with several classical array sorting techniques along with an analysis of the complexity of their algorithms. These range from algorithms with poor timing, $O(n^2)$, to the best possible timings, $O(n \log(n))$.

In some cases, these algorithms are presented generically. In other cases, instances of the algorithms are presented so that the algorithm's structure is not obscured by a generic presentation. In those cases, the generic representations are left as exercises with hints pointing out some of the difficulties encountered in creating generic versions of these algorithms.

11.1 $O(n^2)$ Sorts

Sorting methods are usually categorized according to the timing of the algorithm. Sort timings fall into three basic categories: poor sort techniques whose timing is $O(n^2)$; the best sort timings, which is $O(n \log n)$; and a collection of sort techniques that fall between the two extreme categories. This section describes the sorts with poor timing; Section 11.2 describes the middle group of sort techniques; and Section 11.3 describes the best possible timings.

11.1.1 Selection Sort

Each sort technique may be described by its strategy. Once the strategy leads us to an algorithm, the algorithm may be measured and analyzed. The selection sort has a simple strategy, which may be described as follows:

> For each position in the array, starting with the first position, find the object that belongs in that position.

Listing 11.1 illustrates a selection sort. The outer loop **selects** the locations in the array. For each selection, the inner loop searches for the object that belongs in that location. Once the inner loop finds the object, the object is swapped with the object in the **selected** location so that the next iteration of the outer loop will not reselect that object.

It is easy to determine the timing for this sort. If n is the number of objects in the array, the outer loop executes n-1 times. Each time through the outer loop, the number of iterations of the inner loop is completely determined. The first time through the outer loop, the inner loop iterates n-1 time; the second time through the outer loop, the inner loop iterates n-2 times. Each time through the outer loop, the number of iterations of the inner loop is one less than the number of iterations of the same loop during the previous iteration. This leads to the total number of iterations of the inner loop as

$$(n\text{-}1) + (n\text{-}2) + \ldots + 3 + 2 + 1 = O(n^2).$$

Since this is the largest timing component in the algorithm, the algorithm's timing is $O(n^2)$.

Frequently, when reviewing the timing of algorithms, it is not always easy to get a firm handle on the algorithm's timing. When that occurs, there are three

Listing 11.1. Generic selection sort algorithm.

```
generic

   type Array_Range is (<>);
   type Object_Type is private;
   type Array_Type  is array (Array_Range range <>) of Object_Type;
   with function Precedes ( left, Right: Object_Type ) return boolean;

procedure Select_Sort ( The_Array: in out Array_Type;
                        left_end : in     Array_Range:= Array_Range'first;
                        Right_End: in     Array_Range );

-- generic Select_Sort body

procedure Select_Sort ( The_Array: in out Array_Type;
                        Left_End : in     Array_Range:= Array_Range'first;
                        Right_End: in     Array_Range )     is

   function "<" (Left, Right: Object_Type) return boolean renames Precedes;
   function pred (IX:Array_Range)return Array_Range
                                               renames Array_Range'pred;
   function succ (IX:Array_Range)return Array_Range
                                               renames Array_Range'succ;

   Selected_Index: Array_Range;
   Extra         : Object_Type;

   begin -- of sort
   for Outer_Index in Left_End .. pred(Right_End) loop
      Selected_Index:= Outer_Index;
      for Inner_Index in succ (Outer_Index) .. Right_End loop
         if The_Array(Inner_Index) < The_Array(Selected_Index)
           then Selected_Index:= Inner_Index;
         end if;
      end for;
      if Selected_Index /= Outer_Index then
         Extra                     := The_Array(Outer_Index);
         The_Array(Outer_Index)    := The_Array(Selected_Index);
         The_Array(Selected_Index):= Extra;
      end if;
   end loop;
   end Select_Sort;
```

cases that are usually discussed, the algorithm's worst timing case, the algorithm's best timing case, and the average timing for the algorithm. The worst-case timing provides an upper bound on the algorithm's timing, and the best case provides a lower bound on the timing. Sometimes, the average case is an easy one to determine. The selection sort, because of the simplicity of its algorithm, is unusual in that all cases have the same timing characteristic, $O(n^2)$.

11.1.2 Insertion (Bubble) Sort

The sort strategy of the insertion sort is as follows:

> For each $i \in [2,n]$, assume the object in locations 1 through $i-1$ are in order. **Insert** the ith number into position so that objects in locations 1 through i are in order.

The simple algorithm that appears in Listing 11.2 performs this strategy. If the objects in array positions 1 through $i-1$ are in sorted order, the ith object is placed in its correct position by comparing it to the object in the position preceding it. If these two objects are not in the correct order, they are swapped and a new comparison is made. This process proceeds until either no swap occurs or the ith object is "bubbled" up to the first position in the array.

The inner loop in Listing 11.2 is a `while` loop controlled with two conditions. As a result, the timing of the sort depends on the organization of the data. An upper bound may be observed by assuming that each time through the outer loop, the object being "bubbled" in the inner loop bubbles up to the first location in the array. The first time through the outer loop, the inner loop iterates at most 1 time. The second time through the outer loop, the inner loop iterates at most 2 times. The total number of iterations of the inner loop is at most,

$$(n-1) + (n-2) + \ldots + 3 + 2 + 1 = (n-1)*n/2 = O(n^2).$$

This bound is realized in the worst-case scenario, which is achieved if the objects were placed in the array in reverse order.

On the average, each time through the outer loop, the inner loop would bubble objects halfway up between the object's initial location and the first location in the array. This leads to an inner loop timing of

$$(n-1)/2 + (n-2)/2 + \ldots + 3/2 + 2/2 + 1/2 = n*(n-1)/4 = O(n^2).$$

From this we may observe that both the worst-case and the average-case timings are the same order of magnitude, and the average-case timing of the inner loop takes half the time of the worst case.

The best-case timing is achieved if the inner loop in Listing 11.2 does not iterate. This is realized when the objects in the array are initially in order. The timing for the algorithm is bound by the timing of the outer loop, $O(n)$.

Listing 11.2. Bubble sort algorithm.

```
generic
   type Array_Range is (<>);
   type Object_Type is private;
   type Array_Type  is array (Array_Range range <>) of Object_Type;
   with function Precedes ( Left, Right: Object_Type ) return boolean;
procedure Bubble_Sort ( The_Array: in out Array_Type;
                        Left_End : in     Array_Range:= Array_Range'first;
                        Right_End: in     Array_Range );

-- generic Bubble_Sort body

procedure Bubble_Sort ( The_Array: in out Array_Type;
                        Left_End : in     Array_Range:= Array_Range'first;
                        Right_End: in     Array_Range )     is
   function "<" (Left, Right: Object_Type) return boolean renames Precedes;
   function pred (IX: Array_Range) return Array_Range
                                     renames Array_Range'pred;
   function succ ( IX: Array_Range ) return Array_Range
                                     renames Array_Range'succ;
   Continue_Looping         : boolean;
   Inner_Index, Inner_Plus_1: Array_Range;
   extra                    : Object_Type;
   begin -- of sort
   for outer_index in Left_End .. pred(Right_End) loop
      Inner_Index    := outer_index;
      Inner_Plus_1   := succ (outer_index);
      Continue_Looping:= true;
      while Continue_Looping and then
         not (The_Array(Inner_Index) < The_Array(Inner_Plus_1))
         loop
         extra                     := The_Array(Inner_Index);
         The_Array(Inner_Index)  := The_Array(Inner_Plus_1);
         The_Array(Inner_Plus_1):= extra;
         if Inner_Index = Left_End then
            Continue_Looping:= false;
           else
            Inner_Plus_1:= Inner_Index;
            Inner_Index := pred(Inner_Index);
         end if;
      end loop;
   end loop;
end Bubble_Sort;
```

The best-case timing leads to a special case. Suppose each object is at most k positions from the location where it finally belongs. In this special case, for each object the number of iterations of the inner loop is bound by k for each iteration of the outer loop. Thus, for this case, the algorithm would bound by $k*(n-1) = O(n)$. This is an important observation that leads to the strategy for the Shell sort.

11.1.3 Timing Characteristics

Table 11.1 lists the timings for the selection and bubble sorts. Although both sorts have poor timing characteristics, for the bubble sort the best-case timing and the special-case timing, observed in Section 13.1.2, demonstrate that we should not be so quick to dismiss the bubble sort as a poor sort method. The special case leads to the Shell sort, which first attempts to place objects close to where they belong and then performs a bubble sort.

Table 11.1. $O(n^2)$ sort timing characteristics.

Sort Method	Best	Average	Worst
Selection	$O(n^2)$	$O(n^2)$	$O(n^2)$
Bubble	$O(n)$	$O(n^2)$	$O(n^2)$

11.2 Better Sorts

Although these sorts are referred to as "better," not "best," they are worthy of study for several reasons. First, their algorithms are relatively easy to implement in any programming language, because the algorithms are not very complex. Second, the timing characteristics of these sorts almost mimic the timing of the best sort techniques. The Shell sort is not intuitive in that it is composed of three nested loops! One might think that three nested loops would have worse timing characteristics than two nested loops. However, the timing of an algorithm depends on the combined timing characteristics of each of the nested loops.

Both of these sorts, the Shell sort and the quicksort, share the indication that the sort timings could be in the neighborhood of $O(n \log n)$. In fact, the quicksort, discovered by C. A. O. Hoare, has an average timing of $O(n \log n)$. However, the Quicksort has a potential timing problem that keeps it from being considered as one of the best. But the probability of an occurrence of a poor timing anomaly is substantially reduced with a slight modification of the algorithm.

11.2.1 Shell Sort

A generic Shell sort algorithm appears in Listing 11.3. The approach taken with this algorithm may be described as follows:

> Try to put each number close to where it belongs, and then do a bubble sort.

This approach is accomplished by attempting to overcome a shortcoming in the bubble sort. That shortcoming is that the bubble sort moves objects by moving them only one location at a time. The approach taken with the Shell sort is to compare numbers that are a fixed distance apart and swap pairs of numbers the specified distance apart that do not satisfy the linear ordering. This process is performed several times using successively smaller distances.

Listing 11.3. A generic Shell sort.

```
generic

   type Object_Type is private;
   type Array_Type  is array (positive range <>) of Object_Type;
   with function "<" (Left_Side, Right_Side: Object_Type) return boolean;

procedure Shell_Sort ( Object      : in out Array_Type;
                       No_Of_Objects: in      positive  );

-- Sort Body
procedure Shell_Sort ( Object      : in out Array_Type;
                       No_Of_Objects: in      positive ) is

   Inner_Index: natural;
   Distance   : natural:= No_Of_Objects / 2;
   Extra      : Object_Type;

   begin -- of Shell_Sort
   while Distance >= 1 loop
      for Outer_Index in 1 .. No_Of_Objects - Distance loop
         Inner_Index:= outer_Index;
         while Inner_Index > 0 and then
            not (Object(Inner_Index)
                  < Object(Inner_Index+Distance)) loop
            Extra               := Object(Inner_Index);
            Object(Inner_Index):= Object(Inner_Index+Distance);
            Object(Inner_Index+Distance):= Extra;
            Inner_Index:= Inner_Index - Distance;
         end loop;
      end loop;
      Distance:= Distance / 2;
   end loop;
   end Shell_Sort;
```

The algorithm in Listing 11.3 initially sets the distance at half the size of the array. The inner pair of loops is a bubble sort that bubbles groups of objects. Two objects, *a(i)* and *a(j)*, are in the same group if and only if

$$|i-j| = 0 \ (\text{mod distance}).$$

The algorithm interleaves the sorting of the groups of objects. With the distance equal to 5, there would be five groups of objects, indicated by the sets of indices,

1, 5, 9, . . . ,
2, 6, 10, . . . ,
3, 7, 11, . . . ,

and

4, 8, 12, . . .

Figure 11.1 (i) illustrates the shell sort with a distance of 5, which produces the result in Figure 11.1 (ii). This, in turn is processed with a distance of 2, producing the result that appears in Figure 11.1 (iii), which may now be processed with a distance of 1 and sorting the array.

Timing the Shell sort is a challenge. In fact, the best that has been accomplished in timing the Shell Sort is the observation that its timing falls somewhere between $O(n \log n)$ and $O(n^{1.5})$.

To get a handle on the timing of the Shell sort, first observe the number of iterations of the outer loop. Since `distance` is halved each time the loop iterates, the number of iterations of the outer loop is bound by $O(\log n)$. Under ideal circumstances, if each time through the outer loop, each object is at most some fixed distance *k* from where it belongs, the inner pair of loops would be a bubble sort with time bound by $O(n)$. Therefore, the total timing of the algorithm is bound below by $O(n \log n)$.

Although no useful theoretical upper bound has been found for the Shell sort, experiments with the algorithm have indicated that the upper bound is substantially less than the $O(n^2)$ of the poorer sorts and might be close to $O(n^{1.37})$. The sort timing does seem to depend on the selection of successive distances used in the bubble sort implemented by the inner pair of nested loops. In particular, there should be log *n* values used for the successively decreasing distances. Each distance should be approximately half the previous distance. The best possible timing for the Shell sort seems to be achieved if the successive distances are

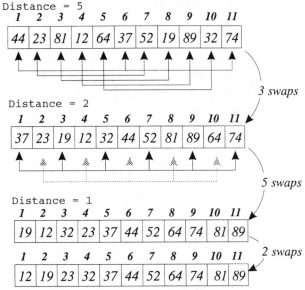

Figure 11.1. Shell sort illustration.

relatively prime. That is, the sequence of distances

$$1, 2, 4, 8, 16, \ldots, n/2$$

will normally produce poorer timing results than a sequence like

$$1, 2, 3, 7, 17, 31, \ldots, n/2.$$

Experimenting with various sets of distances is left as an exercise.

11.2.2 Quicksort

The quicksort is called a distributed sort technique. It lends itself to a recursive algorithm that sorts a piece of the array at a time. The approach taken by the quicksort is as follows:

> Given a key object, determine where it belongs. In the process
> of determining where it belongs, place all objects that precede it

to the left of where the key belongs and place all the objects that follow it to exactly where the key object belongs.

Listing 11.4 contains an example quicksort algorithm. This version of the procedure contains a recursive sorting algorithm. The algorithm is straight-forward. An object is selected and placed into the variable `Key_Object`. As part of the selection process, the location 1 in the array is vacated. The main looping structure of the algorithm is a `while` loop that contains two other loops. The two inner loops work in tandem, one incrementing `Right_Index` down from the high end and the other incrementing `Left_Index` up from the low end.

Since the loop begins with location 1 available, the first inner loop searches from the high end of the array, decrementing the `Right_Index`, until it finds an object less than the `Key_Object`. When it does, that object is moved into location 1. The second inner loop now searches up from the left end, incrementing `Left_Index`, until an object greater than the `Key_Object` is found. When an object is found, it is moved to the location previously vacated and indicated by `Right_Index`. This process continues until `Left_Index` = `Right_Index`, at which point the `Key_Object` may be placed back into the array.

After being processed by the algorithm, the array may be considered as being composed of three components:

a.   That part of the array with indices in the range

```
[Left_End, Left_Index)
```

contains those objects whose values are less than or equal to the value of the `Key_Object`.

b.   The `Key_Object`, which does not have to be moved because it is in the correct position relative to all other objects in the array.

c.   That part of the array with indices in the range

```
(Right_Index, Right_End]
```

contains those objects whose values are greater than or equal to the value of the `Key_Object`.

If either or both of parts **a** and **c** contain more than one object, the algorithm is called to recursively sort those parts of the array.

Listing 11.4. Quicksort algorithm.

```
generic

   type Object_Type is private;
   type Array_Type  is array (positive range <>) of Object_Type;
   with function "<"
            ( Left_Side, Right_Side: Object_Type) return boolean;

procedure Quick_Sort ( Object           : in out Array_Type;
                       Number_Of_Objects: in      positive   );

procedure Quick_Sort ( Object           : in out Array_Type;
                       Number_Of_Objects: in      positive ) is

   procedure Recursive_Quick ( Object    : in out Array_Type;
                               Left_End,
                               Right_End: in      positive ) is

      Left_Index : natural    := Left_End;
      Right_Index: natural    := Right_End;
      Key_Object : Object_Type;

   begin -- of Recursive_Quick
   if Left_End < Right_End then
       Key_Object:= Object (Left_End);
       while Left_Index /= Right_Index loop
          --| Move the Right_Index <--
          while Right_Index /= Left_Index and then
                not (Object(Right_Index) < Key_Object) loop
             Right_Index:= Right_Index - 1;
          end loop;
          Object(Left_Index):= Object(Right_Index);
          --| Move the Left_Index -->
          while Left_Index /= Right_Index and then
                not ( Key_Object < Object(Left_Index) ) loop
             Left_Index:= Left_Index + 1;
          end loop;
          Object(Right_Index):= Object(Left_Index);
       end loop;
       --| Left_Index = Right_Index and ...
       Object(Left_Index):= Key_Object;

       if Left_End+1 < Left_Index then
           Recursive_Quick (Object, Left_End, Left_Index-1);
       end if;
       if Right_Index+1 < Right_End then
           Recursive_Quick (Object, Right_Index+1, Right_End);
       end if;
   end if;
   end Recursive_Quick;

   begin -- of Quick_Sort
   Recursive_Quick (Object, 1, Number_Of_Objects);
   end Quick_Sort;
```

Timing the sort involves a careful look at the timing of each recursive call and determining the number of recursive calls. The time for each recursive call is bound by the sum of the number of iterations of the two inner loops. Since one loop starts at the `Right_End` and iterates down and the other loop starts at `Left_End` and iterates up until the two indices are equal, the timing for one recursive call is bound by the size of the piece of the array being processed.

To arrive at the timing for one particular case, assume that during each recursive process the `Key_Object` that is selected is placed close to the middle of the piece of the array being processed. In this case, an array of size n is split into two arrays whose size is approximately $n/2$. Each of these pieces is split into two pieces of size $n/2/2 = n/4$. This splitting continues until each piece contains a single object and the recursion halts. The depth of this splitting, under our assumption that during each recursive call, `Key_Object` comes very close to splitting the piece of the array in half, is log n. The sum of the length of all the pieces processed yields the order of magnitude of the timing;

$$n + (n/2 + n/2) + 4\,(n/4) + \ldots + =$$
$$n + n + \ldots + n \qquad \{\text{there are log } n \text{ "}n\text{"s}\}$$
$$= O(n \log n).$$

This case happens to illustrate the best-case timing. For the quicksort, this also happens to be the average-case timing. Unfortunately, the worst-case timing for the quicksort is $O(n^2)$. This case may be arrived at by considering the quicksorting of an array that is already sorted. This is left as an exercise for the reader.

Fortunately, there is a way to keep the quicksort away from its worse-case result. This method involves the use of a random number generator. Assume `Random` is a package containing an integer random number generator,

```
. . . := Random.Integer (Left, Right);
```

that returns a random integer in the interval [`Left`, `Right`]. The random number generator is used to select the location from which the `Key_Object` is chosen. Swap this value with the value in the first location,

```
R_Index:= Random.Integer (Left_End, Right_End);
Key_Object        := object (R_Index);
object (R_Index):= object (Left_End);
```

and then use the rest of the algorithm in Listing 11.4.

The selection of the object whose location must be determined during each iteration of the recursive process has a major impact on the eventual timing of the algorithm.

11.2.3 Timing Characteristics

The timing characteristics of the Shell and quicksort methods are summarized in Table 11.2. Although precise theoretical timing results are not available for the Shell sort, there is substantial information that indicates that in practice it is an excellent sort. I saw one example many years ago where an updating process based on a bubble sort was replaced by a Shell sort. As a result, a program that ran in about 1.5 hours took only 10 minutes after the Shell sort was installed.

The average timing for the quicksort makes it a prime candidate for basic array sorting. However, in practice, several variations are employed. First, the use of the random number generator to select Key_Object dramatically reduces the probability of a worst-case scenario. Next, rather than having the recursive process continue subdividing the array down to single object pieces, a practical algorithm goes down to somewhere between 20 and 40 objects and reverts to a simple sort, like a bubble sort, for these small pieces of the array. The claim is that although a simple sort, like a bubble sort, might have poor theoretical timing, in fact the algorithm overhead on small array pieces outweighs the actual results when compared to a bubble sort on small pieces. That tradeoff is typically encountered in the range of 20 to 40 objects.

Table 11.2. Better sort timings.

Sort	Worst	Average	Best
Shell	??	??	??
	$O(n^{1.5})$ >=	?? >=	$O(n \log n)$
Quicksort	$O(n^2)$	$O(n \log n)$	$O(n \log n)$

11.3 *O(n* log *n)* Sorts

Three sort methods are discussed in this section, the heapsort, the mergesort, and a "realworld" variation of the mergesort, called the polyphase mergesort.

11.3.1 Heapsort

The heapsort was presented in Section 7.2.1. The timing for each phase of the heapsort is easily bound. During the first phase, $n-1$ nodes in the tree are processed to order the heap. The sifting up of each node is bound by the length of the longest path in the tree, log n. Therefore, the timing of phase one is bound by $(n-1)$log n.

During phase two, $n-1$ nodes are pruned from the heap and sifted down. As in the first phase, the sifting process is bound by the length of the longest path in the tree, log n. Hence the second phase is bound by

$$(n\text{-}1)\log n.$$

Therefore, the timing, T, of the entire heapsort satisfies

$$T <= 2(n\text{-}1)\log n = O(n \log n).$$

11.3.2 Mergesort

The approach taken by the merge sort may be described as follows:

> Given two ordered collections of objects, merge them together as a single ordered collection of objects by comparing the first object in the one collection with the first object in the other and removing the object that would be placed first by the ordering function from its collection and placing it into the rear of the newly formed collection. Continue this until all objects are placed.

To illustrate, consider the two ordered collections of integers

12, 25, 36, 44, 62

and

    <u>8</u>, 27, 33, 52, 59

The mergesort would compare the two values underscored and move the smaller value to the rear of the new collection being formed:

    New Collection   Old Collections
                      <u>12</u>, 25, 36, 44, 62
    8   (i)
                      <u>27</u>, 33, 52, 59

As a result, the numbers 12 and 27 are compared and 12 would be moved. As the process continues, the new collection is formed

                      <u>25</u>, 36, 44, 62
    8, 12   (ii)
                      <u>27</u>, 33, 52, 59

                      <u>36</u>, 44, 62
    8, 12, 25   (iii)
                      <u>27</u>, 33, 52, 59

and the process finally produces the ordered collection

    8, 12, 25, 27, 33, 36, 44, 52, 59, 62

Figure 11.2 illustrates how a mergesort might work on an array of 12 objects. The merge process initially views the array as 12 collections of 1 object. These 12 collections are merged two at a time into six collections of 2 objects. The six collections of two objects are then merged into three collections of four objects. At this point, the merge process would merge two of these collections together and form an ordered collection of eight objects. Finally, the collection of eight is merged with the remaining collection of four, forming the ordered collection of objects.

    The mergesort timing may be observed as follows: The total timing of the merge algorithm is the same order of magnitude as the number of times objects are moved from one of the old ordered collections into the new ordered

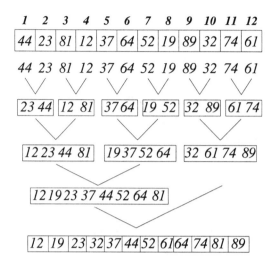

Figure 11.2. Mergesort illustration.

collection.   Following the levels of successive merges, as illustrated in
Figure 11.2, at the first level, *n* objects are moved from *n* collections of one
object to *n/2* collections of two objects. This requires *n* moves, hence is bound
by *O(n)*. At the next level, *n/2* collections of two objects are merged into *n/4*
collections of four objects. The timing of this level is also bound by *O(n)*. In
fact, the timing at each level is bound by *O(n)*. Hence, the total timing of a
complete merge process is bound by *O(number of levels * n)*. Since the goal at
each level is to halve the number of collections, the number of levels is of order
log *n*, producing the timing bound *O(n log n)* for the mergesort.

A complete merge algorithm is normally composed of two processes. The
first process is the merging process, described above. The merge process is
continued until one of the two collections is empty. At this point, the merge
algorithm must take the objects remaining in the nonempty collection and place
them at the rear of the new collection.

The merge algorithm does not lend itself well to array processing. Typical
array implementations of the mergesort use two arrays and move the objects from
one array to the other in performing the merge process. Merging does lend itself
to processing lists and queues of ordered objects.

11.3.3 Polyphase Merge

The mergesort lends itself well to merging ordered collections of objects. The polyphase merge is a practical version of a mergesort. Many sort processors made available in operating systems are based on the polyphase mergesort. The polyphase merge is best described as if the objects are stored on magnetic tapes. The minimum resources required for a polyphase merge are three tape drives or the ability to manipulate three sequential files at one time. An assumption made in performing a polyphase merge is that the number of objects to be sorted, n, is so large that all the objects cannot be placed in memory at the same time, but the memory is sufficiently large to place some number k of objects, $k > 2$, in memory at one time.

Under these assumptions, the polyphase merge operates as follows:

> First, k object are placed in memory and sorted. This sorted collection is placed on one of two tape drives. This process continues until all objects are placed into a sorted grouping s on two tapes. Next, one sorted group from each of the two drives are merged and placed on the third drive. When all the groups are processed from one of the tapes, groups on the other two tapes are merged and sorted groups are placed on the remaining tape. This process continues until a single ordered collection appears on one drive.

Figure 11.3 illustrates the operation of the polyphase mergesort. First, the objects collected on tape A are read into the computer, k objects at a time, and the sorted group is placed on one of the other two tape drives. When this processed is completed, a number of sorted collections appear on tapes B and C. Tape A is now available. The collections on tapes B and C are merged and placed onto tape A until one of the tapes B or C is emptied. At this point, the collections on tapes A and C are merged onto B. This process continues until a single collection is formed.

An obvious question that arises is: How many ordered collections must be initially formed and how should they be placed on the two available tapes so that the merging process may easily bounce back and forth among the drives and produce a single collection on one drive? The answer to this question may be obtained by working backwards. One collection on one drive is obtained by merging one collection, each from the other two drives.

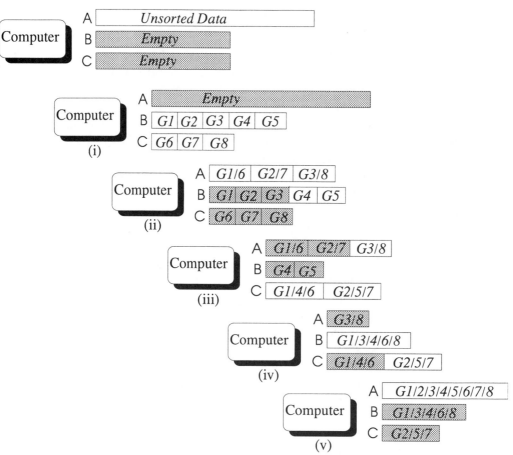

Figure 11.3. Polyphase illustration.

Table 11.3 illustrates the number of groups on each drive during each phase, starting with the last phase and working backwards. The number of ordered groups on each tape during one phase is arrived at by taking the larger number and assuming that this number was formed by merging that number of groups from the two other tapes. As a result, at the beginning of each phase, the number of groups on two tapes must be two consecutive Fibonacci numbers. This guarantees that the polyphase process leads directly to one group on one tape.

During the initial phase, if the number of ordered groups of numbers does not equal two consecutive Fibonacci numbers, then null collections may be added to one of the tapes to start the process correctly.

Table 11.3. Polyphase collections.

```
                    A     B     C

                    1     -     -    (1)
                    -     1     1    (2)
                    1     -     2    (3)
                    3     2     -    (4)
                    -     5     3    (5)
                    5     -     8    (6)
                   13     8     -    (7)
                    -    21    13    (8)
                           . . .
                  F(i)  F(i-1)  (i)
```

Although the description above illustrates the polyphase merge using three
tapes, or sequential files, the process may be performed with t tapes, merging t-1
at a time. It is an interesting exercise, and is left as one, to determine the number
of groups of ordered objects that must be placed on t-1 tapes to guarantee that
the merge leads to one ordered group on one tape.

11.4 Explorations

1. Verify the performance characteristics of the bubble sort by running it with
   several sets to observe its performance with random sets of data and data sets
   where the numbers are almost in order.
2. Experiment with the following variation of the Shell sort: In a Shell sort,
   instead of simply dividing the previous distance by two (50, 25, 12, . . .),
   create a predefined set of distances. Check the performance with various sets
   of predefined distances, and verify whether a choice of predefined distances
   maximizes the number of distances used that are relatively prime to each
   other. For example, would the set of distances (1, 2, 3, 7, 17, . . .) produce
   better timing results than (1, 2, 4, 8, 16, . . .)?
3. A random number generator is used with the quicksort to avoid the possible
   anomaly of $O(n^2)$ timing. Assuming a random number generator is not
   available, devise an alternate plan to avoid $O(n^2)$ timing. Build your
   algorithm and test it.
4. Build and test the mergesort procedure described in Section 11.3.2.
5. Build and test a polyphase mergesort that uses three sequential files to
   simulate the three queues.

6. The following three tables of data contain samples of the loop counts required to sort 100, 200, 300, 400, and 500 objects from each of five data sets. One of these five data sets is a random set of data, and another is a set of data where each object is almost where it belongs. The three main data sets are one set in order, one in reverse order, and one of identical objects. Determine which data set is which. Also, guess at the sort technique represented by each of the three collections of data. Provide rationale for your choices as to which data set is which and which sort technique is represented by each set of data.

Set 1	100	200	300	400	500
Data #1	509	1210	2112	2811	3514
Data #2	769	1830	3112	4251	5614
Data #3	509	1210	2112	2811	3514
Data #4	663	1526	2487	3472	4215
Data #5	957	2266	3480	4527	5861

Set 2	100	200	300	400	500
Data #1	726	1712	2718	3608	5012
Data #2	616	1650	2495	3556	5877
Data #3	324	745	1186	1686	2031
Data #4	636	1544	2496	3619	4857
Data #5	589	1515	2244	3412	5398

Set 3	100	200	300	400	500
Data #1	99	199	299	399	499
Data #2	5049	20099	45149	80199	125249
Data #3	99	199	299	399	499
Data #4	398	791	1192	1582	1956
Data #5	2669	9985	22523	39495	62879

12

Search/Update

Different methods of organizing information lead to various method of seeking objects. Chapter 7 described several important search and update methods based on tree structures. This chapter describes several classical search and update techniques based on array access. Each technique depends on a particular array organization method and involves tradeoffs between the algorithm that organizes the data and the algorithm that searches for information. **Searching** is the seeking of a particular object in a structure. In this chapter, the structures happen to be arrays. **Updating** refers to the process of adding one or more objects to a structure.

Search and update combine with sorting to form the foundation for organizing and retrieving information. Searching takes advantage of the method of data organization to locate information. Updating is inserting, or deleting, a few objects in the organized collection. The sequential search algorithm is included to illustrate searching and updating a collection of data that is not ordered. The bisection method takes full advantage of ordering. The block sequential and address calculation methods demonstrate two array-ordering techniques that do not directly employ a linear ordering of the objects in the array. Each of these methods has tradeoffs between the searching and updating processes.

12.1 Sequential Search

Given an array of objects, a sequential search simply starts at the first location and searches sequentially until the object is located or until it is determined that the object is not in the array. Listing 12.1 illustrates a sequential search process. If n objects are in the array, the average search time is $O(n/2)$. If the object is not in the array, the search processes the entire array and hence is $O(n)$ time.

There are some advantages to a simple sequential search. First, no sorting of the objects is required. Second, updating the collection of objects takes only a constant amount of time to place the new object at the end of the array and updating the count of the number of objects.

Removing an object, once its location is known, may be quickly accomplished by placing the last object in the array in the vacated location and resetting the count of the number of objects.

There is one serious disadvantage to the sequential search. Its timing is $O(n)$. The other search techniques described ahead are substantially faster. If one expects to perform a very large number of searches, the other techniques offer substantial advantages over a sequential search.

Listing 12.1. Sequential search algorithm.

```
generic

    type Object_Type is private;
    type Array_Type is array (integer range <>) of Object_Type;

function Linear_Search ( Look_For : Object_Type;
                         The_Array: Array_Type) return integer;


function Linear_Search ( Look_For : Object_Type;
                         The_Array: Array_Type) return integer is

    begin -- Linear_Search
    for Index in The_Array'range loop
       if Look_For = The_Array (Index) then
           return Index;
       end if;
    end loop;
    raise constraint_error;
    end Linear_Search;
```

12.2 **Bisection Method Search**

The **bisection method search**, also called **binary search**, assumes the collection of objects has been ordered. This method selects the object at the center of the array range being searched and determines the relationship of that object to the object being sought. Depending on whether the object being sought precedes or follows the object at the center of the array range, the algorithm uses this result to bisect the search range and recursively continues the process.

Listing 12.2 illustrates a recursive version of the bisection search algorithm. This process cuts the search space in half during each recursive call. If the array contains n objects, the search is bound by $O(\log n)$ recursive calls. This timing bound may be derived by observing that each recursive call reduces the search space by one-half. The original space was of size n. The number of recursive calls is bound by k, where k is the integer for which $2^k <= n < 2^{k+1}$. Hence, $k = O(\log n)$.

Listing 12.2. Bisection search algorithm.

```
generic

   type Object_Type is private;
   type Ordered_Array is array (integer range <>) of Object_Type;
   with function "<" ( Left, Right: in Object_Type ) return boolean;

function Bisection_Search ( Looking_For: Object_Type;
                            The_Array   : Ordered_Array;
                            Last_Index  : integer         ) return integer;

function Bisection_Search ( Looking_For: Object_Type;
                            The_Array   : Ordered_Array;
                            Last_Index  : integer         ) return integer is

   Left   : integer:= 0;           --The_Array (Left) < Looking_For
   Right  : integer:= Last_Index;--Looking_For <= The_Array(Right)
   Middle: integer;

   begin -- Bisection_Search
   while (Left+1) < Right loop
      Middle:= (Left + Right) / 2;
      if The_Array (Middle) < Looking_For then
         Left := Middle; -- The_Array (Left) < Looking_For
       else
         Right:= Middle; -- Looking_For <= The_Array (Right)
      end if;
   end loop;
   return Right;
   end Bisection_Search;
```

The obvious advantage to the bisection is its very fast search time. This search time is a major advantage when a very large number of searches are expected with very few updates. The only apparent disadvantage is updating. Whether objects are inserted or removed from the array, the time to update the array is $O(n)$. This disadvantage is not a problem if only a few updates are expected. If updates are expected to be relatively frequent, then the search methods discussed in Sections 12.3 and 12.4 are more appropriate.

12.3 Block Sequential Search/Update

If a large number of updates are expected, since the bisection method search requires a sorted array, each update requires $O(n)$ time. It would be desirable to have a method of searching and updating where the search and update times are about the same order of magnitude and still reasonably fast. The block sequential method does just that.

The block sequential search requires an initialization. Assume k blocks are used in this search method. This method requires a collection of n representative objects. The representative objects are sorted and placed one per block into the first location of each block. Figure 12.1 illustrates an initial configuration for a block sequential search. The representative objects are sorted. After the sorting, the first object is placed in the first block, the second object in the second block, and so forth. Each object is followed by a sentinel value, the algorithm recognizes as a sign that there are no more objects in the block.

With this setup, the search and update algorithms share a common piece of code that locates the starting point for the algorithm. Given a value x, regardless of whether x is being sought or being placed in the array, the algorithm first compares x to the first object in each block until x is less than the object at the beginning of one block. When it is, the algorithm then backs up and sequentially searches the previous block until x is located, an object greater than x is located, or all objects in the block have been searched. At this point, if the algorithm was searching for x, it can report on the result of the search. If the algorithm was an update, the algorithm may place x at that point in the block and move all objects down one, including the sentinel object. Figure 12.2 illustrates a block sequential structure after several objects are placed into the structure.

In either case, the search or update time is the time required to find the block plus the time to search through the block. Hence, it is bound by

$$O(n/k + k).$$

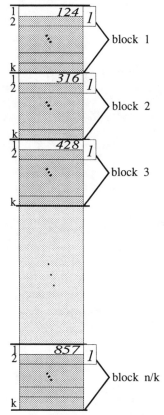

Figure 12.1. Block sequential setup.

The update time is $O(k)$; hence, the update time is bound by

$$O(n/k + k)+O(k) = O(n/k + k).$$

Since the timing is represented as a function of n and k,

$$T = n/k + k,$$

calculus may be used to determine the minimum value for the function. The minimum is achieved when $k = \sqrt{n}$ and produces a timing $T = O(\sqrt{n})$.

Although the block sequential search/update has the desirable attribute that both the search and update times are of the same order of magnitude, it does have its drawbacks. For example, if the initial set of values used to initialize the

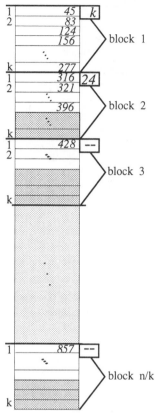

Figure 12.2. Block structure after inserts.

blocks is not representative, a block may overflow. Therefore, the support should contain a method for handling block overflow or for reorganizing the blocks. Overflow handling, or block reorganization, could become time consuming.

Specifications for a block sequential search/update package appear in Listing 12.3. The private types `Collection_Type` and `Access_Type` hide details of the representation of the block sequential structure. A `Collection_Type` object must be initialized by passing an `Init_Array_Type` array containing representative objects to the `Initialize` procedure. Once initialized, the other procedures update the structure by inserting and deleting objects and searching through the structure. Block overflow may occur because of an unusual distribution of the objects placed in the structure, or because of a poor choice of objects used to initialize the array. The operation of the `reorganize` procedure is left as an exercise.

Listing 12.3. Block sequential specifications.

```
generic
    Block_Size      : positive:= 50;
    Number_Of_Blocks: positive:= 50;
    type Object_Type is private;
    with function "<" ( left, right: Object_Type) return boolean;
package Blk_Sqtl is
    type Block_Seq is private;
    type Object_Access  is private;
    subtype Block_Range  is positive range 1 .. Number_Of_Blocks;
    type Init_Array_Type is array (Block_Range) of Object_Type;

    procedure Initialize ( Structure :     out Block_Seq;
                           Init_Array: in      Init_Array_Type );
    procedure Insert ( An_Object: in     Object_Type;
                       Structure: in out Block_Seq );
    procedure Delete ( An_Object: in     Object_Type;
                       Structure: in out Block_Seq );
    procedure Reorganize ( Structure: in out Block_Seq );
    function Get_Access ( Object   : Object_Type;
                          Structure: Block_Seq ) return Object_Access;
    function Get_Object ( Object_ptr: Object_Access;
                          Structure : Block_Seq ) return Object_Type;
    procedure Update ( Object     : in      Object_Type;
                       Object_ptr : in      Object_Access;
                       Structure  : in out Block_Seq);
    generic
        with procedure Process ( Object  : in out Object_Type;
                                 Continue:     out boolean );
    procedure Block_Iterator ( Block: in out Object_Access );
    function First (Object_Ptr: Object_Access) return Object_Access;
    function Last (Object_Ptr: Object_Access) return Object_Access;
    function Pred (Object_Ptr: in Object_Access) return Object_Access;
    function Succ (Object_Ptr: in Object_Access) return Object_Access;

    Block_Filled, Object_Not_In_Block, Object_Update_Error,
    Not_Initialized, Structure_Error, Block_Error: exception;
private
    subtype Xtd_Sub_Block_Range is natural range 0 .. Block_Size;
    subtype Sub_Block_Range    is Xtd_Sub_Block_Range range 1 .. Block_Size;
    type    Sub_Block_Array    is array (Sub_Block_Range) of object_type;
    type    sub_Object_Access   is
        record
            Number_In_Block: Xtd_Sub_Block_Range:= 0;
            Item            : Sub_Block_Array;
        end record;
    type Block_Seq     is array (Block_Range) of Sub_Object_Access;
    type Structure_Ptr is access Block_Seq;
    type Object_Access is
        record
            Structure    : Structure_Ptr      := null;
            Block_Number : Block_Range;
            Object_Number: Xtd_Sub_Block_Range:= 0;
        end record;
end Blk_Sqtl;
```

The `Get_Access` function provides access to individual objects in the structure. `Get_Object` obtains the value of the object at the location indicated by the `Object_Access` parameter. Searching to see if an object, `x`, is in the structure is performed as

```
x = Get_Object(Get_Access(X, Structure), Structure)
```

where `Structure` is a `Collection_Type`.

Frequently, users of a collection require alternate methods of accessing a structure in an exhaustive fashion. The package specifications support two types of exhaustive access, one through the entire structure and one through a block. The `generic` procedure `Block_Iterator` allows a user to instantiate the iterator with a procedure and apply the process to an arbitrary block. Through the function, `First`, `Last`, `Pred`, and `Succ`, users may sequentially process the objects in the structure. A user may use `First` or `Last` to begin at one end or the other of the entire structure, then use `Pred` and `Succ` to sequentially process the objects.

Note that objects in the structure may be modified with either the `Update` procedure or the procedure used to instantiate the `Block_Iterator`. However, an exception would be raised if the attempt to update an object changes the order of the object in the structure.

The `private` declarations in Listing 12.3 illustrate the structures that represent the block sequential structure. The structure is an array of blocks. Each block is stored in a record containing a count of the number of objects in the block and an array of `Object_Type`. As objects are inserted or removed, the count for the block contained in the record is updated. Building the body of the package is left as an exercise.

12.4 Address Calculation Search/Update

There are many search update scenarios where the universal set of potential objects is very large, M, but the actual number of objects, m, in the collection is relatively small and the size of the target array, n, where the objects are placed is sufficient, $n > m$, to hold the actual number of anticipated objects. This set of circumstances lends itself to the address calculation techniques.

The address calculation search update process attempts the impossible, a search update method that takes a constant amount of time for each search or update. The desired ideal may be approached under certain circumstances. These circumstances typically require some knowledge about the distribution of expected values as well as a value that will not be in the distribution. In general, the address calculation function requires

1. a linear ordering function for the collection of objects,
2. a cumulative distribution function for the collection of objects,
3. a "null object," an object not expected to be in the collection should be known.

Figure 12.3 illustrates the basic concept, namely that there is a direct connection between the value of the object and the object's location in the array. This object-to-array-index association is normally achieved with a cumulative distribution function. A **cumulative distribution** function, C, satisfies

$$0 <= C(x) <= 1$$

and $x_i < x_j$ if and only if $C(x_i) < C(x_j)$. The cumulative function value may then be mapped onto the array range.

A cumulative distribution function may be derived from a probability distribution function. A **probability distribution** function, f, satisfies

(1) $f(x) > 0$ for all x, and

(2) $\int_{-\infty}^{\infty} f(x)dx = 1$.

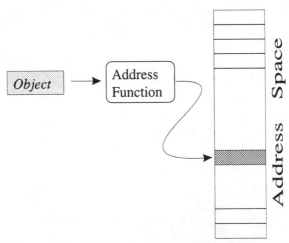

Figure 12.3. Address calculation concept.

Then the cumulative distribution function, C, is

$$C(x)= \int_{-\infty}^{x} f(x)dx.$$

The simplest cases of the address calculation method involve linear ordered objects, like ranges of numbers. Figure 12.4 illustrates the case where the objects are numeric values over a fixed range and the expected values are uniformly distributed over the range. If these values are placed in an array of size n, then the relationship between the values and their anticipated positions is linear and is given by the equation of the straight line

$$y = m(x - First) + 1,$$

where the slope m is given by

$$m = (Last - First)/(n - 1).$$

The address calculation method works best if the size of the array is substantially larger than the anticipated number of objects. Also, the support algorithms must expect worst-case possibilities, including that two or more objects might correspond to the same address.

The address calculation algorithm described in this section assumes there is a null object. The array is initialized with the null object to indicate that all positions in the array are available. Both searching and updating use the same

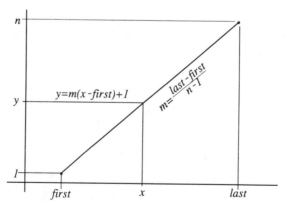

Figure 12.4. Address function for numeric objects.

address calculation function to locate the possible position of an object. If the space indicated by the address calculation contains a null object, then that space contains no object, and an update process could directly place the object in that location. However, if there is an object in that space, it might not be the one being sought. If the location is occupied by another object, a sequential search is made from that location until the process is resolved.

The heart of the address calculation approach is the `address_of` function that appears in the package body. The function, which appears in Listing 12.4, uses the `distribution` function from the package's instantiation. The `address_of` function expands the value returned by the distribution function to the range `1..an_array.size`. The function also tests for anomalies and adjusts them to the desired range before returning the value.

To illustrate a typical distribution function, assume the objects being manipulated are uniformly distributed in a specified range, as illustrated in Figure 12.4. The distribution function for this example is given by

```
function Uniform ( Object: in float ) return positive is
    begin -- Uniform
    return (Object-First_Object)/(Last_Object-First_Object);
    end Uniform;
```

The address calculation function determines where an object should be placed in an array. However, two or more objects may have the same address, which is referred to as an address **collision**. Address calculation packages must have a strategy for resolving collisions. There are many potential collision resolution strategies. This section describes two, chaining and linear searching. Other strategies are discussed in Section 12.5, on hashing.

Listing 12.4. The `Address_of` function.

```
function Address_Of ( Object  : float;
                      An_Array: adrs_calc_array) return positive    is

    Answer: integer;

    begin -- Address_Of
    Answer:= integer (float(An_Array.size - 1)
                    * distribution (Object));
    if Answer < 1 then
        Answer:= 1;
    end if;
    if Answer > An_Array.size then
        Answer:= An_Array.size;
    end if;
    return Answer;
    end Address_Of;
```

The chaining approach does not require a `Null_Object`. In the chaining approach, the array is an array of lists and the address calculation function computes an index into an array of lists. Each list is a list of the objects in the structure with the same address calculation result. Building this type of address calculation package is left as an exercise.

The second approach uses the address calculation as if it is an approximation of the location of the object, and linear searching and insertions are made relative to the calculated address. The `Is_In` function, in Listing 12.5, illustrates the search strategy. The algorithm is fundamentally a selection structure that first tests for a potential `Illegal_Object` exception. The next two alternatives test whether the computed address contains a `Null_Object` - in which case the function returns `false` - or the object being sought - in which case the function

Listing 12.5. An address calculation `Is_In` function.

```
function Is_In ( Object : float;
                 Ad_Array: adrs_calc_array) return boolean is

Index: positive:= Address_Of (Object, Ad_Array);

begin
if Object = null_Object then
    raise Illegal_Object;
  elsif Object = Ad_Array.Item (Index) then
    return true;
  elsif Null_Object = Ad_Array.Item (Index) then
    return false;
  elsif Object < Ad_Array.Item (Index) then
    while Index > 1
         and then Ad_Array.Item(Index) /= null_Object
         and then Object < Ad_Array.Item (Index) loop
       Index:= Index - 1;
    end loop;
    if Ad_Array.Item (Index) = Object then
        return true;
      else
        return false;
    end if;
  else
    while Index < Ad_Array.size
         and then Ad_Array.Item(Index) /= null_Object
         and then Object > Ad_Array.Item (Index) loop
       Index:= Index + 1;
    end loop;
    if Ad_Array.Item (Index) = Object then
        return true;
      else
        return false;
    end if;
end if;
end Is_In;
```

returns true. The two remaining alternatives search sequentially in one or the other direction depending on whether the object at the location indicated by the address calculation is either greater than or less than the object being sought.

The structures of the insert and remove algorithms have similar complexity. Listing 12.6 illustrates the Insert algorithm for the address calculation search. This algorithm first tests for an exception. If none is raised, it searches in both directions, starting at the index computed by the address calculation. The search proceeds until a Null_Object is found or until there is no space available in the array. If a Null_Object is found, the new object is bubbled into the array so that the linear ordering is maintained. This requires two loops, one to bubble up from Low_Index and the other to bubble down from High_Index depending on where Null_Object was found. Completing the Insert procedure is left as an exercise.

Listing 12.6. An address calculation Insert algorithm.

```
procedure Insert ( Object  : in      float;
                   Ad_Array: in out Adrs_Calc_Array) is

Index     : positive:= Address_Of (Object, Ad_Array);
Low_Index: positive:= Index;
Up_Index : positive:= Index;

begin
if Object < first_Object or Last_Object < Object then
    raise illegal_Object;
  else
      while   Ad_Array.Item (Low_Index) /= Null_Object
              and Ad_Array.Item (Up_Index) /= Null_Object
              and Low_Index /= 1
              and  Up_Index /= Ad_Array.Size loop
        if Low_Index /= 1 then
            Low_Index:= Low_Index - 1;
        end if;
        if Up_Index /= Ad_Array.Size then
            Up_Index:= Up_Index + 1;
        end if;
      end loop;
      if Ad_Array.Item (Low_Index) = Null_Object then
          -- bubble new Object in from below
          . . .
        elsif Ad_Array.Item (Up_Index) = Null_Object then
          -- bubble new Object in from above
          . . .
        else
            raise Constraint_Error;
      end if;
  end if;
end Insert;
```

12.5 Hashing

One class of objects that lend themselves to an address calculation-like strategy is strings. Various calculations may be performed on the bits patterns that form the characters in the string to create an address from the bit pattern. This address may be used in ways similar to the address calculation search. **Hashing** is the application of address calculation strategies to strings. There is one fundamental difference between hashing and address calculation. Address calculation might use the linear ordering of the objects, and objects of similar value associate to close addresses. Hashing, on the other hand, makes no attempt to associate any possible string ordering to the positions where the objects are placed into the array.

A discussion of hashing must address three topics:

1. the desirable traits of hashing functions,
2. hashing methods,
3. collision resolution.

One obvious trait that hashing functions should have is that the function should distribute the collection of potential strings in a relatively uniform way into the target array. Other desirable traits have to do with the way certain strings are distributed relative to each other. For example, the hash function should take strings that are similar, like **bat**, **bit**, **but**, and **bite**, and compute different target values for these strings. One reason why this trait is desirable is that many applications involve situations where users may use similar strings or strings using the same symbols but in different orders, like **pat**, **tap**, and **apt**.

These problems may be resolved with string hashing by the classical methods of forming hashing functions. These methods normally involve various manipulations of bit patterns of the characters by pattern shifting and various boolean and integer arithmetic operations of the bit patterns.

To simplify the discussion of these methods, assume the hash function must compute an array index in the range $0 .. 2^k-1$. This range of 2^k values may be represented with exactly k bits. For the illustrations ahead, assume $k = 10$ hence, the range would be $0 .. 1023$.

One hashing method is **folding**. Folding takes the string of characters and views it as a string of bits. If the string has n characters, there are $8n$ bits. These $8n$ bits are collected together in groups of 10 bits. If the last group of bits does not contain 10 bits, it is padded with zeros or ones. These groups of 10 bits are **folded** together with a boolean operation, like **exclusive or**. The result is a

hashed 10-bit pattern, which may be viewed as an integer value in the range *0 .. 1023*.

The folding method works well when the table size is a power of two. If the table is of size *n*, with a range 0 .. *n*-1, the hashing-by-division method works well. If the string of characters is viewed as a binary value, *S*, the hash function *h* is defined as

$$h(S) = S \bmod n.$$

This method works well, but certain values for *n* should be avoided. Specifically, *n* should not be even because the hash function would map strings whose value is even onto even indices and strings that are odd onto odd indices. That is, one bit in the string plays a significant role in determining the possible corresponding indices. This is not desirable.

In general, the value *n* selected for a division method should be prime. However, certain primes should be avoided. Research into the selection of *n* has shown that nonprime values of *n* may be good choices if *n* contains no small primes less than 20. Other poor choices for *n* are

$$n = p^k \pm 1,$$

where *p* is prime and *r* is the radix of the character set. For Ada 83, *r* = 128. For Ada 95, *r* = 256.

There are two popular hashing methods based on multiplication. One, called the **mid-square** method, takes bit patterns and squares them. The purpose of this method is to randomize the bits used to form the hash value. For example, suppose the strings being hashed are formed as strings of uppercase alphabetic characters. This represents only 26 of the 127 available character patterns. Further, these 26 patterns are sequential, not distributed, in the ASCII scheme. However, if each 8-bit pattern is viewed as an integer value and that value is squared, the result is a 16-bit pattern:

$$b_{15}b_{14}b_{13}b_{12}b_{11}b_{10}b_9b_8b_7b_6b_5b_4b_3b_2b_1b_0.$$

The middle of this pattern,

$$b_{10}b_9b_8b_7b_6b_5b_4,$$

produces a value that, when compared to the original, has better scattering over the range of possible values. The drawback to this approach is that if the key begins or ends with a long sequence of zeros, the new key obtained by the mid-square method may also contain a long sequence of zeros.

Another multiplication method that appears to avoid the problems of the mid-square method is the hash function given by the equation

$$h(S) = \text{truncate } (n *((c*S) \bmod 1)),$$

where S is the string, n is the size of the array, and c is a real number, $0 < c < 1$. Naturally, the choice of c is critical. Knuth has found that

$$c = \frac{2}{1+\sqrt{5}} = 0.61803398...$$

is a good choice.

Hashing functions are usually formed through some combination of the methods shown above and other methods of manipulating the bits. As long as the function may be rapidly computed and satisfies the performance criterion, it is acceptable. Hashing is similar to the address calculation method described in Section 12.4, except that no ordering is maintained. However, once the hash function is applied, the hash package must address collision resolution, handling strings that hash to the same array location. There are a number of techniques for addressing collision resolution: linear search, chaining, and double hashing. Linear probe is similar to the linear search method employed in the address

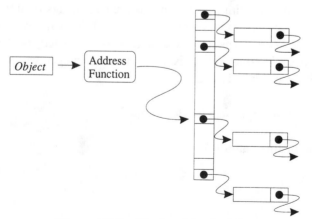

Figure 12.5. Hash with chaining

calculation package described in Section 12.4. Chaining is illustrated in Figure 12.5. In this method, the hash indexes into an array of lists. Each list is a list of the strings whose hash result is the index into this list. Building a hash package with chaining is left as an exercise.

Because of the many applications that require the manipulation of strings, there is substantial literature expanding on the hash methods described here, as well as many other variations, including double hashing and perfect hashing. Readers are encouraged to search the literature, including several articles and texts, including Smith's, which contains a very thorough presentation on hashing.

12.6 Evaluation

The sequential search, presented at the beginning of the chapter, serves as a baseline and should not be considered a serious search/update strategy. The bisection method is a very fast search technique, but updating is relatively expensive. If little or no updating is expected to be performed, the bisection method should be given top consideration.

The block sequential method is an excellent compromise when both searching and updating are intermingled. The block sequential method is an array equivalent of the first fast disk access method called the **indexed sequential access method (ISAM)**. ISAM has been superseded by methods based on the tree restructuring concept described in Chapter 7.

The address calculation method is an excellent method when the data distribution is well known or the size of the array is larger than the expected number of objects. However, if for any reason one expects substantial contention between objects for the same target, the method could become a timing disaster.

Hashing is the premier method for handling tables of strings. The only real alternative is the dictionary tree approach described in Section 7.5. Various hashing methods with chaining are very successful. Also, chaining may be accomplished with arrays, thus avoiding the potential overhead of dynamic storage allocation. There is very interesting literature on perfect hashing functions, which are very useful when there is a predefined collection of search strings. This is very useful for speeding up compilers, where the programming language's reserved words, or lexical symbols, are predefined.

12.7 **Explorations**

1. Implement and test the block sequential search package.
2. Review the probability and statistics literature, and form a taxonomy of cumulative distribution functions. Evaluate various possible applications of the address calculation function where the linear distribution would not be appropriate. For one of these applications, determine which distribution function in your taxonomy is most appropriate for the application under consideration. Provide rationale to defend your selection of a distribution function to represent the application.
3. Implement and test a hashing function.
4. Search the literature on perfect hashing functions and implement a perfect hash for Ada's lexical symbols.

References

1. N. Abramson. *Information Theory and Coding*. McGraw-Hill, New York, 1983.
2. ACM/IEEE-CS Joint Curriculum Task Force. *Computing Curricula 1991*. New York: Association for Computing Machinery, 1991.
3. G. M. Adel'son-Vel'skii and E. M. Landis. An algorithm for the organization of information. *Soviet Mathematics Doklady,* **3**(4):1259-1263, 1962.
4. A. V. Aho, J. E. Hopcroft, and J. D. Ullman. *The Design and Analysis of Computer Algorithms*. Addison-Wesley, Reading, MA, 1974.
5. A. V. Aho, J. E. Hopcroft, and J. D. Ullman. Data Structures and Algorithms. Addison-Wesley, Reading, MA, 1983.
6. B. Allen and I. Munro. Self-organizing search trees. *Journal of the ACM,* **25**(4):526-535, 1978.
7. K. Appel and W. Haken. Every planar map is four colorable. Part I: Discharging. *Illinois Journal of Mathematics,* **21**(3):429-490, 1977.
8. K. Appel and W. Haken. The solution of the four-color map problem. *Scientific American,* **237**(4):108-121, 1977.
9. K. Appel, W. Haken, and J. Koch. Every planar map is four colorable. Part II: Reducibility. *Illinois Journal of Mathematics,* **21**(3):491-567, 1977.
10. S. Baase. *Computer Algorithms: Introduction to Design and Analysis*, 2nd ed. Addison-Wesley, Reading, MA, 1988.
11. D. W. Barron. *Recursive Techniques in Programming*. McDonald, London, 1968.

12.   R. Bayer. Symmetric binary B-trees: Data structure and maintenance algorithms. *Acta Informatica,* **2**(4):290-306, 1972.

13.   J. Beidler. Building on the Booch components: What can be learned when modifying real world software tools for educational use. *Proceeding of Tri-Ada '92.* Orlando, FL, November 18, 1992.

14.   J. Beidler. Structuring iterators to encourage reuse. *Proceeding of Ada-Europe, Paris,* June 1994.

15.   J. L. Bentley. Multidimensional binary search trees used for associative searching. *Communications of the ACM,* **18**(9):509-517, 1975.

16.   J. L. Bentley and J. H. Friedman. Data structures for range searching. *ACM Computing Surveys,* **11**(4):397-409, 1979.

17.   J. L. Bentley. How to sort. *Communications of the ACM,* **27**(4)287, April 1984.

18.   J. L. Bentley. Writing Correct Programs. *Communications of the ACM,* **26**(12)1040, December 1983.

19.   G. Booch. *Software Components with Ada.* Benjamin/Cummings, Menlo Park, CA, 1987.

20.   G. Booch. *Software Engineering with Ada.* Benjamin/Cummings, Menlo Park, CA, 1987.

21.   G. Booch. *Object-Oriented Design: With Applications.* Benjamin/Cummings, Redwood City, CA, 1991.

22.   G. Brassard and P. Bratley. *Algorithmics: Theory and Practice.* Prentice-Hall, Englewood Cliffs, NJ, 1988.

23.   W. H. Burge. *Recursive Programming Techniques.* Addison-Wesley, Reading, MA, 1975.

24.   J. L. Carter and M. N. Wegman. Universal classes of hash functions. *Journal of Computer and System Sciences,* **18**(2):143-154, 1979.

25.   G. Chartrand and L. Lesniak. *Graphs & Digraphs,* 2nd ed. Wadsworth & Brooks/Cole, Pacific Grove, CA, 1986.

26.   W. Cheney and D. Kincaid. *Numerical Methods and Computing.* Brooks/Cole, Monterey, CA, 1985.

27.   D. Cheriton and R. E. Tarjan. Finding minimum spanning trees. *SIAM Journal on Computing,* **5**(4):724-742, 1976.

28.   P. Coad and E. Yourdon. *Object-Oriented Analysis.* Yourdon Press, Englewood Cliffs, NJ, 1990.

29.   J. Cohen and M. Roth. On the implementation of Strassen's fast multiplication algorithm. *Acta Informatica,* **6**(4):341-355, 1976.

30.   N. H. Cohen. *Ada as a Second Langauge,* 2nd ed. McGraw-Hill, New York, NY, 1996.

31.   T. H. Connen, C. E. Leiserson, and R. L. Rivest. *Introduction to Algorithms.*
        McGraw-Hill, New York, 1990.

32.   E. W. Dijkstra. *Structured Programming.* Academic Press, New York, 1972.

33.   E. W. Dijkstra. *A Discipline of Programming.* Prentice-Hall, Englewood Cliffs,
        NJ, 1976.

34.   J. L. Eppinger. An empirical study of insertion and deletion in binary search trees.
        Communications of the ACM, **26**(9):663-669, 1983.

35.   R. W. Floyd. Algorithm 245: Treesort 3. *Communications of the ACM,* **7**(12):
        701, 1964.

36.   B. A. Gailer and M. J. Fischer. An improved equivalence algorithm.
        Communications of the ACM, **7**(5):301-303, 1964.

37.   Z. Galli and G. F. Italiano. Data structures and algorithms for disjoint set union
        problems. *ACM Computing Surveys,* **23**(3):319-344, 1991.

38.   M. R. Garey and D. S. Johnson. *Computers and Intractability: A Guide to the
        Theory of NP Completeness.* W. H. Freeman, New York, 1979.

39.   D. Gries. *Science of Programming.* New York: Springer-Verlag, 1981.

40.   J. Guttag. Abstract data types and the development of data structures.
        Communications of the ACM, **20**(6):396-404, 1977.

41.   C. Hoare. Quicksort. *Computer Journal,* **5**(i):10-15, 1962.

42.   J. E. Hopcroft and J. D. Ullman. Set-merging algorithms. *SIAM Journal on
        Computing,* **2**(4):294-303, 1973.

43.   E. Horowitz and S. Sahni. *Fundamentals of Computer Algorithms.* Computer
        Science Press, Rockville, MD, 1978.

44.   D. A. Huffman. A method for the construction of minimum-redundancy codes.
        Proceedings of the Institute of Radio Engineers, **40**:1098-1101, 1952.

45.   D. W. Jones. An empirical comparison of priority-queue and event-set
        implementations. *Communications of the ACM,* **29**(4):300-311, 1986.

46.   D. E. Knuth. *The Art of Computer Programming, Volume 1, Fundamental
        Algorithms.* Addison-Wesley, Reading, MA, 1973.

47.   D. E. Knuth. *The Art of Computer Programming, Volume 3, Searching and
        Sorting.* Addison-Wesley, Reading, MA, 1973.

48.   D. E. Knuth. *The Art of Computer Programming, Volume 2, Seminumerical
        Algorithms* 2nd ed. Addison-Wesley, Reading, MA, 1981.

49.   D. A. Lelewer and D. S. Hirschberg. Data compression. *ACM Computing Surveys,*
        19(3):261-296, 1987.

50.   G. S. Leuker. Some techniques for solving recurrences. *Computing Surveys,*
        12(4):419-436, 1980.

51.   B. Liskov and J. Guttag. *Abstraction and Specification in Program Development.*
        McGraw-Hill, New York, 1986.

52.   R. Morris. Scatter storage techniques. *Communications of the ACM*, **11**(1):38-44, 1968.

53.   M, H. Overmars. *The Design of Dynamic Data Structures, Volume 156, Lecture Notes in Computer Science*. Springer-Verlag, Berlin, 1983.

54.   C. H. Papadimitriou. *Computational Complexity*. Addison-Wesley, Reading, MA, 1994.

55.   C. H. Papadimitriou and K. Steiglitz. *Combinatorial Optimization: Algorithms and Complexity*. Prentice-Hall, Englewood Cliffs, NJ, 1982.

56.   G. Polya. *How to Solve It*. Princeton University Press, Princeton, NJ, 1943.

57.   W. Pugh. Skip lists: A probabilistic alternative to balanced trees, *Communications of the ACM*, **33**(6):668-676, 1990.

58.   R. L. Rivest. On self-organizing sequential search heuristic. *Communications of the ACM*, **19**(2):63-67, 1976.

59.   R. L. Rivest, A. Shamir, and L. M. Adleman. A method for obtaining digital signatures and public-key cryptosystems. *Communications of the ACM*, **21**(2): 120-126, 1978.

60.   F. S. Roberts. *Applied Combinatorics*. Prentice Hall, Englewood Cliffs, NJ, 1984.

61.   S. Roberts. *Thinking Recursively*. New York: John Wiley & Sons, 1986.

62.   R. Sedgewick. The analysis of quicksort programs. *Acta Informatica*, 7:327, 1977.

63.   R. Sedgewick. Implementing quicksort programs. *Communications of the ACM*, **21**(10):847, 1978.

64.   R. Sedgewick. *Algorithms*, 2nd ed. Addison-Wesley, Reading, MA, 1988.

65.   R. C. Singleton. An efficient algorithm for sorting with minimal storage: Algorithm 347. *Communications of the ACM*, **12**(3):185, 1969.

66.   D. L. Shell. A High Speed Sorting Procedure. *Communications of the ACM*, **2**(7): 30-32, 1959.

67.   D. L. Shell. Optomizing the Polyphase Sort *Communications of the ACM*, **14**(10): 713-719, 1971.

68.   H. F. Smith. *Data Structures: Form and Function*. Hartcourt Brace Jovanovich, New York, NY, 1987.

69.   D. D. Steator and R. E. Tadan. Self-adjusting binary search trees. *Journal of the ACM*, **32**(3):652-686, 1985.

70.   D. D. Steator and R. E. Tarjan. Self-adjusting heaps. *SIAM Journal on Computing*, **15**(l):52-69, 1986.

71.   D. F. Stubbs and N. W. Webre. *Data Structures with Abstract Data Types and Pascal*, 2nd ed. Brook/Cole, Pacific Grove, CA, 1989.

72.   J. Vuillemin. A data structure for manipulating priority queues. *Communications of the ACM*, **21**(4):309-315, 1978.

73.   J. Westbrook and R. E. Tarjan. Amortized analysis of algorithms for set union

with backtracking. *SIAM Journal on Computing*, **18**(1), 1989.

74.   J. W. Williams.   Algorithm 232: Heapsort.   *Communications of the ACM*, **7**(6):347-348, 1964.

75.   N. Wirth. *Algorithms + Data Structures = Programs*. Prentice-Hall, Englewood Cliffs, NJ, 1976.

Index